T0339785

CONTROVERT
OR
ON THE LIE
AND
OTHER PHILOSOPHICAL DIALOGUES

CONTROVERT

OR

ON THE LIE

AND

OTHER PHILOSOPHICAL DIALOGUES

Nicholas J. Pappas

Algora Publishing
New York

Library of Congress Cataloging-in-Publication Data —

Pappas, Nicholas J.
    Controvert, or, On the lie : and other philosophical dialogues / Nicholas J.
Pappas.
        p. cm.
    ISBN 978-0-87586-651-2 (trade paper: alk. paper) — ISBN 978-0-87586-652-9
(hard cover: alk. paper) — ISBN 978-0-87586-653-6 (ebook) 1. Truthfulness and
falsehood. I. Title. II. Title: On the lie.

    BJ1421.P37 2008
    177.3—dc22
                            2008023823

Front Cover: Life Decisions by Noma
© Images.com/Corbis

Printed in the United States

For my Jamies

TABLE OF CONTENTS

I. Controvert, Or On the Lie

Persons of the Dialogue:

Extrovert

Introvert

Critic

Director

An Interlude with a Critic

Extrovert: Why, Director, it's Introvert. But who is that he's with?

Director: A stranger, by the looks of him.

Extrovert: Oh, I suppose that I deserve that irony from you — I didn't think you knew him either. Look. He's stopped off in that store, but Introvert's outside. Let's talk to him and find out who the stranger is.

Director: Alright.

Introvert: Good evening, brother. Hello, Director.

Director: What luck to find you here, my friend. I saw a sight today I meant to email you about. While waiting for the bus, right over there, a lovely woman sat upon the curb, just taking in the beauty of the day. A man approached and spoke inanities. From what they said, I guessed that he must work with her. A woman sitting with me on the bench just shook her head and said: "She'd rather be alone. Her body language says it all. She sits there smiling nervously and offers him encouragement. Disgusting, isn't it?"

Critic: You see that sort of thing quite often, no?

Director: Enough, I guess. But still it makes me wonder every time I witness it. I cannot understand why she can't find the inner strength to stop the act, if that is what it really is.

Introvert: Oh, how rude of me! I should have introduced you. Critic, this is Director — and this is Extrovert, my brother.

Extrovert: Critic? You're the one who writes the column for The News?

Critic: The same.

Extrovert: Whatever makes you come to Town?

Introvert: We're on our way to see an opera, Extrovert.

Extrovert: What opera's that?

Introvert: The Magic Flute.

Director: You mean the one where two set out upon a quest, directed by the Queen of Night, to save another from the clutches of an evil man?

Critic: Indeed, that is the one.

Extrovert: You really must enjoy your work!

Critic: It's not as fun as you suppose. Some people seem to think that all I do is gallivant about from play to play, enjoying every minute of the day. Tonight's performance certainly will be at best but poor. The politics — of course, the only thing that really counts — will be quite good, however. My review will stress —

Extrovert: Excuse me. How can you already know what things you'll say?

Critic: Your brother, Introvert, knows nothing of the literary world, it seems.

Extrovert: That may be true. But I am sure that people think reviews appraise performances for what they are, and not what critics judge before they've seen the show.

Critic: How charmingly naïve! Why, Director, he's so unlike the woman that you say you saw.

Extrovert: The people shouldn't be misled.

Critic: I think I'll let the implications of that slide.

Director: What implications do you think there are?

Critic: I'll say, if you insist. It's clear he thinks that I mislead my readers, making me some sort of evil man. That really doesn't bother me. It's natural for him to think that way. Your friend and I belong to different camps.

Director: What camps are those?

Critic: I'd rather not embarrass Extrovert.

Extrovert: No need to worry, Critic. I would like to know what camps you mean.

Critic: Alright. So, Director, although your friend will probably deny this fact, I'm sure you see that he exists as party to the ruling class. He sees hypocrisy in my reviews. But if he were to learn to see with better eyes, he'd know that an unmasking of the values that support the ruling clique is all that I'm about whenever I set out to write. A literary leader helps inform the people's tastes, and taking off the masks of those in power helps to educate their palates, as it were.

Extrovert: Why, you don't think they know their tastes?

Critic: With art they can't discriminate, my friend.

Extrovert: If we belong to different camps then how am I your friend — and why do you suppose that people can't decide about the things they like?

Critic: "Potential friend," I should have said — you may decide to leave the camp you're in. It's possible you'll come to see the nature of the ones who lead you now, and that it differs from your own. However, you may also, later in your life, become recalcitrant — and then you'd surely be an enemy — an older version of the character you now possess, but with some present latent tendencies victorious and tyrannizing in the pilot's house within your soul. And yet the elasticity of youthful souls sometimes surprises me. I take the hopeful (not the optimistic) view. As for your question on the people's tastes, they cannot always see what follows from their likes politically. My job is making these things clear.

Extrovert: You call your column "Art Review." "Political Review," I think, is more the thing. Why don't you call it that? At least you'd make disclosure of your full intent. Who knows? Your writing might become more powerful that way.

Critic: Some people think my writing is effective as it is.

Extrovert: But do your readers know that you decide what you will say, essentially, before you've even seen the show?

Critic: You seem to think that I am doing something wrong. It's wrong to help the ones who can to see?

Extrovert: If that is what you really do, then why must you affect that you are doing something else?

Critic: I have to give the readers what they want, if I intend to keep on publishing within the main stream press. They do not want to read a column called "Assumptions of Your Politics Revealed." Who knows? Perhaps I may one day decide to do exactly this, and be content to end my days obscurely, Extrovert. For now I choose to write the "Art Review" because it seems to me to be the means to work my ends the best. But I must say I think that you're too hard on me. I think you overestimate the variation possible within the arts. The matter of the actors' job may be disposed in one small paragraph. (They get enough attention as it is.) Direction, casting, lighting, setting — all of these I cover thoroughly, of course, and do not judge them in advance. But all of this will only take a rather small amount of space — and isn't really what the readers want to see. They want to hear about the juicy things — the intrigues we associate with politics. For this, a knowledge of the context and intent of what goes on must be obtained by long and careful study, well before the curtain's drawn. Political conditions and maneuverings make all the difference in the arts. I don't believe that there is any use in art that's only for the sake of art itself.

Extrovert: But even if it's as you say, do you ignore the variation possible in works of art themselves? Each year so many books, and films, and plays come out!

Critic: There's nothing new beneath the sun, my friend. All art is variation on the timeless themes, the fundamental questions of our lives. A talent that can work these themes to good effect cannot remain obscured for long — unless it chooses this is best. So why should I concern myself with being first to find that someone new has come along? Ability will rise, eventually, and when it does I'm quick to offer praise — when it's deserved.

Extrovert: But you do more than praise. The people wouldn't follow you and set their tastes according to your words if all you did is praise. You also blame — and I would like to know if there is anything preventing you from blaming great ability instead of giving praise. In other words, I want to know what guarantee the people have that you will lead them right.

Critic: The only guarantee they've got is their own pleasure, friend. They like to read my articles.

Extrovert: But they don't know the politics behind your words!

Critic: Oh my! You really think that everyone must give a full disclosure every time of where one stands on everything? Perhaps I ought to attach a list of all my friends and what they think, as well, in order to assure everyone that there is no conspiracy to take control of civilization, eh?

Extrovert: Why, I'm not saying that at all! But facts of relevance must be disclosed!

Critic: Oh ho! The "relevant facts" it is? What facts are those?

Extrovert: I think it should be obvious to everyone, don't you?

Critic: Well, I disclose the facts as I see fit. But why you keep your true opinion in, I cannot see. You clearly think that I'm a liar. Manfully you struggle, hiding scorn for me. Suppose, however, failure to disclose the facts that someone, somewhere just might think are relevant does constitute a lie indeed. I stipulate this controverted point. Yet lying is not the worst that humans do.

Extrovert: I'm well aware that there's no shortage of the bad within this world. But you would make it seem that lying isn't wrong — and that is what I'm questioning.

Critic: A lie's not always wrong. That doesn't mean I think it's always right, you know.

Extrovert: Then when's it right?

Critic: Consider that young woman Director observed this morning. She was lying, right?

Extrovert: Well, I don't know. I wasn't there.

Director: Since I'm the one who brought this up I think it only fitting I should answer here. It's clear to me that I was in the presence of a lie.

Critic: Now why do you suppose this was?

Director: Perhaps to keep their talk polite.

Critic: By this you mean that one will lie to make the other think the conversation is enjoyable, when anyone who isn't blind can see it isn't true? Now why would one do that?

Director: I meant it when I said I wonder that myself.

Introvert: Perhaps she acts like that because she fears.

Critic: What is it that she fears?

Introvert: I think that she's afraid of what will happen if he knows that she does not enjoy his company.

Critic: You mean that her position's such that he holds power over her? So what would happen if she were to let him know she doesn't want his company?

Introvert: Well, I don't know.

Critic: But surely you must have some notion, right?

Introvert: I'd guess she fears that she will lose her job, or something that's along those lines, like never rising in the ranks.

Extrovert: Well, if that's true then she's a fool. The only power that he's got is what she lets him have. Why, I've got bosses I don't like and I don't coddle them!

Critic: But you're a party to the ruling class. It's harder for the dispossessed. This poor young woman probably can't bear the strain that's put on her. Oppressed, she's forced to lie about the way she truly feels. It's thus she saves some face.

Extrovert: But how can you describe that act of hers as saving face?

Critic: I stand corrected. Face is less important than the soul — and that's the thing her little lie protects.

Extrovert: Her soul? That little lie you talk about is just the thing that kills the soul!

Critic: Oh no, my friend. You see, our souls are nourished by the power of the state. That poor girl's soul is about to starve. She has no share in power.

Extrovert: What? That's nuts!

Critic: (I thought that this would lead to little good. Yet I go on in hope of shedding just a little light.) The soul that has no power has no voice. Without a voice a soul will shrivel up and die. The fringes of society must struggle desperately to keep in contact with the power structure of the state in order to sustain their voice. Why, it's a noble struggle that they wage. Pathetic, too — a tragedy. The unjust distribution of the power of the state has made it necessary that this woman lie to save her voice — to save her dignity — to save her soul.

Extrovert: That doesn't seem so dignified to me!

Critic: I didn't think you'd understand. With more than your fair share of power —

Extrovert: More than my fair share? Ha, ha! What power have I got? I'm taking orders all day long!

Critic: Regardless of your rank, you're nonetheless a party to the ruling class, and thus a detriment to those beyond the pale. You fail to understand the nature of my work. You're judging by a different standard, one that people of your sort —

Extrovert: What sort is that?

Critic: It's nothing you can help, of course. It's this that makes for tragedy. All you can do is try to make amends for power not deserved by speaking on behalf of those less fortunate in this regard.

Extrovert: I hardly think that I'm to blame for someone else's lack of dignity. But even so, I'm curious to hear your thoughts concerning what exactly I should do.

Critic: Perhaps you'll try to understand the things they have to say, and not condemn them out of hand. I think that you'd do well to start with that.

Extrovert: Condemn them? Who's condemning them? I pity them! I don't believe, however, all — or even most — not even any — have to lie! And even if some did, I'd rather help the honest ones!

Critic: I think you overestimate the honest in this world. I wouldn't be so quick to judge, if I were you.

Extrovert: I hope I'm not too quick to judge! But surely you'd agree integrity is best? I almost can't believe I'm asking you this question!

Critic: Integrity. Now there's a word I thought you'd introduce. Integrity requires a healthy dose of dignity. The woman we've been speaking of is trying desperately to keep her dignity. The human with integrity allows the others dignity as well. The ruling party fails to understand this fact. Beware my friend. Participation in a system that denies an opportunity for dignity destroys one's own integrity. Consider yourself warned.

Extrovert: But how can what I do or so say take someone's dignity away? That's up to each of us alone! Besides, integrity confers the dignity, and not the other way around. A dignity without integrity is merely affectation — false! Integrity involves a fundamental honesty!

Critic: This argument has now become a tautological affair. As I have said, society can put a human being in a place where lies are necessary. It is very sad.

Extrovert: But no one really forces anyone to lie! There's always choice! Or do you think so poorly of us all you won't allow us that?

Critic: I see us as we are. We really haven't got much choice to any meaningful degree. We're products of the interplay.

Extrovert: The interplay? Of what?

Critic: Biology and politics. A very few can recognize this fact.

Extrovert: Then why give voice to the unfortunate? What difference does it make?

Critic: It keeps alive a small degree of hope — and that is really all there is to say.

Extrovert: You'll just dismiss the argument like that, as if you've won the point?

Critic: I think the point's been made quite clear.

Director: Much more than clear, if you ask me.

Critic: I thought that you would see.

Director: I have a question, though. In your opinion, what the woman did amounted to a lie that's white, not black?

Critic: That's right.

Director: I've often wondered how to tell the difference. I have tried for many years to learn, but it would seem that no one knows.

Critic: I'll tell you how I differentiate the two — necessity's the thing. A lie is white when necessary, black when not.

Director: I've thought of it this way before, but it's the notion of necessity that gives me pause.

Critic: Necessity reserves itself for higher things. The problem with most people is they think of lies exactly wrong. The lies of innocence aren't for the little, meaningless affairs. Profound significance alone can justify the lie. The noble lie is white because it's necessary for the highest things.

Extrovert: But all you're saying's that it's necessary that one lie because it's simply necessary! Being justified like that is more excuse than justice!

Critic: Drawing out distinctions such as that you move within a world of words and not of facts. Excuses, when they're truly justified, are based on perfect reason. Reason shows us whether lies are ever right, or white, or innocent — or what you will.

Director: The question here, it seems, is what is the highest thing the lie of innocence must serve. Am I correct to think you think that lying serves our dignity?

Critic: You are.

Director: Well, if you think it serves our dignity, I'd also like to know if you believe that lies like that are just.

Critic: I do, of course — when dignity is properly conceived — but hope we don't concern ourselves unduly with these verbal niceties. It's clear that we must know that justice is a matter not of logic but experience — of knowledge of ourselves and how we fit within the world, and not some rigid code. The truth is evident to those who're strong enough to take it undiluted.

Director: I don't like to think I sound as though I'm weak, but I would like to ask you one more thing. It seems to follow that you think that all the other lies must be unjust.

Critic: Of course. But we would find it tedious to spell these things all out at length. A few will understand without the need of point by point articulation of the whole of what's been said — as long as they don't think too much about the things of little consequence that always rear their heads.

Director: The things of little consequence? Do they include the strange idea that justice is a matter of necessity? The consequences of that notion in the larger world in which you cast your articles may well indeed be close to none, but for an individual the import may be very great, you know.

Critic: I take it you would rather not have justice be a function of necessity.

Director: I don't believe it can be.

Critic: It can for those who dedicate their lives to serving moral principle.

Director: What's this? But that implies a qualified necessity — which is to say there's no necessity at all.

Critic: There is, when one considers that necessity is subdivided in two types. The first necessity is merely physical. The second sort is that which flows from principle. The first of principles that leads to justice by necessity is one of simple choice — it's whether one is moral or one's not. It's not so hard for us to understand it when I say it boils down to just one thing — the good of others, or one's own. A moral man, when rightly understood, is dedicated to the good of others, Director — and it's from this that he derives his dignity.

Director: So moral men will lie? They'll tell white lies for others' good and their own dignity?

Critic: They will, when necessary.

Director: Am I right to think that you believe that this "necessity" will never cause another harm?

Critic: You are, when it is really necessary that they lie.

Director: Then let me get this straight with one more question, *Critic*. Lies are white when they prevent a harm to others?

Critic: Yes, that's right.

Director: Suppose a man is acting crazy with a gun. Is it alright to lie to him to take the gun away, assuming that it seems he'll cause harm to others?

Critic: Yes, that's one example.

Introvert: It's not obvious to me, however, that it's simply right to lie although a harm seems imminent. I think the answer here depends on whether he is really crazy and about to cause a harm, or only full of bluster.

Extrovert: Either way, we've got to take the gun away because we can't afford to take the risk. So, in a sense, it doesn't matter if he's really crazy then or not.

Introvert: Of course it does!

Director: You mean that if this man is not in fact insane, he's acting as he does for some good reason, right? But if that's true then what is it that makes him seem insane?

Introvert: Most people would say that it's the fact that he's not listening.

Director: Not listening?

Introvert: To reason, Director! But what if what they're calling reason's really not?

Extrovert: And waving guns around is reasoned argument? That's nothing but brute force.

Introvert: The way some people put their words to use amounts to — or disguises — force. They want the ones to whom they speak to cower, not to listen.

Director: That's because the things they say are false?

Introvert: I think it is.

Critic: Why, that's not why they want the man to cower. They are clearly of the sort who do not think of others' good.

Extrovert: Has everyone forgotten that this man is acting crazy with a gun?

Director: So how are we to stop his acting crazy? Reason, lies, or force?

Introvert: I can't believe it's ever right to lie, or threaten force, before we've tried the way of reason first.

Extrovert: The way of reason to a man who wields a gun? Alright, but even then I think that we should threaten force — and even use it, too — before we tell a lie! Why lie, when that will only make us baser men, without a guarantee the lie will work?

Critic: You wouldn't even lie in order to prevent a harm?

Extrovert: Well, can't the lie result in harm instead of good?

Critic: Not once you've learned to see beyond the propaganda of the ruling clique.

Extrovert: How's that got anything to do with this? What sort of propaganda do you mean?

Critic: The ruling party makes all things appear more complicated than they truly are, in order to obscure the truth about who benefits from things the way they are. The ruling party's colors always show — to those who recognize the markings. Someone with an understanding of their lies can find a way to lie himself to bring the man who's acting crazy (if he's not beyond all hope) right through the maze of all these ruling lies, convincing him to set the gun aside. One day, if he persists in questioning, he'll learn the meaning of the lie that saved him from the ones who only think of their own good.

Extrovert: You mean to say that once you see the truth about who benefits from what, regardless of the things the leaders say, you're free to lie, and that is well and good?

Critic: That's right. So very few can see the truth for what it is and act on it. It's likely that the crazy man began to see truth but failed to act.

Extrovert: He failed to benefit himself by stealing power through the use of lies?

Critic: That isn't what I said.

Extrovert: But that's sure what it seems you meant!

Critic: The power is to be used for others' good. I'm not implying that one's free to lie on any whim. With knowledge comes restraint. The dignity belonging to the ones who use their power well is born of this. The same is true of those who do not have but strive to gain their proper share of rule. You think that I'm encouraging barbarians to use the power they've obtained for spoil? They hardly need encouragement. Barbarity's defined by lack of dignity.

Director: I have to ask you, Critic — dignity, is it the end itself? Or is it good for something else?

Critic: It's good for something else. Our health requires that we have dignity. We need our dignity as much as we need food.

Director: Yet dignity is gained through taking part in rule?

Critic: Political society is natural to us. We form society to meet our needs. Without community there is no dignity. So it is only natural that dignity is gained through taking part in rule.

Director: I see. But is it pleasant to have dignity?

Critic: It is, but pleasure only comes when dignity has been obtained. The having, not the gaining or the maintenance is always pleasant, Director. The latter two are much like exercise, that in and of itself may not be pleasant all the time.

Director: I wonder then what sort of exercise or training's best. For physical well-being one may walk, and run, and hike, and climb — one swims, one stretches — myriad devices supplement these basic forms of exercise — and I expect it's much the same for mental health.

Critic: Why, yes, indeed.

Extrovert: It's true. One finds so many exercises that enhance the memory

Director: But what of all the muscle of the mind that gives it strength and quickness? Books, and films, and conversations all must serve to build and tone the brain.

Extrovert: That's true.

Director: Well, I, for one, enjoy variety in mental exercise. Don't you? The stimulants available delight — and all the choices almost make my head begin to spin.

Critic: Oh yes, I'm quite aware of what you mean. When I first started out I felt so overwhelmed by all there was to learn my head was nearly spinning all the time.

Director: Well, given your experience I'm wondering if you can help us understand.

Critic: I'll do my best, of course.

Director: It's clear to us that one must train the mind. It's also clear that dignity is part of mental health, and that it's something we must train ourselves to have. So now we've got to ask exactly how the lie can serve to train our minds. What benefit results from lies? You'd do us good to teach us this.

Critic: I'm happy to oblige. Ability to lie confers a mental flexibility that serves oneself and others well. A lie can get one out of narrow scrapes, and it can help another do the same. Not everyone will understand the truth — and often those who do rebel. What other choice is there but lies when faced with this? The lie's essential to the few of us who think. It's just a tool we keep within our box, to use as we see fit. The training of our minds is not complete until we learn the proper use of lies.

Director: A tool conferring flexibility? You mean to say that practicing with lies is like the stretching martial artists must perform to stay in fighting shape?

Critic: Oh, Director, when drawing a comparison between the health of body and the health of mind one ought not take it too far. We must recall that this is only metaphor. There is a fundamental difference we must understand. The healthy functioning of bodies is a private thing — but mental health involves community. A desert island may allow a man alone to keep his body firm — but mental health's not possible in long-term isolation. Intercourse with others keeps your sanity intact — but physical exertion is emphatically a solitary thing. Now what of lies? Our mind's imbalances arise when power rests with those who are not wise. A distribution that is thus unjust is what we've got to fear. When those who have a greater share than they deserve are lording over those who lack their proper share of power we will have a need for lies — if only as relief.

Introvert: But doesn't lying introduce a tension in the soul?

Critic: A psychic tension's better than a loss of dignity.

Extrovert: I still can't see that lying serves one's dignity. To cringe and fawn, pretending that you really like a thing you hate — what good is that? Suppose you lose your job because you will not paste a phony smile upon your face. So what? I'd say your dignity's enhanced!

Critic: This noble vision that you conjure's of a piece with all the propaganda that the ruling clique churns out. It only makes the situation worse. To take that woman once again, she knows she can't resist presumptuous men of power openly and hope to make her way in life. And yet the lie within your noble vision plants itself within her soul. It works to animate her feelings to resist — and make her fight a battle she will surely lose. She's torn between a loss of dignity and guilt. No matter what, she feels she's doing wrong — or failing to perform her full share of the right.

Extrovert: But moral courage isn't just an empty lie! It's not some myth! It's real — as real as you or me!

Critic: Your moral courage keeps the poor distracted from political solutions to their plight. The hypocrites will praise the actions bolstering their rule.

Extrovert: Do you deny the worth of selfless sacrifice?

Critic: Oh no, good man, I don't deny its worth at all! I fully see that there is gain in sacrifice — it's only that the gain does not belong to those who make it. Benefits accrue to people "in the know," the ones who see the ruling lies and aren't afraid to act on them.

Extrovert: It's obvious that sacrifice won't benefit the ones who give — by definition! Benefits will flow, at times, toward the rich, of course — but surely that's not always so! Consider all the children who are born in poverty. Their mothers sacrifice themselves in order that the children have a chance to live in better days. Why, do you think that there's no moral worth in that? The children benefit — and then the mothers, indirectly, benefit — and not the rich.

Critic: I am afraid you've got it rather wrong. The mothers do not sacrifice themselves — they sacrifice their children — to the ruling class. They teach their children all the "virtues" of the ruling clique, the virtues that will make them tools in bolstering their "betters'" rule. The ruling class, when wise, will always honor mothers doing so. The mothers gain respect, and are contented with this wage.

Extrovert: Ridiculous!

Director: Hold on a minute, Extrovert. The thread of argument is now obscure. The issue might be rendered clear if Critic tells us if the membership in ruling groups is always simply good. I hope he'll tell us what he really thinks.

Critic: Why, Director, of course I'll tell you what I really think. The answer's yes — it's always good to rule — and further, Director (because you are a man who's bold in questioning), not only is it good to be within the ruling class — the source of all our good lies here. Most people won't admit this openly. They're all in competition for the rule — and there's the issue of the propaganda that's in play. It's difficult enough to see through all the boasting and the smoke — and then one must discern who has the strength and what they do with it. How many lives are spent in chasing for the rule — and in the wrong direction, wasting efforts that would be more fruitful otherwise? Those in the ruling class will not admit the truth about their situation. Those who do are persecuted by their own. The rulers endlessly complain about the bitter dregs they swallow as the price of place, when truth is that they find it very sweet. But is it good to be a party to the rule? The very question makes one laugh. It's evidence of propaganda's victory. Oh, Director, it's good to be a member of the ruling class — the only good we know, in truth. The sooner we all own this fact the better off we'll be. We must accept as necessary evil we can't help. To know the truth about the rule will put us in a better place to make the choice of lesser ills. Our lives will not be perfect then — we'll have our share of suffering, of longing, and of sorrow — senseless pain will wrack our bones, and fear will chill our hearts — but we'll have less of that the more we see the truth. It's for enlightenment that we must struggle. That is something, yes.

Director: You are a man of candor, Critic. I can see the passion in your gaze bespeaks your honesty — and I suspect that you are one who would endure so many painful struggles bringing this enlightenment. Yet there's a thing we cannot understand. Please lend your generosity to see if you can help us see. You say that rule is pleasant. Rulers say, however, that it's not. So let's assume they lie. Is that because their dignity's enhanced if others think their rule has cost them pains? Why, you yourself have said that proper rule confers a dignity that makes one's rule worthwhile. But if they're being honest when they say it isn't pleasant, one would have to think that they aren't ruling right — or have I got it wrong?

Critic: You've got it very wrong — as wrong as wrong can be. They lie because it's to their benefit. They've got to watch that others don't get envious. If they can keep the monster jealousy in check, then there are fewer people who will hate them for their rule. By keeping hatred at a minimum the peril to themselves is less. With lessened peril they enjoy to full extent the pleasure that their rule provides.

Director: But from this reasoning it seems the pleasure of the rule defines the rule's success.

Critic: There's nothing wrong with taking pleasure in a job well done.

Director: Then let me see if I have found the basis for the lie. Enjoying one's success requires security, and this will only come through lies — is that the thing?

Critic: Of course — deception is the basis of security.

Director: Assuming, then, that they've obtained security through lies, what else might keep the ones who rule from tasting all the sweeter fruits that come of what they do?

Critic: A guilty conscience sometimes steals within their hearts and rots those fruits upon the vine — or else it makes them pluck them off before they're ripe. The ones who're born to rule must quickly learn to overcome the scruple that they're taught to feel.

Director: But who today is teaching scruple such as this?

Critic: We all are, Director, because we all would rather rule than let another take our place.

Director: I wonder, then, if teachings such as this require lies.

Critic: Of course. The ones who are not born to rule will argue that it's wrong to think that one is ever born to rule, while harboring within their heart of hearts the notion that it's they themselves who're truly born to rule — and that the only way for them to right the wrong that comes of others' failure to acknowledge this is using every means they've got to put themselves into their "proper" place. The lie's a fundamental tool that people such as this will use — they always have, and always will.

Director: So if the lie they tell about it being wrong to think that there are those who're born to rule succeeds in entering the heart of one who is, then he'll feel guilty for his lot, and fail to act the way a ruler should — and this will mean, in part, that he'll decline to lie? Is that the way they fight with lies?

Critic: It is. They seek to make the proper rulers lose their stomach, Director.

Director: It seems to me they want the rulers to discard their arms, if what you say is true — but this assumes that we must take it that the lie is simply part of rule.

Critic: Well, don't you think we do?

Director: It's not so clear. You would agree that parts partake in qualities pertaining to the whole?

Critic: Of course.

Director: And rule is pleasant when it serves a proper dignity?

Critic: It is.

Director: So lies are pleasant, too, if we make use of them to serve our proper dignity. We can't be sure of what to make of why you smile here — but surely we can see that if a ruler grows in strength his pleasure, too, will grow — and so he'll need to lie the more in order to protect himself from jealousy — if what you say is true.

Critic: Of course it's true. Our rulers always lie to those they rule. They lie to other rulers, too. They want to rule an ever growing sphere, expending effort to secure themselves an ever greater pleasure, Director.

Director: But they won't limit their desire for rule. It's clear that if they don't then they will be at war with all who don't accept them as their kings. They'll seek to grow their base and shrink the number of their peers within the apex of the state. The few will wish to come to be the one. In order to succeed at this they'll strive to conquer all their equals, right? But once they've conquered them then they're no longer peers — and then they'd have to stand alone — but stand on those they rule with legs that aren't accustomed to such shaky ground. It seems that this is where the lie that's told for rule must lead. I think you know what all this means. If rule is simply pleasant, everyone will seek to rule. Not only will they seek to rule, they'll seek to gain a sole and total rule. They will employ whatever means might lead them to this end. They'll use the lie, of course. They'll lie to anyone — including all their friends.

Critic: Perhaps.

Director: Perhaps — but how perhaps? You smile again? What reason can we see for this determined hedge? You mean that even rulers have their trusted friends?

Critic: Of course they do — like every other must.

Director: But can they really think that friendship's sweet if they consider that to rule's the source of every human good?

Critic: There is no necessary contradiction there, as you are well aware.

Director: But that would mean that friendship must derive from rule.

Critic: You've reached the point where you will have to answer your own questions, Director. We'd hate to think you lack the courage for the argument's concluding phase.

Director: I'd like to think I'm brave enough for that. The argument implies that friendship must exist between the ruler and ruled, who'll lie to one another — or between ambitious strivers who would rule — or else between those men who jointly rule — but how can any of this be? Are lies the basis of all friendships? Must we hide our pleasures from each other? Friends should surely share. So, no — I won't assert that such a friendship can exist and still be true. Then what about a friendship based on hopes to gain the rule? I'm not so sure about a friendship based on that. If they obtain their goal then they'll become just like the other rulers, entering a competition for the sole and total rule. But what about the friends who'd rule together, sharing in their pleasures? This would seem to be the best — but only if it's true that rule is pleasant. Still, they'd have to learn to limit their desire for rule, if only not to trample one another while they slake their power lust. But if it's true that rule's the source of all the human good, then how can they forgo to further their own good by setting limits on how much of it they'll gain?

Critic: There is a danger that you'll take this all too far. We've got to put it in perspective. Friends will sometimes lie, but still they are our friends. The world is not a perfect place.

Director: But are they friends the moment when they tell each other lies?

Critic: But now we're quibbling, Director.

Extrovert: We are not quibbling, Critic. No — a real friend, good and true, will never tell his friend a lie! A friend can't lie and still remain a friend! Of course, the friendship might resume once they have gotten past the lie. But at the time the lie is told the friendship is dissolved and has to be reformed or lost.

Critic: A friendship's not as fragile as we think. There may be chaos in your view, you know.

Extrovert: But would a friend who lies repeatedly remain our friend?

Critic: I think it all depends upon the nature of the lies.

Extrovert: The nature of the lies? Well, I, for one, believe that every lie's the same.

Critic: But it's quite obvious that there are different sorts of lies. Some lies are subtle, some are blunt — some lies succeed, and others fail — some lies are quite transparent, some are most opaque — some lies concern gross fact, some lies concern one's feelings.

Director: Which of these should we allow our friends to use on us?

Critic: That, too, depends.

Director: Does it depend on whether we detect a pattern to the lies?

Critic: Of course — and also on the sort of pattern that it is.

Director: As long as there's no threat to rule contained in it?

Critic: That's right. But do you think that we are so naïve? The ruler and the ruled both benefit when rule's maintained. The tension that exists because we all desire the rule will foster creativity — which fosters growth. Is that so bad? Should we decide to throw that all away because we want to practice brutal honesty? To rule is sweet. To lie in furtherance of one's rule is sweet. To gather friends that bolster up one's rule is sweet. To hope to one day rule is sweet. Shall we go on? The woman that you say you saw today, although she suffered pains because her conscience (grounded in a noble, propaganda lie) rebelled — beyond that pain, held sweetly in her soul the hope of future rule. Should we deny that hope from her? To leave her where? Her only chance at dignity — at good — is there, in future hope. But now it's time to go. It's gotten very late.

Introvert: I'm sorry, Critic, but I think I'm going to stay and skip the opera.

Critic: Well, you must suit yourself, you know.

The Music of the Principles

Extrovert: I'm sure that Critic hasn't been stood up for quite some time. I wonder if he's mad at you. He's very hard to read. I hope it's not a problem for that teaching job. I just can't see the reason why he says that some are forced to lie. I think he can't admit he's wrong. He says it's right to lie in cases of necessity. But necessary why? For what? For rule? I disagree. There's no necessity. A ruler who can tell the truth is best — and strongest, too. The weak depend upon the lie. But is it right for men of stronger character to ever lie? Suppose they say they're lying for the greater good. That seems alright when kept abstract, but every time particulars arise it's never very clear. Can something that must come from lies be good? It seems to me that good's contaminated by a lie. And what about preventing harm? Can lies do this? I can't see how — because you can't be sure they'll work — or if they do, you can't be sure the lies won't set in motion things that lead, eventually, to even greater harm.

Introvert: But what do we take harm to be?

Extrovert: Well, how about a broken neck?

Introvert: That's almost certainly a harm — but not in every case, as when the other choice is death — or when the injured man thus comes to see the light about the way he lives and learns to be a better man. At times an injury can shock a man enough to make him see himself for what he is. Of course, it need not take a broken neck — at times a loss of money is enough to make him think.

Extrovert: Of course. The point is that we've got to know if trying to prevent a harm we're only going to make it worse.

Director: Is there a type of harm admitting of no worse?

Extrovert: There is — a conscience that's not clear.

Introvert: But there are those, you know, who say that conscience is imagined anyway, a thing that one must think away or just ignore.

Extrovert: The ones who talk like that have guilty consciences. They've done something they knew was wrong, and now they want to make it seem alright. They're wicked liars, Introvert.

Introvert: But doesn't that depend?

Extrovert: On what?

Introvert: On whether what they thought was wrong is really wrong.

Extrovert: Well, harming innocents is always wrong.

Introvert: But how do we confirm they're really innocent? And how do we confirm that what we've done was wrong or right? Some people pray on others' sense of guilt, you know. Perhaps we're only fooled to think that what we've done is wrong.

Director: We'd better take this one thing at a time. The question of one's guilt or innocence will only complicate the argument.

Extrovert: That's true. To harm is wrong, and justice calls for punishment of those who harm — and punishment that's just is never harm but only right.

Director: If that's the case, suppose there is a man upon whom justice smiles (and not because he's done something that he has hidden from the law). Suppose, however, that he has bad conscience over some imagined wrong he thinks he's caused.

Extrovert: Well, any pain of conscience from imagination that's run wild all goes for naught, I'd say. Some people are too hard upon themselves.

Introvert: Perhaps — but that assumes the question only deals with harm and nothing else. We've also got to think of working good — not just commission but omission, too. A man might keep from causing harm — but he might also keep from doing any good.

Director: Well, is it right to lie in order to achieve some higher good?

Introvert: I think it all depends on what we think is good.

Director: To save a lot of time (for now, at least), since that can be a very complicated question, Introvert, I'll guess that you are wondering about a problem something much like this, involving good and harm. If tortured conscience (using that example as the worst of harm) can prompt a man to change his way to lead a better life, the fact of all that pain turns out to be the spur toward good. The question of the goodness of a thing — whatever thing — depends on actions subsequent. In other words, the fate of all things present both controls and is controlled by all the things existing in the past (if it is right to say that they exist, as though they were in present time). This means, of course, that all the present things are hostage to the future, too. Is this the sort thing that troubles you about the goodness or the harmfulness of things?

Introvert: It is.

Director: Now, as you've said, we're sometimes fooled. It seems that we're most often tricked about the facts. Without a detailed knowledge of events and their results we cannot know if necks have snapped, or funds been lost, or someone's happy or depressed.

Introvert: Of course.

Director: The latter's most important, no? There's no amount of health or wealth that takes away the blues.

Introvert: That's true.

Director: We call this mental health.

Introvert: We do.

Director: Then we should focus here. Well, let's review before we start. Our question is about the lie. We want to know if it is ever right to lie. Should we tell lies to gain some good? Should we tell lies to stop some harm? It's hard to know what's good and what is not — so how are we to know if it is right to lie? Are we so sure that we will reach our end of stopping harm or causing good? Regardless if we use the means of lies or not, we're never wholly sure that we'll accomplish what we set ourselves to do. So if we have to choose a place to start, should we assume it's better that we aim at working good or stopping harm?

Extrovert: More harm is caused — by far — by those who try to do another good than harm is caused by those who seek to stop a harm. So if we have to err, let's err in working to prevent a harm.

Director: Alright. Well, what's the worst that we can do to someone else?

Extrovert: The worst that we can do is ruin someone's joy.

Director: And how do we do that?

Extrovert: We take away the things they love.

Director: Besides external things, what other objects are there for one's love?

Extrovert: Well, there's a healthy love of self, I think — a love of one's own virtue — one's own worth.

Director: And how could one attack another there to take those things away?

Extrovert: I guess he'd have to lie and make the person think the self or virtue that he loves is false.

Director: If someone really knows himself, it seems to me that he must be immune to this attack. And isn't there a danger to the liar trying to work this harm? If he succeeds he might regret the ill he's wrought and suffer from bad conscience. No, it's not as simple as it seems.

Extrovert: That's right. But don't forget the ones who have no conscience, Director.

Director: That's just a way of speaking, Extrovert. Why, don't you think that all of us have conscience — whether good or bad?

Extrovert: I'm not so sure we do.

Director: Well, what is conscience but the knowledge that the thing one does is right or wrong?

Extrovert: That's true — it is exactly that.

Director: You mean to say, then, that some people have no thoughts at all about the things they do?

Extrovert: Some people act like animals.

Director: Then they're not human, right?

Extrovert: That's true.

Director: So now that we are clear we're speaking of just human things, I wonder if I'm right to think that you believe that when the conscience has gone bad there comes the greatest of all pains, and that you'd readily admit that healthy conscience isn't pleasure, but the absence of that pain?

Extrovert: I think that's fair to say.

Director: Now, let's recall that we've implied that pain is not the sole criterion of harm, since pain of conscience, as we've said, can cause a man to change for good — and so it cannot simply follow that we'll keep our conscience clear by merely trying not to cause another pain, correct?

Extrovert: That's right. We've got to keep from causing others harm, not pain. And so if there's a pain that we can cause to prompt a man to change his evils ways, I'd say that we deserve bad conscience if we fail to cause that pain to stop the harm that evil doing surely brings.

Director: And that's because we know that pains are sometimes clearly necessary, right?

Extrovert: That's absolutely right.

Director: So we can see the reason why we must distinguish pain from harm. If pain's identical to harm, then truth and lies are morally equivalent, depending on effect — on whether truth can be the source of pain as much as lies. So yes, we surely must distinguish pain from harm. And there is nothing radical in this. It seems that everyone makes use of this distinction every day. A teacher causes students pain by making them work hard. The teacher doesn't have bad conscience over this.

Extrovert: Of course he doesn't.

Director: Don't we think the teacher's even good for doing as he does?

Extrovert: We do.

Director: Implicitly distinguishing a pain from harm, a doctor and a trainer take the same approach.

Extrovert: They do.

Director: The doctor and the trainer cause a pain the body feels. Is it the same with teachers, Extrovert? Or do they cause a different sort of pain?

Extrovert: They cause a mental sort of pain.

Director: It's pain that comes from exercising what we'd call the muscles of the mind?

Extrovert: That's right. A good example's that it's painful when we work to learn a foreign tongue. But once we've learned it fluently it's pleasant to converse in it.

Director: Now, how would you describe the pain of conscience? Mental, as with learning?

Extrovert: Yes, but somehow different. Learning seems to me to pain a portion of the soul, while conscience makes the whole thing sear.

Director: But what if conscience were a call to learn a basic thing, a fundamental fact of soul? We know that learning's not just memorizing facts, but questioning opinions held, then putting them to proof, and recomposing thought around the knowledge newly won from these investigations, right?

21

Extrovert: I guess that's right. I'd never thought of it like that. But does that mean the pain of conscience is the same as that which comes when learning, only more intense?

Director: Well, if it is we've got some questions we must ask. Is mental effort, in and of itself, the cause of pain? Or is it changing what we think by forming mind to principle that causes pain? But then again, perhaps composure of the mind, when lost, results in pain? Or are these three essentially the same?

Extrovert: I think that lost composure of the mind creates a pain as great as that of conscience, Director — regardless if the two are basically the same. But mental effort, by itself, is not the cause of pain. It's only when we think too hard that we must suffer. Minds that fall from harmony, however, always suffer from a mental dissonance — which may well be exactly what bad conscience is. The pain increases with the clash of mental notes.

Director: And what's the cause of this? A decadence from principle?

Extrovert: Exactly so. A man must act on principles he knows are sound or else he loses mental harmony — and that is torture to the soul.

Director: So what's the price that men would pay to keep their harmony?

Extrovert: A man who's worth his salt won't even ask the price.

Director: He'd toil and strain?

Extrovert: No doubt.

Director: He'd take great risks in holding fast to what he knows is true?

Extrovert: He would.

Director: He'd lie?

Extrovert: He'd what?

Director: He'd lie in order to maintain his mental harmony?

Extrovert: Of course he wouldn't!

Director: Didn't you assert a man who's worth his salt will keep his harmony at any cost?

Extrovert: I did! But lies will make for dissonance!

Director: I see. Well, I suppose that if they do it's got to be because the principle one acts upon when lying clashes with another principle.

Introvert: But what if someone lies from instinct, not from will?

Director: That's awful, don't you think? To act from instinct means to act without a choice. Will conscience bother those who act involuntarily?

Introvert: It might — if they believe they should have acted with resolve instead.

Director: But you don't think that mere resolve can soothe the conscience.

Introvert: No, I don't.

Director: Then is the thing that matters if we're moral — serving others' good, as Critic says?

Introvert: Perhaps. But Critic thinks that everyone will lie and scheme so they might rule. So how he thinks that anyone will ever act for others I can't see.

Director: You really cannot see the way? The reconciliation of the things he says involves the competition of the rulers for the good of others. That's the way to square the principle of rule and working for a good that's not one's own. It works because the good's supposed to be to rule, that's all.

Introvert: But what about the lies that rulers tell?

Director: Well, what about them, Introvert?

Introvert: I thought they lie and say they're helping others when they're not.

Director: That's certainly a possibility. But there's another, one that's more effective.

Introvert: What?

Director: The rulers' good is lost — a sacrifice to others' good.

Extrovert: So they're not lying when they say that rule's not pleasant? Those who say these things must lack a harmony of soul, if they still strive for rule.

Introvert: A harmony of soul? They've hardly got the mind for that. The mind's an instrument that must be strung with expert care.

Director: Is playing on it, once it's strung, much easier?

Introvert: It's even harder, I would say.

Director: And how are we to stand in judgment of performances upon this instrument?

Introvert: Well, that's the hardest thing of all. It takes a subtle ear to catch the faintest notes and hear the ones that aren't in key.

Director: Then let's lay out the first things first, before we move to subtler things. So what comprise the strings of soul?

Introvert: The principles one holds.

Director: I see. And what's the first, the lowest string?

Introvert: Well, if we follow on the path that we've laid out, I think it's got to be to cause no others harm. That takes a great restraint that's only possible with strength of soul.

Director: Alright. So here's the lowest string — no harm. Then lying would be right if that's the way to keep from causing harm. You know the saying that the truth will always hurt?

Introvert: Of course. But how are we to know when stopping harm is only an excuse to lie for other things? We'll need a second principle.

Director: I think you're right, my friend. And what's the second string upon our instrument?

Introvert: I'd say it's got to be to recognize a thing or act for what it is. If it is ever right to lie then we must recognize the act as virtue when it's right, and vice when wrong. In proper praising, all we do is recognize an act that's good for what it really is — to praise in any other way is merely flattery. And when we blame we recognize an act that's bad for what it is. To call a virtue "virtue" is an act of praise — to call a vice a "vice" is blame — to call a vice a virtue's flattery, and virtue vice is evil.

Director: What's the principle in play? To recognize all things for what they truly are? If that's the case, it seems we have our string. But is it only things pertaining to our praise and blame, or is the principle a broader one than that? I ask because if we must offer praise and blame that's based on truth, we've got to know the truth itself before we start.

Introvert: I think that's fair to say that we must know the truth entire, and that the second string's the string of truth — and only honest souls can play this string.

Director: Then we have got our strings, and each one plays a double note — to harm no others, which involves restraint — and truthfulness, involving honesty. Now, let's suppose that there's no more nor less than these two strings with which to make our mental harmonies (at least for now). Would lies be part of any tune we'd play?

Extrovert: They can't, because they'll always sound like notes belonging to a different key. Our second string is tuned to truth, and any other note must ring out false.

Director: Is that the case no matter if we add some other, higher strings?

Extrovert: A thousand strings would fail to drown the sound produced by one false note against our second string.

Director: Are we agreed that there's no way to lose the second string and substitute some other string instead, a string that doesn't clash with telling lies?

Extrovert: We are. We'd have no way to know if we are causing harm if we don't know the truth — and that still holds if we decide to change the lowest string to working good instead.

Director: So as our instrument's composed, regardless of the principle that's strung upon the lowest string, we still have got to have a principle of truth. But what if people using different instruments, the sort that are not strung with truth, begin to play. You said a thousand strings would fail to drown the one false note. But what about the other way around?

Extrovert: Well, then I think the truth will have a hard time being heard — but there are those who'll hear our notes and try to learn to change their tune.

Director: And what if there are many players playing true but one lone instrument that's playing false?

Extrovert: It's still the same. A million instruments can't fully mask the sounding of single a note that's out of key.

Director: Not even if the instruments are all the same?

Extrovert: That wouldn't matter, Director.

Director: It wouldn't matter? Well, if all the instruments are one then surely we would notice if an instrument is playing differently than all the others, right? But tune can be an odd phenomenon, my friend. It's quite precise. A string's in tune or not. The quality of "tuned" involves no more or less — it's yes or no. A string that's very close to proper resonance is nonetheless a string that's out of tune. A string that's tuned is neither taut nor slack. Yet coming into tune's a matter less of quality than quantity — of more and less, of loose and tight. Now how do strings, or principles, go slack or taut?

Extrovert: Well, when it comes to harming none, the string goes flat when harm is done through negligence (and in the case of causing good, the negligence results in failure to perform the good we should).

Director: And how does it go sharp?

Extrovert: When harm is done intentionally.

Introvert: I think it's something different, Director. I think the string goes sharp when someone thinks he's causing harm but really isn't causing it at all.

Director: You mean to say that if a trainer pulls up short, and doesn't bring his student to his optimum degree of excellence, because he doesn't want to cause him harm by training him too hard, although there really is no danger here of that, you'd say his string has gone too tight? Yet if he trains his charge too hard, and tears his muscles down — so far they can't grow back — he's let the string go flat? The trainer needs to know the trainee's nature very well — and so our second string, the string of truth, must be involved. Like good musicians, it is best for him to loosen up before he plays, to get familiar with his charge, before he sets to training earnestly. He ought to run through all the scales, reviewing what he knows about the proper intervals between the notes for every key, until he's certain that he knows which key will show his charge to best effect. He'll have to watch the way his charge reacts, and calculate exactly what potential he has got. In other words, he'll have to see his charge for what he is. But tell me what you think of this. Suppose the trainee's heart is set on being an Olympic champ. The trainer sees, however, that the trainee doesn't have the stuff it takes for that. I wonder if you think it's ever right to flatter his desire.

Introvert: Of course I don't. That's only cruel.

Director: Well, let's suppose the trainer tells the truth — and still the trainee fails to hear. He begs and pleads, harassing day and night. He claims that his desire is evidence of his potential. Is the trainer wrong to turn this man away?

Introvert: Of course not, not at all.

Director: Well, should he seek to soften up the blow by offering excuses that aren't true? Perhaps he'll say he's got too many trainees as it is. Would that be better, Introvert?

Introvert: To tell the truth's the only thing to do. It's not a favor if he leads the young man on.

Director: Then truly this involves the proper tuning of the second string. But there's a problem with our metaphor, my friend. We've seen the way our first of strings goes slack — we've also seen how it goes taut. Now, on the second string, with truth and honesty combined, a lapse of honesty must make the note fall flat. But what will make the string go taut? You see the trouble now? So there's the rub. We said the elements of truth are two — both truth and honesty. But these things differ, much as pain and harm. Now, truthfulness is knowing what is true, while honesty is saying what you think is true. The only time the string of truth goes taut, it seems, is when it's time to lie but honesty prevails. So don't you think it's better that each string consist of just one principle, not two? Our second string is truth itself, and nothing more — for what is honesty without concern for truth? And as for honesty, why isn't that a principle belonging to a higher range?

Introvert: I see your point.

Director: And don't you think we've got to get the lower matters right before we move to higher things?

Introvert: Of course.

Director: Well, what about our first and lowest string?

Introvert: We made it compound when we said it takes restraint to keep from causing harm.

Director: Restraint must presuppose desire — desire to harm, my friend. But do we want our fundamental string to presuppose a lust for something bad? Is that the basis of our instrument? What sort of player have we got in mind?

Introvert: I take your point.

Extrovert: But aren't we tempted, one and all, to work some harm at times?

Introvert: If so, it's due to forces operating on us, making us desire a thing we know is wrong. The pressure of that force can drive us on, against our will.

Extrovert: But then it cannot really be desire.

Introvert: But healthy men will never want to see another harmed!

Director: Well, is our instrument for those who're healthy or for those who're sick?

Introvert: The instrument we build should be for healthy men.

Director: So if it's true that healthy men do not desire to work another harm, it seems we've got to make a change in how our lowest string is strung.

Introvert: You're right. For healthy men, there's no restraint involved in working no one harm.

Director: So now our strings are simple — working no one harm, and truth. But don't we have the order wrong? Are we to know we're working harm if we don't know the truth about the things we do? We'd made the point before but failed to note that we had got the order wrong.

Extrovert: You're right! Our fundamental string must be the truth. The second string will follow from the first, of course.

Director: Alright. Consider that the change is made. Is this enough, or do we need some other strings?

Extrovert: I'm sure that there are more that we might add, but what we've got's enough for now. Let's see how it holds up just as it is before we complicate our music with another string.

Director: So now that we have got construction of the basic instrument and tuning down, it's time to cover other skills. It's good to have an instrument well made and tuned, of course — but only when we know the way to play. Well, on the lowest string the opposite of truth will sound false notes — and on the second string each harm must do the same. In either case, an expert knows that something's wrong — that there's a note that's out of place, or else that there is dissonance within the key, or failure to produce a proper harmony in chords. Now, experts are particular in following each principle, exactly to a "T." The truth's the truth, with no exceptions, right? To harm no other means to cause no harm to anyone at all — not even to oneself.

Extrovert: But why would someone do a thing like that, unless you mean unknowingly? We never harm ourselves intentionally — we only harm another knowingly.

Director: To harm another knowingly we'd have to play upon the first but then ignore the second string, correct? If our concern is lies, and if they're ever right, and whether they must always cause some harm, or whether there are lies that don't — then we should focus on the first, and not the second string, if only for the sake of learning what we must or mustn't do in order to avoid or cause a harm. Let's look a little closer. Truthfulness requires knowledge, yes? Expanding on our metaphor, — which has its limits — greater knowledge means a greater range of pitch. A greater range requires dexterity. Dexterity across the range allows a man to play the note the score demands, no matter where it falls. That's what it takes to sound the proper note right at the proper time.

Introvert: But not all music makes good use of one's full range!

Director: Why, Introvert, that's true. If, for the greater part, you're asked to play a narrow sort of tune, what should you do in order to maintain your range with virtuosity?

Introvert: I think that you must practice on your own — alone. But if you're overheard by those who only play the standard score, they'll sense a weirdness in your art — and this will disconcert, and they'll cast doubts on you.

Extrovert: Although you play the standard music without flaw? You'd think they'd want to learn a music that is strange, if only to increase their range!

Introvert: They may at first, but lose desire when they discover that they lack the skill it takes to play a note they know they must.

Director: A note they know they've got to play? The thing you say's impossible, my friend.

Introvert: Impossible?

Director: Again, our metaphor reveals itself as falling short of truth. You see, this instrument of which we speak is one where knowledge and ability go hand-in-hand. You cannot know a note's required if you don't have the skill to play.

Extrovert: Ability to read the score confers ability to play?

Director: In this case, yes.

Extrovert: Then we will have to teach them how to read.

Introvert: Well, what's the analog to this? If one has knowledge of the truth, then that confers ability to... what? To speak? To say? To teach? Suppose that one can state the truth. That doesn't mean that he can teach the truth to all. What if the students cannot learn?

Extrovert: Well, what of that? The teacher's skill does not depend upon the students' gifts. I wonder if the question really is with whom to share the truth. I do not hesitate to say I think it's only best to share with friends.

Introvert: But that's not always true. At times a stranger's best to hear a thing.

Director: What things are best to share with strangers, Introvert?

Introvert: It's hard to say. But I suppose they're things your friends won't understand.

Extrovert: But friends should understand — that's why they're friends!

Introvert: Oh, I agree, of course. But still, while friends may understand a great amount there's always something more.

Extrovert: You'd lie to them about this "something more?"

Introvert: Not lie — but neither share. There'd be no point.

Extrovert: Not even if directly asked?

Introvert: That's where it gets quite hard — that's where the friendship's really strained. Should friends expect to share all things? Perhaps with time it's possible — but only over time — and then I'm not so sure the friendship could endure once all's been said!

Extrovert: Well, don't upset yourself because of this. You shouldn't lie — but nothing says you've got to share all things. It's not as though you're in a court of law where you have sworn to tell the whole truth, Introvert. You're being much too strict. Besides, a court of law demands the truth entire, it's true — but only for the truth that's relevant!

Introvert: The court of conscience asks for more than that.

Director: You mean that conscience — once it's clear a certain note's been etched upon the score — cannot condone a failure to perform?

Introvert: I do.

Director: Then one must play wholeheartedly, it seems.

Introvert: But sometimes playing seems perverse — and this prevents one's heart from being fully in the tune. I mean, suppose you see a note your friends can't see. You know that if you play the note your friends won't understand the reason why you're doing what you do — and if you fail to play you know you haven't done your part — and so you're torn — and this is why you'd seem perverse. Your friends will see that something's clearly wrong — but not have any clue to what it is.

Extrovert: But why should you concern yourself with playing notes you really do not want to play? I mean, if there's a thing that you don't want to do, then no one's got the right to make you play — regardless who's conducting, as it were.

Introvert: But there's a duty to the author of the score — if only out of loyalty — or gratitude — for all the beauty that he's wrought!

Director: I think we'd better know the score quite well before we go that far, before we feel compelled to make ourselves comply — don't you?

Introvert: Agreed. But let's assume the score is known by heart.

Director: Alright, but let's be clear about this metaphor of ours. The score's the world, this here and now, with all that it contains.

Introvert: That's just the sense in which I took your words.

The Political World

Extrovert: So, who composed this great big symphony that we should show him gratitude?

Introvert: That's not an easy question, brother.

Extrovert: Why? Because we're only speaking in a metaphor? Well, some would say it's God.

Introvert: That's true. And some would say Big Bang. But I'm not only speaking of the world of nature.

Extrovert: Oh? What other world is there?

Introvert: The world that man creates.

Director: Political society? Then let's get to the point. I think you think refusing what's demanded by the score of nature leads to something different than one's failing to perform the thing the state demands — whenever they are unaligned. Correct?

Introvert: Correct. I do. You can't fool nature but you just might fool the state. With nature you must play or pay — and there's no choice. But with the state it's always possible a lie will work.

Extrovert: You mean if told to play a G you'd play the A but lie and say you played a G?

Introvert: That's right.

Extrovert: I didn't think your conscience would allow for that!

Introvert: You're right to raise that point, of course, but wrong to laugh. The conscience isn't merely natural, you know. It is, at least in part, political.

Director: In part?

Extrovert: Oh, Introvert! A conscience that's not natural is monstrous!

Introvert: Man's by nature part political. He cannot reach his full potential if he lives outside society. So that has got to mean his conscience is, at least in part, political — as far as it's concerned with what takes place within society. My point is just that this must make the question of the lie emphatically political. When unjust laws or tyranny attempt to force the sounding of a note that's false against the score of nature — which will always make the well-made instrument sound best — we've simply got to know the thing to do.

Extrovert: That's not so hard. We strive to change the laws and fight the tyranny as best we can!

Introvert: And what if things have gotten to the point where we can't free ourselves without a fundamental change within the state? There comes a time when we must think of starting things afresh. A new regime might be the only way.

Extrovert: It comes to that at times, it's true.

Director: And what has that do with lies? You'd better be specific, Introvert, before you venture out upon an ice as thin as this.

Introvert: I'm sure you've heard it said that new regimes require the use of lies.

Director: You're right — I have. But do you think that this is true?

Introvert: I think a new regime must operate to some degree on faith — and this implies a limitation on the truth. All faith begins where knowledge ends. Regimes must have their laws. The judgment of the founders frames the laws. But judgment's founded on evaluation of existing circumstance. All circumstances change. But laws — at least the basic laws — can't change without a new regime. A founder — if he's wise — can see his laws won't be obeyed unless he says they're absolutes. He knows his laws are limited, but speaks of them as if they're always true. In other words, he lies — because he understands the limits of the law — and there are very few who do.

Director: It must be terrible to live like that — if what you say is true. But might a founder not believe wholeheartedly his laws embody truth entire?

Introvert: He might — but then he can't be truly wise.

Extrovert: So you believe a noble lie is necessary?

Introvert: I would rather that it weren't. But how can founders make the people see the truth? The truth takes time, but politics is always rushed. Persuasion, full and true, requires we speak with every individual, addressing all concerns. Yet need — or opportunity for change — arises suddenly. So I don't think it's possible for there to be a founder truly wise who doesn't lie. He'd have to know all relevant political detail — and that's what every single person thinks — and people change their minds! So he has got to do a lot of guessing, but pretend he knows — because the people must believe he acts from knowledge if they're going to put their faith in him.

Director: Well then it seems affairs like this would take a deal of luck. Is it the same not only with a founder of a brand new state but also with the ruler of a state that's old?

Introvert: I think that rule must always take a deal of luck, for all the reasons that I've said.

Director: So founding states requires luck, and ruling states requires luck — and what about correcting states gone bad? Does that take luck?

Introvert: I think it does — and skill, of course.

Director: So if there's someone with the skill and luck it takes, regardless if he's founding, fixing, or just keeping on the course already set, I'd like to know exactly why you think he's got to lie. Can't luck replace the lie, effectually? You've said that new regimes require some faith. But I would think that if that's true, considering the things we've said about the need for luck, then every age of state requires a bit of faith.

Introvert: That's very true.

Director: Then every age of state is essentially the same, as far as need for faith is concerned. But now to turn the focus back to our main point — does faith itself necessitate the lie? Is that the source of what you think?

Introvert: I think it does — and is, whenever it's a faith that isn't natural, a faith that isn't true, but one that takes its bearings from or for the state. An able man who holds a faith that's true won't lie.

Director: You mean to say an able man who holds a faith that's natural, and therefore true, won't lie?

Introvert: That's right — when he is strong enough to live his faith. The trouble starts, I think, when others start to place their faith in him (and here's the root of politics). He doesn't want to disappoint. He's tempted to play notes the people want to hear, and not the notes he knows he must. Now some would say that he should play the notes he must to calm the savage crowd — then play the proper notes alone, or only to his chosen friends. But then I think the man becomes divided. Why should he play tunes he doesn't really love except to do so when he absolutely must? The sweetest songs will nauseate the player when his heart lies elsewhere. Slowly, he will find the means to play the songs the people want to hear as seldom as he can — and then he must be tempted to forgo the people's songs entirely. But when he gives that effort up he's crossed the line to tyranny.

Director: It's tyranny because he fails to play the soothing songs? How strange. But if a tyranny evolves exactly as you say, then tyrants favor those who play the tune of nature, right? I think that this is what you'd like to see, my friend. So are you arguing in favor of a tyranny? Do you desire to be a member of the tyrant's chosen few?

Introvert: Oh no! I think the tyrant has gone wrong in letting others place their faith in him! That sets him down this awful path!

Director: Is that the lie the tyrant tells that works his doom? He's saying, in effect, "Have faith in me and you'll do well?"

Introvert: I think that that's exactly what he says. I also think, however, that at first he must believe it's true — but later come to see it's not — and only when he's gone so far that there's no turning back. It's then he really starts to lie.

Director: So if we're not a member of his chosen few, that means he's lying to us, right?

Introvert: And more — especially if he detects that we are privy to the truth. He'll want to kill us, Director, if we don't lie as well.

Director: And that's the note that's false that we can't play? So now the question has to be what note to play. Perhaps a different sort of lie is right. You've said it's possible a lie will work in order to avoid a note that's false. Is that the thing to do?

Extrovert: But if we lie to him what does that do to us? We might ourselves become the thing we hate! If we convince ourselves it's right to lie, what happens in the end? We might begin to lie about the motives of our acts! We might be speaking of the greater good but really only thinking of ourselves!

Director: Well, if you want to know if one who talks about the greater good is really thinking only of himself, it's best for you to speak with him apart — without the noise of politics — to hear if false notes sound within his tune. An expert might perceive a note that's sour amongst the crush of politics — but you are only starting out, my friend.

Extrovert: But selfish men like that would never give you opportunity to question them alone!

Director: Well, if that's true then you have got good reason for your doubts. But let's suppose you speak with one of them apart and find a man who holds a faith that's true — a man who plays his instrument quite well. It isn't likely that he'd be a tyrant, right?

Extrovert: Of course!

Director: Well, that is good — but doesn't necessarily imply that he is truly wise. Your brother wants the wise to rule.

Introvert: That's right — it takes a special sort of man to solve the prime political dilemma. How will he give everyone what he deserves? When everyone has got what's right for him there is no need for lies. All notes ring true. The music's simply good. But there is dissonance when people do not get what they deserve. But who can know what everyone deserves and then confer those things? To know in full detail would take omniscience. Then to have the power to distribute rightly all the goods the state provides would take a tyranny that's absolute. And that's the reason that I think the state requires the use of lies. It isn't possible to make the music fully good in any other way.

Director: Is it so hard to know if someone's done good work, deserving payment on fair terms?

Introvert: If only that were all it takes!

Director: But don't transactions just like this make up the bulk of daily life?

Introvert: That may be so in day-to-day affairs. But there is more in play than trade. The state must always keep an eye out for the safety of the group. When there's a danger to the state, the people all begin to think that they deserve more say in what to do than's right.

Director: But is that really true? You mean to say that you don't think the people know who's best to lead? Why, if the people were upon a ship that entered troubled waters they would seek the pilot who had navigated waters such as that before. And if the people started getting sick they'd search both high and low to find a doctor who could make them well. The same is true if neighbors threaten war. The people want a general who will win.

Introvert: A lot of people seem to think they know the job of generalling although they've never fought a war.

Extrovert: But don't you think they'd see the truth that, even though they might be good at something, if another comes along whose better then it's he who has to lead?

Good the Enemy of Better?

Introvert: But people have a tendency to crack when under stress. They fail to choose the better choice. Besides, with stress or not, you know that there's a reason why they say that good's the enemy of better.

Director: Introvert, I don't know what to say to that. What do you think that saying means?

Introvert: It means the good are jealous of their betters, Director. It seems to me the center of the question's here. While I'm not sure that there's a need for lies, there might be need of something that resembles them. The better, when denied because of what they are, might have to learn to hide themselves from those who're not as good. What else can someone better do when he who rules denies or fails to see his worth, and then attempts to dominate by means of rules and laws? A better man who won't submit to rule by lesser men is always marked as dangerous. At best, they'll think he's gone insane. At worst, they'll think that he's a heretic or witch. It seems to me that he has got no choice except to live as a fugitive or find a way to veil himself from envy's sight.

Extrovert: But what's the cost of doing that? You'd only reinforce the ruler's prejudices. Life is hard, at times — but hiding out can only make it worse.

Besides, you know false modesty's as bad as arrogance. When rulers do not know the proper way to play their instruments — to know and act upon the truth — then we must teach them how, or drive them from their rule.

Introvert: And if they do not learn and we can't muster up the force it takes to bring them down?

Extrovert: Then still we shouldn't hide. They need to see it's best to let the better lead — and that the better are not cowards.

Director: Why might they think they have to keep the better men in check?

Extrovert: I think they just assume that might makes right, and that the better ones are fools who can't or won't accept this fact. They simply grab as much as possible. They do not have the sort of pride that won't allow the use of any means. They think that every starving man would lie, or steal, or kill for bread. They're not aware that some still have a pride too strong for that — a pride that even overcomes the love of life. A few still stand on principle and choose a painful death above a shameful act. To some extent, I have to say I think that Critic's right. Our need for dignity's the highest need we've got. I only disagree with him on how it's won. To lie destroys one's dignity.

Director: You think a man who lies for food has switched a better thing for worse?

Extrovert: That's right. To some the truth's a greater thing than food.

Director: And dignity is more important than the truth?

Extrovert: That's not the way I'd put it, Director.

Director: Well, maybe honesty is greater than the truth?

Extrovert: That doesn't make much sense. You can't be honest without truth.

Director: So which is greater, Extrovert, the raw materials or what they serve to make? Are bricks and wood superior to homes?

Extrovert: The home's the greater thing, of course.

Director: You can't have homes without the bricks and wood, just like you can't have honesty without the truth. So what's the problem here? It seems to me that honesty is greater than the truth.

Extrovert: I guess you're right. It just sounds odd.

Director: That's not surprising, Extrovert, because the question here is what's the worth of truth, and there are very few who ask this question earnestly — and then set out to know. I think that many ask themselves the question, "What is truth?" But do they really want to know?

Extrovert: But how can we set to know the worth of truth when truth is what we use to value everything?

Director: You act as though you weren't aware that many people do not set their values to the tune of truth. Their instruments are calibrated differently, it seems. Their scales are false.

Extrovert: Well, that's because they do not know the truth. The standard of all things is truth, so any other way of measure must be false — and that is all there is to say. The "value" of the truth in valuing is that it works.

Director: Then that's its value, Extrovert — the truth's expedience, the goodness of the policy of honesty. You know, I think I see the thing your brother sees between the good and better, as he says. I think he means to say that good upholds a standard that is not the truth.

Introvert: That's right. The question then is why be honest to the ones who do not use the truth to do their valuing, to make their judgments — if it means that we will come to harm when we submit to standards other than our own?

Director: We'll come to harm? I thought we said the value of the truth's expedience?

Introvert: It is, but we'll expose, by virtue of our standard, falsity in those who claim that they maintain a different standard than the truth — and they will want to take revenge.

Director: I see. Well, what's the standard that these so-called "good" maintain?

Introvert: They say their standard is the good of others. Once they've set this as the end they justify their every act, their every means — and these include, of course, quite shameless means — against this lie.

Director: And do you think they never really think of others' good?

Introvert: I know they don't, though some of them believe they do.

Director: And do you think that those who rally to the truth should also lie and claim a standard other than their own, that they should hide within the Trojan horse until they get within the city walls?

Introvert: I'm only open to the possibility that sometimes that's the thing to do. Besides, how else can we persuade them if we do not use their terms?

Director: Take care, my friend. There is a danger here of entering a maze from which you won't return to ever see the light of day again. Are you aware of what you risk in taking steps like this?

Introvert: I think I am. These people won't back down. How can they? If they do, their own supporters start to turn on them. They've backed themselves into a corner. Talking in their standard's terms it might be possible for one to demonstrate how they can get themselves out of that spot without provoking harm. They always talk about how people have to get the things that they deserve — it's just that they assume dessert will follow from the use of wily means. Adherents to the standard of another's good assume they know what everyone deserves. They really don't believe in free exchange of services and goods, although at times they say they do. They factor in a weight for "moral worth," and they demand that others do so, too. Of course, the only "moral" that they praise is loyalty to any cause that lends support to their own wealth. So they demand that others value this and thus ensure a payoff for themselves and all the ones who serve their cause.

Extrovert: But if we hide within the Trojan Horse and lie to them, by saying that we hold the standard of another's good and not the truth, aren't we the same as them — the bearers of a standard that we do not rally to ourselves?

Introvert: I think that we can find a way to handle things so that we keep ourselves distinct from them. We might adopt their standard, use their formula — but with a meaning of our own. The good of others? Everyone must have an instrument that's made and strung and played the proper way! If that's the truth, then that's our meaning — if it's not, our meaning changes as we learn. It's not a lie — it's honesty in our belief. We will not lie in speaking of another's good. We'll tell them what we really think. And we will care if they do well or ill, unlike the others telling them they act for their own good. We do not act on their behalf, we simply tell them what we think. We'll bring the better of the good to see. They'll find their leaders always lie to them. But all we need to do is make them think. The implications of their leaders' words will do the rest — once they are understood. The closest of the inner circle see the difference that there is between the promised things and what is really done. The children of the leaders know this best. The ones with natures that are good — the "betters," as it were — will slowly come to see what standard truly flies, and what it means in practice. Gradually, they'll change the meaning of the words they use themselves and, with great effort, bring them closer to the truth.

Director: That method seems to me to almost certainly precipitate a crisis, Introvert.

Introvert: That may well be. It has to come in any case.

Extrovert: All this by way of showing them the nature of their standard?

Introvert: Yes. We simply show them what it is, and what is possible. Then they decide themselves.

Extrovert: That sort of work is dangerous.

Introvert: It is, and this is why we have to operate from knowledge, slowly — by degrees. The better ones who'll understand the import of our words depend, by luck of birth, upon the "fruits" of reason that has taught that "moral" men deserve their wealth. In changing how they reason they will have to deal with all the leaders of the "good" who seize the goods of those they deem immoral — those who don't support the standard that they claim. They seize the goods they have no proper right to claim. But we will only seek what's rightly ours.

Director: You sound as though you mean to claim much more than wealth.

Introvert: I do, of course.

Director: It's hard to see exactly what you mean. But let's consider only money, for right now. Supposing that we hear about a man with lots of cash who has no knowledge of its proper use. He is a fool. What principle would say that we should take his wealth and give it to another man who knows its use?

Introvert: A principle of knowledge, *Director.*

Director: Is that a variation on the theme of others' good?

Introvert: It is in its effect. They'd confiscate the goods with peace of mind, and say that what they do is good and right.

Director: But isn't there some truth in what they say?

Introvert: Well, that's the question, Director.

Director: It isn't good to have a thing but not to know its use, correct?

Introvert: If one misuses it, that's true; but if one makes no use of it at all then that is neither good nor bad.

Extrovert: But isn't that a waste?

Introvert: It is, indeed.

Extrovert: And you don't think that waste is bad?

Introvert: I don't, as long as "waste" is not "destroy." To use a thing improperly destroys. To leave a thing alone is only that. If you don't know the way to drive you'd better leave the engine off.

Director: Is it the same with wealth?

Introvert: It is.

Director: So money's not a special case.

Introvert: It's not, but may be harder than the rest because its uses are complex.

Director: I see. With something simple, then, it's easier? A fishing pole's a simple thing.

Introvert: Indeed.

Director: We always know its proper use?

Introvert: The fishermen sure do.

Director: Well, what about a compass? That's a simple thing. So, do we always know its proper use?

Introvert: The navigators always know.

Director: Economists will know the proper use of cash?

Introvert: Not always.

Director: What's the difference?

Introvert: Everyone has got to know the use of wealth, at least to some degree. A currency is meant to be a universal mark of value. Everyone should know the value of a dollar, but they don't.

Director: The value of the dollar shows the value of the thing it buys?

Introvert: It should, but it's all relative to what the people with money want.

Director: You mean it's not the value absolute.

Introvert: That's right. The truth of something's value's often quite unclear. They say that money is the root of evil. That's not really it — it's valuing a thing improperly.

Director: To value something properly you've got to know exactly what it is, which means to take the measure of the thing — to learn its quantities to know its quality.

Introvert: Of course. And that's the only way to know what's good and better, too.

Director: Now, do we always get it right when measuring?

Introvert: Of course we don't.

Director: And do we sometimes lie about the measurements we take?

Introvert: They're those who do.

Director: Now why would they do that? I thought that knowing something's value makes us know its proper use.

Introvert: That's true — or else it just might be the other way around. I think that they're the same, essentially.

Director: Then do they lie because they want exclusive use themselves?

Introvert: That might be it.

Director: The foolish man who doesn't know the use of money doesn't really know what money is?

Introvert: That's right.

Director: But someone knowing money's worth might lie to take it from the fool to use it all himself. So does that mean he's put it to its proper use? Or must he try to teach the fool the truth about his wealth before he does a thing like that?

Introvert: It's better if he does. But it's not clear to me how possible it is for fools to learn.

Director: That's certainly a problem. Let's assume, for now, that he's not capable of learning. He's an imbecile. Or we are imbeciles, because we cannot teach another how to value properly. In either case, instead of taking wealth by naked use of force, it's better to persuade, to have him hand the money over with his full consent to those who know its proper use.

Introvert: It is. But we have got to give the reasons why it's best for all involved. And if he doesn't listen to our reasons, when they're sound, then he's irrational, it seems.

Extrovert: Well, do you think that it's alright to lie to the irrational?

Introvert: I think that it might be alright to lie in order to prevent a harm. Is taking money from a fool preventing harm? That's not so clear. We've got to know what truly constitutes a harm.

Director: Is that the only difficulty?

Introvert: No, the other's how we know that reason's truly on our side. I mean, we might confuse desire for wealth with right. And then we start to lie to satisfy our greed.

Director: Well, I would think that dialogue should show where reason lies.

Introvert: But what if we cannot persuade the fool? What then?

Director: Why, that's what we are asking, Introvert. Is it the time to lie when reason fails? But that assumes that lies have power to persuade. It's this phenomenon that's rather odd. What gives the lie its power? Truth is what persuades — and that which seems to be the truth. Well, what would make a fool take lies for truth except the very thing that makes him be a fool? Illusions, Introvert. Belief in things that don't exist. The lie that casts its line toward imagined things will likely catch its prey.

Extrovert: I think you've got a point. He doesn't even know what money really is, what money really means. So he can't really want the money, anyway. He wants whatever he imagines real. He lives on his illusions. Lies will give him what he really wants. The truth will only take it all away.

Introvert: But I'm not sure that what we're saying's right! When wants are true, they're natural and therefore rational. The fool can't really want illusions, Extrovert. You cannot really want to have a thing you do not understand — and can you understand a thing that isn't true? The wealthy fool's confused, and that is rather sad. He doesn't really know his own desires, and that's the reason why he is a fool.

Extrovert: Confused? I'll tell you what he is. He wants to have his cake and eat it, too! He's lazy! That's the reason why a lie has power over him. A liar sees him eating cake and tells him, sure, just go on eating and you'll still have cake for later when you're done. He would convince him that he'll always have more cake, or that he'll always come across it easily. There is no need to worry now, he'd say. Don't think of winter in the summer's heat. But that's the liar's way. It isn't mine. When fools can't learn I think that men of reason must decide to leave them well enough alone, that's all.

Director: But can't we show the fool that there's a way to make his money grow by placing it with those who know its proper use? But maybe growing's not the only thing. Is that only end of money? Growth?

Introvert: It isn't, Director. The money has to serve a proper cause, a cause beyond itself. The greedy ones don't care at all for money's proper use. They'll lie and lie again in order to obtain more funds and dissipate themselves.

Extrovert: There's nothing we can do to stop them from this waste. A fool's a fool, that's all. We shouldn't give him any more than what he has. Besides, to talk of money's well and good, but I still think the problem of the man who wields the gun is more important to discuss. The harm we want to stop is much more clear. If reason fails to stop the man I say our recourse next must be to force. We must defend ourselves. The violent, greedy, and irrational will overrun us if we fail to stop them cold when they use force. The duty of the better is precisely that.

Director: If we're agreed that force must be the means of last resort, it seems we need a string of self-defense upon our instrument, a principle we hold within our soul to guide our actions here. But, Introvert, what troubles you?

Introvert: I'm not so sure it's better to use force than lies.

Extrovert: You doubt that there's a right of self-defense?

Introvert: Of course I don't. But if we can defend ourselves without the use of force would we be right to disavow these other means without a full consideration?

Extrovert: That depends upon what means you mean, and if they're honorable — and if they'll even work. You'd better be prepared to give it back when someone uses fire in a fight. You won't survive in any other way. And what's the good of mere survival if it comes by stooping down to use the basest means?

Introvert: But if the gunman's really only scared, believing that he's acting in his self-defense, and not aggressive in the least, should we use force on him?

Extrovert: You're too concerned with giving everyone full justice, brother. No one has a right to wave a gun around like that — regardless why he thinks he should. You think that you will speak good reason and allay his fears? The gun's the clearest sign that he's not listening.

Introvert: Should we refuse to try because he has a gun?

Extrovert: You're saying that the use of force on him is wrong as long as he is listening?

Introvert: I am.

Extrovert: That can't go on indefinitely while he has got the gun — assuming someone wants to take the risk to speak with him. So where's the line?

Introvert: We stop when it becomes quite clear that it's impossible to make him stop with words.

Director: And those are either truth or lie, whatever works?

Introvert: A lie will not persuade unless it's cast at an illusion — just as you have said. And if it is, at best it buys some time, creating other problems as it does, until the crazy acting man's illusions have been lost. The power of a lie, of course, is in its seeming truth. But there's a danger that must come when reason is employed to make the false appear as true. The people start to fear the reasoners. They know that something's wrong, but cannot say exactly what it is. If people see us lying to the man who's got the gun, they've got to start to wonder why we wouldn't lie to them. So trust's at stake. And that's the problem if we lie to calm the man who's acting crazy with the gun. He's got to trust enough to open up to what we say. He must be willing to consider that he's wrong. What happens if he sees that he's been duped? We've got to make him see. We've got to make him understand that what he's doing's wrong.

Extrovert: You want to bring his conscience into play?

Introvert: There's all the difference in the world between a reasoned argument and playing tunes on someone's conscience, Extrovert! I am afraid that if we start to lie we might lose sight of this distinction.

Director: Playing tunes on someone's conscience, as you put it — which I take to mean not showing him how he's gone wrong, but rather taking full advantage of some error that he holds about a matter of import — is a perverted use of reason, isn't it?

Introvert: It surely is.

Director: Well, let's consider two non-violent ways to reach the man who wields the gun — the way of reason true, and the perverted way. And for the sake of argument, we shall assume that each succeeds in getting him to put the gun away. Now, what's his motivation in each case? The man perverting reason makes him lose the gun by playing on his conscience — making him feel guilty, which must leave him as a spiritual cripple. Reason shows the other that there is another way. He may fulfill his want, whatever that may be, through means of which he hadn't thought — or thought to be impossible without the gun. Do you agree that this is all the difference in these different ways?

Introvert: I do.

Director: Which way is more effective means to guarantee the man won't ever wave the gun again?

Introvert: The way of reason, Director.

Director: And why?

Introvert: For guilt to work it must be reinforced, and nearly all the time. A rational persuasion, though, requires only that the man can grasp, by efforts of his own, the truth — and nothing else is necessary. Playing on the conscience only leads us to a great police state of the spirit.

Extrovert: If persuasion fails, it's better then that we make use of force instead of mental bullying.

Introvert: But that's a false dichotomy!

Extrovert: Oh, brother! Why must you subject yourself to torture in this way? What other option do you see?

Introvert: That someone with a knowledge of humanity must find a way to talk the gunman down, and that it's his own fault if he cannot — because he cannot see what drives the man who seems insane.

Extrovert: The fault's not yours! I know you're thinking of yourself. You think that you must crack each nut that comes your way? You can't be blamed for what you do not know, but only what you think you know and don't! You think too much!

Introvert: I only think that reason's not just empty words — it has a force its own that men of knowledge have to learn to wield!

Extrovert: Oh, I agree! But only in a certain sense! Our reason only works with those who listen! Guns are means for stopping up the ears and silencing the tongue!

Introvert: And there has got to be a reason why a man would go that way!

Extrovert: Then find it! Find it fast! But if you can't, then rest assured that I won't cower from a crazy with a gun!

Director: So what's the way to find the reason for the gun?

Introvert: We've got to find out what he really wants.

Director: And then we use his own desire to take him down?

Introvert: Perhaps. I mean, we've got to show him how to get the things he wants — but using proper means.

Extrovert: Ah, there you go again! We're all supposed to sit around and wait while you are teaching him the way to live. But don't forget that there can be no proper means to satisfy irrational desire.

Introvert: You shouldn't say "irrational" since all desire's exactly that. Desire's blind, while reason's what we use to see.

Director: But even though it's blind, do you consider that desire is natural?

Introvert: Of course desire is natural. There's no unnatural desire.

Extrovert: What's that? And when a man desires to eat his cake and have it still that's only natural, of course! Then nature's what we've got to fight! Come on! Your "good" are always lazy, wanting things they don't deserve. The better sort must work for everything and only hope to gather in the harvest of the seeds they've sown before the fruits are stolen by the lesser men.

Introvert: You really think that effort is the only difference?

Extrovert: Effort and a dash of common sense.

Introvert: Suppose the better get exhausted from the constant strain, the efforts that they have to make that almost always go unseen. You know that they're not lazy in the least. Suppose the one who's acting crazy with the gun is of this better class but he has reached the point of breaking down. We'll have to take account of this when reasoning with him — and if we don't, our reason's bad. A man will always listen if your reason's truly good.

Extrovert: That's nuts! Are you forgetting that some people are irrational? Sound reason is ignored by many every day. And why is that? If not because of laziness then maybe it's because they are afraid of losing something they possess — a thing they know they don't deserve. And further still, they may be angry at the one who sees the way — the way of reason — to obtain the longed-for end, because they'd have to do a thing that they don't want to do — and not because they're lazy (though that's what lies at bottom here, in my opinion).

Director: Why might they not want to do the thing required by the end?

Extrovert: Oh, how should I know that? They just don't want to.

Introvert: They might think that it's immoral.

Director: So they do not will the means — or should I say they will themselves to drop the means but keep the end?

Introvert: They will themselves to not do something they desire. They fight themselves and what they really want.

Extrovert: Well, if they love the end they've got to court the means.

Introvert: That's why they have to scrutinize their hearts.

Director: But can they really want the end if all the means to it repulse them so?

Extrovert: They must not fully understand the end they think they want.

Director: Well, do you think that ends and means should go together naturally?

Extrovert: Of course.

Director: To want the one without the other's wrong?

Extrovert: It is — and it's the height of unclear thought.

Director: So that would be a way to judge a person's rationality — to see if what he wants and what he does are of a piece.

Extrovert: That's right.

Director: What do you think could make a man become irrational?

Extrovert: You know my answer — laziness.

Introvert: It might just be a lack of knowledge, too. But maybe something else — and something worse.

Director: A thing that's worse than ignorance? What's that?

Introvert: Suppression of the knowledge causing end and means to correspond. A man might fail to use the means he has to get the thing he wants — and he might use those means and yet deny he wants the end to which they point.

Extrovert: All politicians have the latter down — without the pang of conscience, to be sure — and fools are guilty of the folly of the failure to employ their proper means.

Director: What happens to the fools who really want to reach an end but fail to take the proper steps?

Extrovert: They forfeit happiness. They lose their chance at greatness, too. Oblivion's in store for them on death. Our memories of them soon fade.

Director: Then what about the politicians?

Extrovert: They, at least, will have their infamy. That's something, Director — but not the thing for me.

Director: You think that infamy is better than oblivion?

Extrovert: To win a name is hard — and that's the ugly truth. The better people win themselves a name. I've seen enough to know there's virtue even in a villain. Still, the best earn fame for noble deeds.

Director: But let's suppose we prod the ignorant, the fools, and all the lazy ones with reasoned argument, attempting to persuade the squaring of their actions, means, and ends. What manner of reaction do you think we'll get? Will they all strive to win themselves a name?

Extrovert: I'm sure they won't! If you go stirring them you're bound to make them angry, Director.

Introvert: That might be so with many, but it's not the sole response you'll get.

Director: What else should I prepare for?

Introvert: Fear.

Director: Why, people say that fear and anger stand opposed. You really think that if I prod and stir the ignorant, the fools, and all the lazy ones I should expect completely opposite reactions then? An opposite response suggests a different cause — and yet I thought the cause of what would happen here is just my poking into means and ends, to see if everything adds up, if they amount to part and whole.

Introvert: A catalyst initiates a different chemical reaction when it's mixed with different elements. But that in no way means that reason ever fails. It all depends on what we hope for or expect.

Director: Which places all the burden on the shoulders of the reasoner.

Introvert: Exactly where it should be placed.

Director: Then let's proceed to press this weight and think the matter through. The elements in this, our chemistry, are individuals, it seems. If someone stops his ears against our arguments, he's got to be an individual who feels the force or power in those words. I think he's got to feel there's reason there, or else he'd never try to ward off reason's threat with anger or to flee that "threat" in fear. But what's the kind of man — the kind of element — that thinks or feels that reason is a threat?

Extrovert: The kind of man who has a standing that he hasn't earned. The reason that he hears reminds him of this fact he thought he could forget. So anger serves to shout down reason's calling to account, and fear allows the man to run away and think he's only acting in his self-defense.

Director: These sort of men are happy where they stand before we look into their means and ends?

Extrovert: Oh no — I think that they must be quite miserable.

Director: Yet when they hear the voice of reason telling them they're in a bad position they will stop their ears as if we were so many sirens luring them to doom?

Extrovert: They surely will — and then they will entrench themselves to make the matter worse. They're all afraid that they'll be tricked. Suspicious as the guilty always are, they do not want to lose the things they've got and keep a wary watch for any sign of arguments reminding them of what they'd heard from us that set them off. They'll say the man who speaks the truth is false. They're probably the type who lie so much they just assume that everybody else is lying, too. They must assume that everyone is jealous of the things they've got by virtue of their place. It's easier for them to think this way because it's jealousy they feel most deeply in their hearts. They're jealous of the ones who hold a higher place — and for the better sort, the ones who're really worth their weight in gold, they only feel contempt, because they sense that they don't value things with scales the same as theirs. A man's desire bespeaks the character he makes and not his given nature — that's what differentiates the individual.

Director: They clearly think that they're the better sort of man.

Extrovert: Well, that is what they must persuade themselves they are. They want their place and rank beyond all things, deserved or not.

Director: Well, in the case of things, the man who knows their proper use deserves them most?

Extrovert: That's right.

Director: And in the case of power do you think that it's the same?

Extrovert: It is indeed.

Director: And what of honor?

Extrovert: That's a different thing. It goes to those who know the proper use of things, or place, and use them well.

Director: So knowledge that one acts upon should bring both things and place — and honors, too. But won't the thing or place alone suffice? Or must there always be some honor, too?

Extrovert: The honor that's conferred on those who know the proper use of things or place is only natural. It serves to spur the others on to learn. But I agree that problems come from people wanting honors that they don't deserve. They want the honor, not the knowledge and the proper use.

Director: Well, I'd assume that those who hold positions that they don't deserve must have some things they've got to learn to use before they have a chance of learning how to use their place. It seems to me that all positions presuppose a knowledge of the use of certain things. A fisherman, for instance — regardless of his place within the hierarchy of his trade — possesses knowledge of both line and bait, or else he's not a fisherman at all. It seems to me that there's no different proper use of things depending on one's place.

Extrovert: If one's to make a proper use of things belonging to one's place, that's true. But that's not how it always seems to go.

Director: But what about the way that one relates to others? Does the proper way of treating people change depending on one's rank?

Extrovert: The way to treat a man's the same no matter where one stands. To act in any other way is either patronizing, or obsequious.

Director: So there aren't different proper ways of doing things depending on the nature of the person, right?

Extrovert: That's right. I'll never understand how anyone can fail to see that a fisherman must fish, no matter who or what he is.

Director: Of course. Just as the cooks must cook, no matter who or what they are — and critics criticize, no matter who or what they are — and students learn, no matter who or what they are. What happens if you point this out to those who see it differently?

Extrovert: They scorn you as a fool, and then, indignantly, refuse to speak with you again. Your understanding's far beneath their own, they seem to think, and you can't see what noble notion motivates their acts. But they don't know the way to do their proper work, and there is nothing we can do with force or lies or any other thing to make them learn. The only thing to do is call a spade a spade, and drive these people, openly, out from the places that they hold.

Introvert: And if we haven't got the power, what?

Director: Well, maybe we can show them that they've got to face a threat far greater than an argument can ever be. Their false opinions of themselves must surely cause them harm.

Extrovert: But they're not willing to exert the effort that it takes to gain a knowledge of themselves — and I'm not sure they'd like the things they'd see. That's why we've got this problem in the first place, Director.

Introvert: That might be right for many, but I'm sure that it's not right for all. The pressures on some people, causing them to act the way they do, aren't always obvious. Their families and their friends will prop their false opinions up in hopes of getting benefits from their success. They flatter the deluded ones so much, their lies are soon relied upon — and even cherished. Time works flattery into a web so strong the self-deceived are only fit to serve as food for spiders.

Keystone to a Whole Personality

Director: There's little doubt the worst of lies are those we tell ourselves. But do you think the flattered ones must always come to tell themselves the lies they're told?

Introvert: They almost always do.

Director: And what's the ground they've got to stand on when they don't?

Introvert: The truth. But how they might arrive at truth about themselves when faced with all these lies is hard to see.

Extrovert: It's not so hard to see the truth. What's hard is overcoming the desire to think much better of ourselves than we deserve. We tend to give ourselves the benefits of all the doubts — and even where there is no doubt we tend to think there is. We must accept when there's no doubt then brace ourselves to reach inside and tear out any lie that's sprouted like a weed within our soul — for doubt is fertile soil for weed-like lies to grow.

Introvert: But lies like that are deeply rooted, Extrovert. Of course with weeds it's best to pull them out. But don't you think a lie like this is more a keystone to an arch than weed within the ground — an arch that represents one's personality?

Extrovert: Oh no. I think a weed's a better image here because a character that's founded on a lie will creep instead of vault. But if we say your metaphor is best, then we will have to say the structure capped (or founded, for that matter) with the lie is shaky, Introvert, and it must fall if we're to build a better structure in its place.

Introvert: And if the shaky personality belongs to one who rules? Collapse in rulers brings the state and all its citizens to grief — unless provision's made for what's to come before the fall occurs.

Director: Well, let's consider this. If we're to knock a faulty structure down we'll have to do as blasters do before they undertake a demolition. They must make a careful study of the building and the general site. They need to know exactly where to place the charges so the damage is contained, destroying only what must go to clear the ground. Now, if we hope to blast a lie right out of someone's soul, it seems to me we ought to take at least as much precaution. Wouldn't you agree? We'll have to ask, "What sort of man? What sort of lie?" The devil's in the details here.

Extrovert: Of course. We've got to take account of how the man will likely act when put to proof about the lie. Will he react with fear, or maybe anger? What will be the consequences?

Director: If the man reacts with fear, will he let go the lie that grips his soul — or should I say the lie his soul has gripped?

Extrovert: He won't. He might convince himself the lie's a principle that he must stand upon. He'll grow more tense and guarded in his ways. He'll be a nervous coward hoping that he seems to be a principled, courageous man. But he will even fail to fool himself. A brave man stands on principle that's sound, and not on lies.

Director: Well, what about the angry man?

Extrovert: I think he'll also try to tell himself the lie's a principle he must defend. In doing this he'll play the righteous fool.

Director: The cases seem quite similar. If fearful men are only separated from their angry cousins by a difference in the self-assessment of their strength, then all we've got to know is that a man who thinks he's strong enough to challenge any truth will boil with anger when the blasts go off — while one who thinks he's weak will quake with fear.

Introvert: But we must also understand the way they view the principles behind the flattery. An angry man decides the principle is sound, without another thought. The coward starts to think the principle is weak, but fears to contemplate replacing it.

Director: But don't you think that either must suspect that his foundation's weak? Of course, a principle is quite a different thing than strength. Our principles affect the way we use the power that we've got. The prime and truest strength cannot maintain itself without sound principle. A weakened inner principle is bound to run whatever ship a man is piloting aground — and that's because the principle's the rudder to the ship. But what's the thing that really separates the hotheads and the gutless fools — supposing that the principle behind their flattery's the same? Is it their natural degree of strength — or their evaluation of their power — or a difference in their temperament — or something of the three combined? Why, don't you wonder if they differ by their nature or their choice? Could certain principles inhere to someone's nature, Introvert? Or do they merely come from nurture? Either way, we've got to know the way to verify the principle itself — regardless whence it comes. It seems to me that if a person estimates his strength upon a principle, it's got to matter greatly if that principle's correct. Is that the way it seems to you? It also seems to me, however, that it's got to matter if a principle belongs inherently to what one is — if it belongs to one's own kind. But how are we to know what principles belong to certain types? Is this a matter of just idle curiosity? A man might take it on himself to forge a better character through effort of his will. But what if he is operating on some lie? Does all his effort go for naught? What tragedy! Our nature and our character are different things, as Extrovert believes. Our nature's what we have to start with and our character's the thing we make of it. When building character it's necessary that one choose a principle to guide the work. So what's the principle that one should choose in breaking ground but truth?

Extrovert: That's right! The truth is what shall set us free! But it takes strength to live according to the truth. A man is sound of character when he makes choices based upon the truth, and nothing else. It all depends upon the choices that we make. But what we choose, to some degree, of course, depends upon the nature that we've got. Some natures are quite gentle. Some are very fierce. Not everyone who's fiercely tempered loses all control. Not everyone who's gentle natured causes no one harm. And why is this but for the choices that they make in how to live, and whether evil gains the upper hand to rule their lives? So if we want to root the lie right out, our tactics have to change according to the sort of character confronting us. The probability of our success will change, of course, depending on the tactics that we choose, our execution, and the difficulty of the job itself.

Director: What sort of character will give us better odds, in your opinion, Extrovert?

Extrovert: The gentle sort, of course. The fierce are much more difficult. They're much more likely to resist.

Director: Well, is the truth the only charge that we can use to blast the lie? Or is there something special we should save to use against the harder sort?

Extrovert: If there's a thing that's better than the truth for work like this then I am at a loss to know what it might be. The truth is quite a charge! It's very volatile. Accordingly, when bearing truth we must approach our targets gradually — especially the ones who're fierce. They're sensitive to truth. We must reveal the truth to them a little at a time, to see how they'll react. They're apt to lose their temper and attack the messenger, you know.

Director: I would have thought that we'd approach the gentle ones quite gingerly as well.

Extrovert: We will, of course. I can't see any point in getting hurt because of someone else's lie — regardless if they're gentle or they're fierce. We must prepare ourselves for those who'll wage a war against the truth — especially the ones who're fierce, since they're the toughest ones to fight.

Director: I'm not so sure about the way you work the odds. If it is really true that we're at greater risk with those who're fierce, then we might think that our reward for victory against the fierce will far surpass whatever comes from conquering the ones who fear.

Extrovert: That seems to follow, doesn't it? The fierce ones work more harm, by far. So any victory against their sort must work the greatest benefit at large.

Director: Perhaps. But with the gentle ones you think the risk to us is less because they'll bolt? That's what a coward does, correct?

Extrovert: That's right. They flee the argument as soon as fear begins to take a hold of them.

Director: And when they've fled you think that they'll forget the things we've said that made them fear?

Extrovert: I think they'll try, but fail.

Director: And when they think of what we've said it won't be pleasant, right?

Extrovert: To say the least.

Director: So do you think they'll want revenge?

Extrovert: They might, but they might fear too much to ever try. An angry enemy won't hesitate — and that's the reason why we've got to fear this sort the most. Oh, I well know we can't just write the cowards off. I take your point. They're dangerous when left alone to stew and plot. The more the reason not to scare them off when we are laying charges with the truth! We've got to catch them unaware.

Introvert: Your method of approaching gingerly itself appears to be a sort of lie. I mean, you have intention to mislead the one to whom you speak if it appears that he's about to burst in anger or to flee in fear.

Extrovert: I hardly think a prudent method constitutes a lie. But granting that you're right, we said that if it's ever right to lie it's to the ones who act irrational — and it's irrational to stay in places where you don't belong because you've taken flattery to be the truth. When someone holds a rank beyond his skill it's likely that he'll cause some harm — and haven't we considered that preventing harm can justify the lie? But I don't think the method I've described amounts to that. Who doesn't act like this in everyday affairs? It's true we say in court we swear to tell the truth — the whole truth — nothing but the truth. But is it really wrong, when we're not under oath, to offer less than all the truth we know? Come on!

Director: What's this I hear? You say that you don't think each word we speak should come as if it's under oath?

Extrovert: Well, yes, of course — but in a different sense.

Director: What sense is that? You're hoping to deceive? Deception's not a lie?

Extrovert: Deception doesn't slander truth when practiced on the ones who value truth too low or not at all. There can't be any obligation that we share our thoughts with everyone! We only share our inner thoughts with people that we trust. If someone doesn't value what we say, and goes so far as using it against us, I, for one, would say it's wrong to tell him all the truth. There's evil in this world! Discretion saves.

Introvert: Well, do we just abruptly stop revealing truth to someone fierce as soon as he becomes irrational? Or do we start to lie to cover tracks?

Extrovert: We don't — we surely don't! It's not that cut and dry — as you, of all, are well aware. We steer the conversation on to other things — a skill I've seen you demonstrate on more than one occasion, Introvert. That doesn't mean we lie. We simply don't tell all the truth. We'd rather tell it all, of course — whenever that is possible.

Director: But can't you tell the truth entire to everyone? Why, even if a man's not listening it's surely possible to speak the truth to him.

Extrovert: What good is it if he's not listening?

Director: You mean if he's completely deaf?

Extrovert: Not literally, of course — but in a sense I do.

Director: You mean to say no matter what, the truth will not persuade? Is that because the other's not a sympathetic soul?

Extrovert: I think that's more the thing. He might be listening, but truth does not affect him in the way it should.

Introvert: Affect him in the way it should? The truth is only shown through reasoned argument! It may be true to say, "You are not fit for this." But if we cannot demonstrate, then there's no point to what we say. The problem isn't with the listener — it's with the one who does the reasoning!

Director: You mean to say that reasoned argument must bring a sympathy with truth, or else it isn't reasoned argument?

Introvert: I do! So you must know the reason why I'm doubtful of the method Extrovert prefers.

Extrovert: But when persuasion doesn't work you want to play the martyr, that's the thing? You must defend yourself! There's nothing wrong with that!

Introvert: I'll always try to keep myself from harm. But I am also always willing to endure some pain to see if it is possible to help a man to see the lie within his soul.

Extrovert: Well, burning at the stake won't help with that! Take care!

Director: What sort of talk is this? We've got to pull ourselves together, friends. We've got to find the reason that the lie's believed as true to know what we can do to root it out.

Extrovert: The lie's believed because it flatters, Director, that's all. It lets one think one's better than one is.

Introvert: The reason isn't always merely flattery. Suppose one's stuck within the web of lies because one has a secret one can't share.

Extrovert: Like what?

Introvert: A secret that is very deep — a secret that prevents our knowing all the truth about one's personality — the reason one's the way one is.

Extrovert: Oh, how mysterious! We'll have to find the secret out, and once we have we'll let "one" know the jig is up. One listens then, I bet.

Introvert: Or he'll be bent on killing us.

Extrovert: Perhaps, but now we've got some leverage on the man.

Director: We'll always have to keep a watch for deeply buried secrets then, it seems — and have to learn to tell the signs that one exists.

Introvert: For that one's got to know the nature of humanity, and then when something doesn't look quite right one must assume there's more than meets the eye.

Director: The nature of humanity? Why, Introvert, what do you mean? You'd see right through to someone's soul? You'd know when he is lying, then, and when he's not?

Introvert: I think that's possible, don't you?

Director: I want to know what you are saying first. You mean to say if someone asks a stranger if he's ever killed a man, for instance, then you'd know from how he answers if he's telling the truth? Or even if the question's something like, "What do you think about this man?" you'd see the way his soul's disposed from what he says and how he says it?

Introvert: Yes. I'd see the basic fact, although I wouldn't know details.

Director: The basic fact?

Introvert: The truth about the man.

Director: The truth about his character, his personality, and whether he has got a secret that he hides?

Introvert: That's right.

Extrovert: For that you've got to know if he has set his heart on something bad. The objects of the heart define the character, you know.

Introvert: You think that this is something he can choose? The heart's desire is simply what it is. The execution, not the want itself, is what will make a character go bad. It's not desire, it's only how we act on it that counts. The men whose characters are bad have failed to act on their desire as fit.

Director: Is that because they do not understand them very well?

Extrovert: What's there to understand? They want to steal, they steal — they want to kill, they kill. It seems they've got no problem getting what they want.

Introvert: But no one wants to steal for stealing's sake, and no one wants to kill for killing's sake. They do these things for something else they want. The problem's how they go about obtaining what they want. Why, even tyrants who obtain great power get it for the sake of something else.

Extrovert: What tyrants do you know?

Introvert: Potential tyrants.

Extrovert: If it's really possible to see potential tyranny in someone — if it's not potential that's inside us all — then how are we to find out what they truly want but fail to understand? That's how you think you'll help them, right?

Introvert: You ask them simple questions of the sort they think that everyone is too afraid to ask. Who knows? Our questioning might be for them a pleasant change of pace. The way that they react will lead us to the truth.

Director: The basic truth to know about a man is whether something's wrong within his soul?

Introvert: It is.

Director: And questioning reveals this fact.

Introvert: It does.

Director: Like when a doctor probes a wound for tenderness to see if it's infected?

Introvert: Yes.

Director: Suppose that during our examination of his soul he tells a blatant lie. Is that the sort of thing that shows there's something wrong?

Introvert: It does. Unless, of course, it's right for him to lie. A healthy soul will always do what's right.

Director: A man who knows what's right can surely say why he is doing what he does. So if he says it's right to lie, but can't explain the reason why, is that a sign that something's wrong?

Introvert: It is. He cannot really know the thing he thinks he does.

Director: The remedy for such an ill must be to see if there's a way to birth the truth he thinks he bears.

Introvert: I know. He's got to prove he isn't only babbling on about some feeling that he has.

Extrovert: What feeling's that? A sympathy for tyranny, it seems to me! If that's the thing you mean, this man is much too kind.

Introvert: It's not his kindness that's the question here. He feels he needs to know the reason why he feels the way he does. He thinks he knows it's not enough to feel and nothing more. He'd like his head to give articulation to his heart.

Extrovert: Are we to take the inner secrets of the heart, through all one's history, and lay them bare? What good can come of that? Now look, it's only natural if someone knows that something's wrong with someone else's soul to feel a sympathy for him. That's only human. But we can't allow this sympathy to cloud our judgment. Tyrants must be fought, not psychoanalyzed.

Introvert: But don't you want to know the cause of what one feels?

Extrovert: What's there to know? Well, maybe one's potentially a tyrant — that's the reason why one wants to know.

Introvert: And maybe one's afraid. But it may be the feeling that one has is not a sympathy at all, but something else — an indication of a truth one knows, if only in a latent form — because one can't articulate exactly what it is — a truth one has to birth. Just like it sometimes happens in our dreams, one goes to speak about the thing one sees but finds one has no voice.

Extrovert: In dreams like that you're always paralyzed by fear. If that's the case, you've got to conquer it.

Director: Don't people sometimes fail to tell the truth because of fear like this?

Extrovert: Oh yes.

Director: And do they sometimes lie because of fear?

Extrovert: I'm sure they do.

Director: But it's no lie if they believe they know a thing but only have a vague idea of what it is.

Extrovert: They're wrong, but honest, sure enough. They go to bed each night with conscience that is clear.

Director: Perhaps there's hope their honesty will give them opportunity to learn the truth about the thing they think they know. But do you really think they sleep at night — assuming that the thing of which we speak amounts to something that's significant — when only having hazy notions in their heads?

Extrovert: I think a lot of muddle-headed people sleep quite well.

Director: You think that's true if what's in question is their knowledge of themselves?

Extrovert: Most men are never stirred to self-examination, and they rest contented thinking that they're really something that they're not.

Director: Well, should we simply let them sleep?

Extrovert: I think that it depends on whether they hold places that aren't right for them — which is to say, if they are causing others harm.

Director: If we awaken them, and make them see their ignorance, is that enough to spur them on to learn the truth?

Extrovert: It's probably enough to spur them on to persecute the ones who wake them up!

Director: Well, might they not awaken on their own, without our rousing them?

Extrovert: I think that's very rare.

Director: And what would be the cause of that?

Extrovert: Perhaps uneasiness that they've done something wrong. Their consciences might cause them pain and make them see that they've been living in a dream.

Introvert: I think you've got the order wrong. They'll feel no pain until awake.

Extrovert: Then they may never wake unless we sound alarm.

Introvert: Perhaps with most. But there are those who do not need another's prompting, those who see a thing and want to understand, the ones who can't articulate exactly what they see because they do not know exactly what it is. They stir themselves to learn its nature and its cause. And that's the basic fact about these men.

Director: The essence of their personality — their character — their soul — is hunger for a knowledge of themselves and what to do?

Introvert: It is.

Director: Then if they're pregnant with a truth, that truth can only be themselves.

Extrovert: And that means what, exactly?

Director: That they must launch out in the world upon a quest to birth themselves, my friend. But it takes courage to set out, and keep on forging out until delivered, as it were.

Extrovert: You make it sound as though they're animals who go out to the deepest woods to find a place to birth their youth.

Director: Would you prefer to think of what they do as looking at themselves reflected in a pool?

Extrovert: That seems to make more sense.

Director: Alright. Well, as they gaze into the pool suppose a stranger walks right up and throws an object in — a stone or piece of wood, let's say. The waves begin to ripple and the waters are disturbed. The clear, reflective surface of the pool becomes distorted, right? Well, if the splash and ripples represent the type of feelings that distract a man from knowledge of himself, it seems a stranger throwing objects in might give a man a chance to watch and learn the correlations of events to feelings that disturb.

Extrovert: But why a stranger, Director?

Director: So there is no distraction from the learning by some sort of tie or bond of memory. It won't take long to learn this way — supposing that one wants to learn. A certain sort of man might only care to know his waters are disturbed, and never want to bother learning of the sorts of things that cause the waves. He'd simply hope his waters calm back down and pray to never hear a splash again. But, Introvert, the sort that you describe are those who cannot simply let the matter drop until they've learned the cause. They can't forget their ignorance. And that's the way that they begin to long to know, it seems to me.

Extrovert: Calm surfaces can sometimes hide disturbances below. So how are we to know there's not a great big cloud of mud that's swirling at the bottom?

Director: Simple questions are in order, once again, it seems. They should reveal if all is not as it appears.

Extrovert: Okay. Suppose there's something bad that's at the bottom of the pool, a thing that's better brought back up and taken out to keep the water pure. What then? Will simple questions bring it out?

Director: You mean some sort of lie that's at the bottom, Extrovert? We've switched our metaphor, you know.

Extrovert: I'm well aware.

Director: Well, if it's our own pool we simply dive right in, and haul the lie straight up, then cast it out.

Introvert: That's easy if the water's clear and we can see right to the bottom from the top. But if the waters are disturbed the object is obscured and not so easy to bring out.

Director: Then mustn't we remove ourselves from all disturbances and let the waters calm before we dive?

Introvert: But there are some who do not wish to have their waters calmed.

Director: That's true. I do not recommend you try to sound their depths.

Introvert: They're likely unaware there's even anything at bottom, Director.

Director: That might be so — or else they know there's something there but do not care to find out what. But if they are aware of what's within, and if that thing is actually a lie, I wonder if they'd rather it remain that way. To keep it so, and hide it from themselves and others, too, they might prefer that others fill their pool with lies, the sort that splash and keep the waters dark. So tell me, Introvert, does anyone prefer to have within a lie instead of truth?

Introvert: You mean a lie that they themselves create?

Director: Oh no, I mean a lie that someone else throws in. Do you prefer that people lie to you?

Introvert: You're being serious? You know that I prefer the truth!

Director: Do people ever want a lie instead?

Introvert: I think that some are so inclined. There may be something that they want, a thing they think is good and more important than the truth. If falsehood's necessary for this thing, they'll take it — right away. But no one likes when lies are told to him, although he may desire what comes from them.

Director: Let's leave aside for now the question of what sort of things can come from lies, and whether they are truly good or just a bunch of empty hopes. But if another does accept a lie, while secretly detesting it, might stormy waters seem to him a good?

Introvert: I think that's likely, Director. Forgetting all the lies might bring him great relief.

Director: So he will puff and blow and cloud his waters when he can in order that the splashing of the lies might be obscured?

Introvert: He might — or worse.

Director: What's worse?

Introvert: He might accept the lies with deadly calm.

Director: You mean he'd keep his waters clear and undisturbed to notice every lie that someone throws his way?

Introvert: That's right.

Director: What sort of man is this?

Introvert: A monster, Director.

Director: And what's his name?

Introvert: The tyrant.

Tyrant

Director: Why does he accept when lies are told to him?

Introvert: He does so for the sake of something that he thinks is more important than the truth — for power, Director.

Director: So we have come around again to speak of rulers and of their supposed need for lies. What does a tyrant gain by having others lie to him? Is he a special sort of ruler?

Introvert: Oh, he doesn't really gain a thing from all the lies themselves — and he himself will lie a lot like almost all the other rulers do. He differs from the others in that he accepts that people want to share or take advantage of the power that he's got, and lie to him to gain their end. He may not like it, but he doesn't do a thing to stop their lies. He recognizes that he'd do the same if he were them. When he accepts the lies (and doesn't let them know he sees the game they play) he lets the liars feel a sense of false security. Then he sits back and gains an insight into how they operate. He finds this knowledge valuable to keeping up his rule. But sometimes he lets on he knows about the lies, and this instills great fear — which also serves his rule. To let the liars know he knows is nothing more than policy (although he might enjoy to see them squirm) and not an action in accord with his desire for truth. He thinks he's very clever — and he is — and thoroughly enjoys his dominance.

Extrovert: Well, we won't lie to him. We'll let him know right where we stand.

Director: He's sure to see we value truth and honesty. Should we explain to him he doesn't give those two their proper weight?

Extrovert: Ha, ha! I'm sure I'd like to see you try!

Director: Well, maybe while we're at it we can show that power, just like money, never is the proper goal — that both exist for something else's sake, and therefore never make an end themselves.

Extrovert: I'd really like to think that we'd accomplish that.

Director: You think he'll disagree?

Extrovert: Oh no, I think that he'll agree!

Director: That's good! And if we ask him for what sake he thinks that people chase the dollar, what do you suppose he'll say?

Extrovert: I think he'll say it's for the sake of power, Director.

Director: And if we ask him for what sake he thinks that people lust for power, what do you suppose he'll say?

Extrovert: He might just smile silently.

Director: So then we'd have to ask him once again.

Extrovert: And then he might decide to frown.

Director: You mean he'd lie to us?

Extrovert: Of course.

Director: He really thinks that power is the goal?

Extrovert: I think he does but won't admit.

Director: Then if we find that he's unwilling — and we see he's likely to imprison us, or worse, if we persist — instead of asking him these questions, maybe we should tell him what we think. It might be easier for him to listen than for him to speak, considering the place he holds.

Extrovert: You might be right.

Director: Then how shall we explain to him the reason people lust for power?

Introvert: Maybe we should tell him that we think they chase it all for honor's sake.

Extrovert: For honor's sake? A tyrant's not concerned with that!

Introvert: He is, before he gets too far along — and then he cares, like most, about security. So power's sought to gain control of things and make him safe. Security depends on who has got control.

Director: Control? We wouldn't want the tyrant in the cockpit of a plane that's losing altitude. We'd want a pilot in control.

Extrovert: Of course. But tyrants always think it's best when they are in control, regardless of the nature of the task at hand.

Director: Well, what is there that a tyrant knows we would wish for him to keep in his control?

Extrovert: I cannot think of anything.

Director: Well, what about the state? When there is danger, isn't he the one we want to take command?

Extrovert: The tyrant uses danger to promote himself beyond his proper rank. He only makes the situation worse. He needs to keep the tension high. There always has to be a crisis in the state for him to keep his power and his place. But he cannot control the situation he creates. He's forced to change with every movement in the state. Fluidity is the only way that nothing gets a hold of him, that nothing takes him down. He's got no principles, beliefs, or lasting ties to hold him back. He just reacts to everything and never truly has security. He only keeps his place. He's really got no power, then. He's just a slave belonging to the state.

Director: Well, we should show him that if he is just a slave then there's no reason to maintain the tyranny. What will the tyrant say to this?

Extrovert: You can't believe a word he says, so why concern yourself with that?

Introvert: He says he wants the good of others, Director.

Director: But do his actions ever serve another's good?

Introvert: He sometimes brings stability when things are turbulent. He always comes to power in a crisis, but he sees that once it's ended there's no place for him — and this is where the problem lies. In order to resolve the crisis he has got to do some awful things. There's no one else who'll do the things it takes. But doing what he must to make the crisis end he makes it so he can't retreat. The people want a peaceful end but shun the means. The tyrant works the means with zeal — and this disturbs the populace. They do not trust him afterward. His face reminds them of the means employed to gain their end — and they would rather never see that face again, forgetting all the ugly deeds he did by proxy in their name.

Director: Stability's the only good he brings?

Introvert: What other good is there for him to bring? I even have my doubts about stability, depending on the price that's paid for it. It's not a good all by itself — it only makes it possible to seek out other goods. And that's ironic since the tyrant doesn't know the way to seek out his own good — unless his good is fame, or...

Extrovert: What?

Introvert: Our gratitude.

Extrovert: Our gratitude? For what?

Introvert: Security. He feels that people do not understand the things he's done for their own good. The lying, cheating, stealing, killing — everything — must seem to him as all for naught because it's not appreciated.

Extrovert: But who appreciates revolting deeds like that? He's absolutely crazy if he thinks the citizens will show him gratitude for tyranny. You give him too much credit, Introvert. He doesn't really have a noble longing for the people's thanks.

Introvert: But if that's so then why do tyrants long in power love to celebrate their reigns with choruses of children singing praise?

Extrovert: Because they're twisted, evil things. I think they love to see sarcastic statements written large, that's all. A tyrant doesn't really care about his nation's children's future. Granted that he may have been a populist when he began, the things he's done have changed him. When he's old he's nothing but a wicked sensualist or miser, Introvert, existing only to indulge his lusts or greed.

Introvert: Well, when that's true it's just a substitute for gratitude. He's disillusioned, thinking that he should be thanked for all he's done. Debauchery and selfishness is only consolation for the thing he'd rather have.

Director: To know for sure we'd have to ask a tyrant.

Extrovert: That will be the day!

Director: You do not think it's possible to ask a tyrant how he came to be the way he is?

Extrovert: I think that he will be reluctant — at the very least — to give an answer to a question on that score — and even so, it's not a very prudent thing to ask! What purpose does it serve to take the risk to ask a thing like that?

Director: I thought you said that we will openly oppose the tyranny.

Extrovert: I did!

Director: What better way than questioning the tyrant's acts?

Extrovert: I'm thinking of his lack of statesmanship, the things he does in politics, and not the nasty habits he's acquired.

Introvert: One just might drive the other, Extrovert.

Extrovert: Perhaps, but it's too late to change his way in things like that.

Introvert: We cannot know that if we haven't learned some more about him first.

Extrovert: And how are we to learn? You think he'll treat a questioner just like a psychotherapist and pour out all his guts? Suppose we gain his confidence, and speak with him alone — he still might menace us when asked about the things he'd rather hide than bring to light.

Director: But then we'd have to make it clear that there's a line he shouldn't cross with us or he will have to face the consequences.

Extrovert: Consequences?

Director: Sure. We'll let him know we'll leave.

Extrovert: Ah, ha, ha, ha!

Director: We must negotiate from strength.

Extrovert: Oh, ho, ho, ho! That's good! But seriously, I think that once we've marked the line we'll have to tell him that we only hope he doesn't make us use the force at our command.

Introvert: But tyrants use exactly that same argument. They justify their violence when they say they have no choice.

Extrovert: The argument's the same, perhaps — but he tells lies, and we do not. He's not in any danger when he says that he'll be forced. It's only an excuse to take control — exactly what we're trying to prevent! We only use that argument before the clear and present danger he presents.

Introvert: And you don't think that someone who aspires to the tyranny will face grave dangers?

Extrovert: Yes, he will — but that's a different thing entirely!

Director: If both face dangers, why not set aside for now the question of the difference that's between the dangers (danger's danger, to a point, perhaps — a topic for another time), and focus on the difference in the way the two — the "we" and "they" of what's been said — respond to them.

Extrovert: The tyrant doesn't hesitate to lie, while we —

Director: Prefer to tell the truth?

Extrovert: We tell the truth.

Introvert: But don't you think it's possible the tyrant doesn't like, or want, to lie?

Extrovert: Well, if he doesn't like to lie he's taken up a line of work that's not so good!

Introvert: But don't you know that in his private life a tyrant speaks quite boldly? He disdains to lie, and thinks of liars with contempt.

Extrovert: Of course. He has a brutal sort of honesty — he's quite abrupt and rude. He tells the truth to cause another pain, and not because he values truthfulness. Whenever there's a doubt, however, it will be his policy to lie.

Director: Is everyone with such a policy potentially a tyrant?

Extrovert: Yes.

Director: Well, what about our dear old friend Tom Sawyer? He is someone who is in the habit of the lie.

Extrovert: Ha, ha! He is! But that's a different thing again.

Director: A different sort of lie? Or did you mean that he's no tyrant?

Extrovert: He's no tyrant, Director! He's got a sense of humor, after all.

Director: And tyrants don't?

Extrovert: That's right. They're much too serious.

Director: Then maybe Tom has only got a tendency to tyranny.

Extrovert: He's only looking for some fun!

Director: I see. Then maybe he has got potential to support a tyranny.

Extrovert: What's that supposed to mean?

Director: He's very flexible in rendering the truth.

Extrovert: That's true.

Director: Is that a skill in high demand in tyrannies?

Extrovert: I guess it is.

Director: If tyrants lie on policy, they'll need supporters who will do the same.

Extrovert: I think that's true.

Director: Now, what was it that Tom's supposed to be well suited to become when he grows up?

Extrovert: A lawyer! Ah, ha, ha!

Director: Are people trained to make the truth more "flexible" all harmless innocents?

Extrovert: Of course they're not.

Director: Well, let's not be too hasty drawing our conclusion here. Might it not be that Sawyer felt he had to lie?

Extrovert: Perhaps. But why?

Director: Why, can't you hear Aunt Polly hollering? "Now, don't you make me punish you, young man!"

Extrovert: But that is hardly tyranny!

Director: Aunt Polly's in too deep when dealing with Tom Sawyer, isn't she?

Extrovert: He's cleverer than her, for sure.

Director: He's cleverer than most. So then I wonder what you think of one of Tom's most famous lies, the one where he is painting. He pretends that he enjoys the painting of the fence, and he convinces everyone that it's a lot of fun, which makes them want to paint the fence themselves. So he gets out of doing it. What do you make of this?

Extrovert: I think that it is harmless, Director.

Director: The lie produced no harm?

Extrovert: That's right. It's not at all like tyrants' lies. He's only having fun. Besides, it's not like painting fences is a zero sum affair. There is no loser here. They all have fun.

Director: Why, Extrovert, can you be saying that their pleasure proves the lie's alright?

Extrovert: Well, after all, he only lies about enjoying what he does.

Director: The gander's good's not good for every goose, it seems.

Extrovert: But if they work together properly they both get what they want.

Director: And if Tom hadn't lied? If he had said, "I don't enjoy the painting of this fence, but know that you would like it — so it's clear that you should paint the fence and I should watch?"

Extrovert: They wouldn't listen, and they'd surely laugh.

Director: Why's that?

Extrovert: They'd think he thinks he's better than they are.

Director: But would Tom really tell the truth to them when telling them that they'd enjoy the painting of the fence, admitting that he doesn't like to paint?

Extrovert: They wouldn't have much fun if he said that. So, no, he wouldn't speak the truth.

Director: Then what is it that makes them have their fun?

Extrovert: Believing Tom enjoys the work.

Director: I cannot understand the difference here.

Extrovert: You really do not know? They envy him!

Director: I still don't see. But tell me, you've read Twain — what does he tell us Tom enjoys?

Extrovert: Oh, anything romantic — great adventure, I suppose.

Director: A real adventure, or just make-believe?

Extrovert: I think that he prefers the make-believe.

Director: And do you think that he's a fool for this?

Extrovert: Oh, I don't know. The real adventures aren't much fun until they're done — and then we tend to make them greater than they were while reminiscing of our glory days.

Introvert: The thing's the fun then, isn't it? You mean to say that having fun's a reason good enough to lie?

Extrovert: Ha, ha! I can't believe it, but it seems I am! If after I've considered this some more and still it seems this way to me, I'd stress, however, that it's on condition no one's hurt, and everyone enjoys himself.

Introvert: But what if someone gets upset because he knows that someone else is telling lies?

Extrovert: Then that's unfortunate, I guess. C'mon! Now, why would someone get upset to see Tom lie that way? It's funny, isn't it?

Introvert: Perhaps because the fun is not the only reason Tom tells lies.

Extrovert: What other reason has he got?

Introvert: There could be many reasons for his lie.

Director: What's this? Could he be lying earnestly in order to convince the gander that the goose's good is good for it? You've seen a gaggle, haven't you? You really think they're easily convinced to do a thing they do not want to do? Why, surely you must know that nothing's more impervious to reason's council than a stirred-up gaggle! (Maybe we'll except the jackass.) No, they simply will not have it, Introvert!

Introvert: That isn't what I mean.

Director: What do you mean?

Introvert: It's got to do with what you said about a person being in a place that's wrong for him. Tom Sawyer doesn't think that he is in a place that's good for him, and so he lies to free himself from it.

Extrovert: He wasn't having any fun.

Introvert: That's not the thing! I think that Tom is only laughing in relief at having gotten out.

Extrovert: That's right — and now he's having fun.

Director: Did Sawyer think the painting work beneath him?

Introvert: Yes, he did — and I think Twain must think that he's above it, too. He shows us Tom removing to a better place, but does it in a way that makes it seem (to those who cannot understand) as though it's all about the fun.

Director: Is Tom's position tenable?

Introvert: It's not — unless he keeps up with the lies.

Director: The lies get bigger quickly, eh? And that will lead him where?

Introvert: Why, nowhere, fast — or else it may just lead him to support a tyrant. It is as we've said. The tyrant needs some people who will lie for him. (He may disdain to lie himself in matters that are personal, but always needs his lies to run the state.) He'll see that Sawyer's someone skilled in what he needs. He'll try his character to see if he will lie. Perhaps if he can catch Tom in a lie there'll be a chance to blackmail him to do some dirty work.

Director: You seem to say that Tom must find a way to guard his character. Well, how is he supposed to ground himself to keep himself intact?

Introvert: He cannot lie.

Director: That's all it takes?

Introvert: I think that it's a start — a necessary start.

Extrovert: But then he's stuck with painting fences all the time! You said that Tom's not in a spot that's good for him.

Introvert: He'll have to find a better way to get himself into a better spot.

Director: A way that won't imply he thinks himself above the work?

Introvert: That's right.

Director: What sort of way is that?

Introvert: I couldn't say.

Director: Then let me ask you something that I've meant to ask for quite some time. Assuming there are always those like Tom around, do you believe that what he does (or doesn't do) can tilt the scale towards tyranny?

Introvert: Of course. These things are balanced by a hair at times.

Director: I wonder if you think the balance might be tipped by whether Tom, and those like him, believes that it's alright to lie as long as no one's hurt.

Introvert: Of course I do. We're only spared from tyranny (or anarchy) by people's principles.

Director: Is one like Tom concerned with truth, with knowledge?

Introvert: No. He learns enough in order to impress. He loves to wow the other boys with bits and snatches that he's gleaned from books. He gains the reputation of a learned man without a thing to back it up. So he is fit to lead a gang, but nothing more.

Extrovert: That isn't fair to Tom. It's he who knows the truth about the goings on in town. He learns about the murder in the woods, you know.

Introvert: He sees the murder accidentally.

Extrovert: He saw it while adventuring. You know he loves discovery. If not for him, the killers never come to justice.

Introvert: That may be, but Sawyer doesn't set out consciously to learn a thing. A scientific spirit doesn't animate his soul. He stumbles into things. It's only luck that lets him find out something new. And I'm not sure that he's a pure romantic after all.

Extrovert: Why's that?

Introvert: We didn't mention one important bit about the painting of the fence.

Extrovert: Well, what?

Introvert: Tom Sawyer makes them pay.

Extrovert: So what?

Introvert: He's doing this while he's a boy. What sort of things will he demand when he's a man?

Extrovert: Why, money, certainly. There's nothing wrong with that.

Introvert: A tyrant knows the way to play on greed.

Extrovert: Oh, I agree that Tom must be alert to not become a tyrant's tool. But he prefers adventure to base gain!

Introvert: He's young.

Extrovert: You think the older he becomes the greater risk that he'll support a tyranny?

Introvert: I do.

Extrovert: Because of love for money?

Introvert: Yes, in part. His nature's over-generous, so he requires means to keep it up or he'll lose face.

Extrovert: You think that he's a fool.

Introvert: I do — and I won't suffer him.

Extrovert: And you don't think that he will have the wherewithal to get the means, or change his ways, and opt to serve the tyranny instead?

Introvert: I think that it depends on his environment. When all is well, Tom does just fine — he seems quite harmless, even lovable. When tyranny's about to hatch, however, Tom just doesn't have the character to deal with it. His fundamental weakness shows. Perhaps he'll lie to get himself removed from some unlucky scrape. But would he lie to stop the tyranny?

Extrovert: He might. But telling lies is no sign of strength of character. So we can't count on him. More reason why we fight the tyranny ourselves!

Introvert: And if we lack the means?

Extrovert: We fight with what we've got, that's all.

Introvert: Although we know we're bound to fail?

Extrovert: You never know until you try. But if we fail, at least we are examples to the ones who're yet to come. We must prepare to give our lives, our all.

Introvert: You know the tyrant will not hesitate to cover up attempts against his rule. So what if no one knows that we resisted him? I think we've got to wait until we have the means, the force, we need.

Extrovert: We can't allow ourselves to think like that. Consolidated power's harder smashed. We just have got to fight, believing that our efforts aren't in vain. We cannot wait. The people generally do nothing. Silence and complacence are the curses of their lives. They want to keep their property, however small, intact. If that is left untouched then they will keep their mouths shut tight. Of this the tyrant's well aware. He concentrates his lust for wealth upon the rich — the few. He knows that they're his greatest enemies — and those who may be poor but filled with pride.

Introvert: Then they're the ones we'll have to take into our confidence.

Director: If we resist the tyrant openly there is no need for us to lie, correct?

Introvert: That's right.

Director: But taking people into confidence — conspiring — that requires lies?

Introvert: By definition, yes.

Director: To whom?

Introvert: The tyrant and his men, and all of those not in the know.

Director: The use of covert means entails the possibility that any lie that's told might travel far beyond the one for whom it's meant, correct?

Introvert: Of course — and likely, too.

Director: If lying to a tyrant we'd expect that he will act upon the lie.

Introvert: That's right.

Director: But no one else?

Introvert: Well, maybe his supporters, too — but no one else.

Director: If others come to hear of it, it seems that there's a risk that they'll believe and act upon the premise of the lie, and therefore suffer harm.

Introvert: They might indeed.

Director: And do you see a way around this difficulty?

Introvert: There's no problem if we have a thorough knowledge of the men to whom we open up our plans. We'll know that they're dependable, and limit what we say to only what we all agree is best. We'll only tell the tyrant lies that cause no harm to others if believed.

Extrovert: Well, that sure begs the question!

Introvert: None of us will talk. The lie will only spread right from the tyrant's mouth — and who'll believe him, anyway? Besides, the lie we'll tell will likely be a thing he will not want to share, a thing that undermines his rule. We might confess to him, for instance, that we know that there's a plot against his life, but lie and tell him that we do not know exactly who's involved.

Extrovert: And if he hunts to break it up, arresting innocents? I still don't see how lying fights the tyranny.

Director: Well, why not fight by means of truth and not the use of force or lies?

Extrovert: But, Director, the tyrant doesn't value that!

Director: It's my belief he will if he begins to see the truth about himself. I think he'll have no choice.

Extrovert: Why's that?

Director: His vision of himself is the spring of all he does. A tyrant's vision's cramped. We'll open up his view — and what he sees will change the way he acts, or he will suffer harm. The choice is his.

Extrovert: You know that that's an awful risk to take if you're not sure that truth will work. But what if he denies the thing he sees about himself, whatever that may be, and seeks to drown the vision out?

Director: I don't believe it's possible for that to work.

Extrovert: But he might kill you if you're wrong!

Director: Perhaps, but that won't help the problem that I think he'll have. Do you believe that he can kill the truth? Well, I, for one, sure don't.

Introvert: If it is true that friendship is a need that we've all got, and if it's clear that tyrants cannot have real friends, then you are right to say our strength with him is in his wish to have us as his friends. But who would he desire to be his friend? Why, someone who can see him as he really is. And so, if we can really see him as he is, our biggest threat to him is that we'll leave if he won't change his way.

Director: You know that he will try to change us first before he'll ever try to change himself? He'll want to put us to the test.

Introvert: Then we can't budge an inch.

Director: You know that if the tyrant changes he will have to lose all face — at least his public face. That's dangerous to him and us. It's not a simple thing for him to walk away from what he's done, nor is it simple if we wish to walk away once we have gained his confidence. So many hunger for revenge, you know.

Extrovert: Suppose the tyrant chooses rule instead of friends. That's likely, don't you think? I mean, he's made that choice consistently until this point. There's got to be another reason why he'd listen or I think that we're quixotic in our running risks like this.

Director: I think he's going to have his wisdom challenged in a way he can't resist, regardless if he wants us as his friends. A tyrant, at his best, believes that friendship's only possible within a state that's ordered well. In other words, he thinks that friendship's artificial, just like politics. In offering the tyrant friendship — friendship that is true — we demonstrate the fallacy of his opinion. Up 'til now the tyrant thought that he was living as he should. He blamed external factors on his lack of friends. The time in which he lives, he thinks, is wrong — not him. So he must right the time — which means to right the state. It's thus he enters on the path to tyranny. But now he's not so sure about the way he went. He now suspects that friendship's natural. He now begins to see another state exists (if only in the hearts and minds of men), a state that differs, for the better, from his tyranny. He knows quite well the danger that he'll face if he decides to change. He also knows how noble such a change would be.

Extrovert: He's hardly noble, Director!

Director: But isn't that the thing that we desire he be, without a trace of envy on our part of his success?

Extrovert: I guess that's true. But he will have a lot of making up to do.

Director: There is no making up. He must accept that fact. And that's the hardest thing he'll ever do. But he will also have to face the fact that there's no turning back if he begins to travel down this road — and not because of those who'll want revenge. His spirit's bound to sink into the blackest melancholy if he starts out toward this goal and stops before he's reached the end of having friends because he's scared or weak of will. He'll simply have to carry on, no matter what, until he's fully changed and has good friends — or else he will destroy himself. There is no other way.

Questions Concerning the Dubious Virtue of the Lie

Introvert: So we won't lie to tyrants, but we'll lie for fun as long as no one's hurt? That's rather odd. It seems to me it's finally time we talk about exactly what we mean by harm.

Director: But don't you think that we should also know exactly what we mean when speaking of the opposite of harm as well?

Introvert: I do.

Director: So what's the opposite of harm?

Introvert: It must be help.

Director: And help makes better, harm makes worse?

Introvert: That's right.

Director: When someone helps us do we know?

Introvert: We should, but I'm not sure we always do.

Director: Is that because it takes some time before the benefits are known?

Introvert: At least in part.

Director: And is it only partly so because the pain that often comes with help can fool us into thinking that we're being harmed?

Introvert: That's right.

Director: Well, what about the opposite? When someone harms us do we always know?

Introvert: Again, we should, but I don't think we always do — at least not right away.

Director: And what's the cause of this?

Introvert: In part, again, because the harm might only come with time. The pleasure also makes one think that something that's the cause of harm is good.

Director: But there are those, you know, who question whether harm can ever really come from pleasant things.

Introvert: If pleasant things distract one from the more important things, then they will surely lead to harm.

Director: You mean the choice of pleasure causes harm whenever something more important is ignored?

Introvert: I do.

Director: Then for the sake of prudence one had better know the proper rank of things.

Introvert: That's very true.

Director: Do people ever lie about the proper rank of things?

Introvert: Of course they do — just as they do in measuring and valuing.

Director: And this results in what?

Introvert: Confusion of priorities — which leads to harm.

Director: And people being put in places where they don't belong?

Introvert: That, too.

Director: So how should we determine our priorities?

Introvert: We'll have to look back to our instrument and listen for the proper notes.

Director: The lowest string provides the bass on which the melody must rest, and that is truth. The truth is that the better general ought to lead — but sometimes those who're only "good" will say they're better than their betters, thus confusing nature's rank, and making chaos of the best laid plans of state. What sort of melody will that produce?

Introvert: A melody that's not so good.

Director: But this is true not only for positions that one holds, but also things that one enjoys. I mean, the pleasure in all things must lie within the function they perform. To sleep is only pleasant when one's tired, right?

Introvert: That's right. But there are times when one must stay awake in order to achieve a greater end, regardless of how tired one might be.

Director: I see. And that's because the function of that higher thing is more important than one's rest? For instance, if an enemy is on the prowl nearby then one must stay awake until the enemy is gone or safer quarters have been found. Suppose we have a tired friend and we're aware that there's an enemy of his nearby. Would it be wrong to lie and tell him that it's safe and let him fall asleep?

Introvert: Of course, unless we stay on guard for him and let him rest.

Director: We're helping him by keeping him alive? Well, here's the thing. We said that help makes better, harm makes worse. Exactly how's our friend made better?

Extrovert: Ha! To be alive is better!

Introvert: He's already living, so he's not made any better by our keeping watch.

Extrovert: Well, strictly speaking, yes, that's true.

Introvert: Is there another way you'd rather speak?

Extrovert: If I say no then you should tell me what you mean by making better.

Introvert: Better means that one's capacity has grown. He's greater than before. He couldn't do before the things he can do now.

Director: So if he's worse he can't do now the things he could before. But where does pain fit in to all of this?

Introvert: Becoming greater is difficult and always means some pain. No pain, no gain.

Director: But surely we are not to think that growing worse is pleasant, right?

Introvert: Are "we" to think? Are you implying that it's really true that growing worse involves a pleasant lassitude, and that it's necessary that we have most people think the opposite's the case? Well, that would be another sort of noble lie. The opposite would be that growing greater is pleasant. That's the net, I think, with which we catch young lions.

Director: Isn't there a pleasure in the knowledge that one's better?

Introvert: Yes.

Director: So if one's growing better must involve some pain, the question's if the pleasure that one feels will overcome that pain. It's got to be a hardy sort of pleasure, no?

Introvert: I guess it does.

Director: And there are different pleasures?

Introvert: Yes.

Director: Each pleasure has a certain act to which it's properly attached?

Introvert: It does.

Director: So once again it seems the question is of rank. So what's the greatest pleasure, Introvert?

Introvert: It seems it goes along with knowing that one's better, Director — with knowing that one's worthy of the greatest things, regardless if one ever gets those things or not.

Director: But then the question of the ranking of the things one's worthy of arises, right?

Introvert: It seems to me the greatest worthiness is being fit to rule.

Director: To rule at what?

Introvert: At politics.

Director: You mean to be the one who manages the budget, or the one who makes the laws? Perhaps you mean to be the one who judges whether laws are being properly upheld?

Introvert: I mean to know in every case that touches on affairs of state the thing that's best to do.

Director: I'd think that that would take a knowledge of the law.

Introvert: It does, of course — but also takes a knowledge of humanity.

Director: Is that to ascertain the disposition of one's heart — in other words, to know if one is only following the letter, not the spirit, of the law?

Introvert: That's right. The letter kills.

Director: And do the killers lie by only holding to the letter of the law while locking other thoughts within their hearts?

Introvert: They do. Their acts are always lies, essentially, because they contradict their hearts.

Director: So judges of humanity will see when one is wholly true — when heart, and words, and acts are one.

Introvert: They will.

Director: And don't you think that this must be the only sort of greatness there can be — integrity?

Introvert: I do.

Director: But do you think integrity is what a ruler needs?

Introvert: Of course.

Director: To help him help the others be more true?

Introvert: That seems to be the proper function of a ruler, Director.

Director: So how does he assist the others in their quest for truth?

Introvert: By his example — and then it's up to them.

Director: Can rulers such as this make use of noble lies?

Introvert: They can't.

Director: Because they're false examples then?

Introvert: That's right. They're lies themselves if they resort to noble lies. They're fakes.

Director: And only genuine examples ever truly work?

Introvert: If working means to be a beacon to a storm-tossed soul, to bring it safely in to shore, then yes. But there are charlatans who'd run the ship aground.

Director: Now, when a man is true, is leading all he's better at?

Introvert: Why, no. He's better at whatever thing he does because his judgment's better.

Director: That means he's better at deciding, right?

Introvert: That's right.

Director: So let's suppose that he decides he'll run a race. Is it more likely that he'll win because his judgment is improved?

Introvert: Of course it's not improved by that alone. But judgment makes it likely that he'll only enter races where he's got a decent chance to win.

Director: You mean to say that judgment is a sort of prudence?

Introvert: Yes.

Director: And prudent men will do each thing they choose to do the best? I mean, if what we're saying's true, they've got their hearts and heads aligned. What greater strength is there than that?

Introvert: Well, maybe they won't be the best but they'll at least be...

Director: Good?

Introvert: That's right.

Director: So when they talk, they're good at talking, right?

Introvert: They are.

Director: And when they rule, they're good at ruling, right?

Introvert: They are.

Director: And when they tell the truth?

Introvert: They're good at telling truth.

Director: And when they lie?

Introvert: They're also good at that.

Extrovert: But what about integrity? (I didn't want to interrupt, but this whole line of talk has gone astray.) If someone's got a rotten heart what good is it if all his words and thoughts and acts align with that? Is that integrity? A man like that has got no problem lying, even when it means that he will cause great harm.

Director: If harm means making worse, suppose his lying makes another worse at telling lies — or makes another worse at tyranny. What sort of harm is that?

Extrovert: I'd hardly say that that's a harm.

Director: Is being worse at something bad a good?

Extrovert: It is.

Director: Suppose we say it's right to cause a harm to something bad. The question still is whether lying causes harm, but now we have to know what's good and what is bad before we say if someone's wrong in what he does.

Extrovert: But then we don't arrive at crazy notions like the one that says the man who's true is good at lies.

Director: But if the man who's true is good at lies and makes another less a tyrant through his use of them, and this is not a harm but help, because to be a tyrant's bad — because a tyrant isn't truly capable of doing anything at all — except, perhaps, in making things more safe (but we suspect security we purchase thus is false, and hides an underlying situation that has only gotten worse) — then is the notion all that crazy, *Extrovert?*

Extrovert: I thought we said we wouldn't lie to tyrants, Director.

Director: The tyrant's good at sniffing out a lie. Suppose we're better than the tyrant at the lie. What then?

Extrovert: Then don't we run the risk of tyranny ourselves?

Director: If lies are what especially distinguish tyrants then perhaps. I thought we were agreed, however, that it is a love of rule combined with something else that marks out tyrants from the rest.

Extrovert: That's true.

Director: When speaking of our instrument we said that knowledge gives one skill. So what's the knowledge it would take to make us better liars than a tyrant?

Extrovert: Knowledge of whatever thing is lied about, is what we'd need.

Director: The one who has the greater knowledge always tells the better lie?

Extrovert: It seems that way.

Director: And that is all it takes to lie?

Introvert: There's more to it than that. It's not enough to know the truth. A liar must articulate his lie. He needs command of language.

Director: What exactly does that mean?

Introvert: It means the liar's tools of trade are words, and he must master them.

Extrovert: But there's no mastery of words required when one says "no" although the answer's really "yes."

Introvert: But if a one-word liar's questioned thoroughly it soon becomes quite obvious that something's wrong. He has to answer further when he's pressed. He can't just take The Fifth.

Extrovert: But sometimes holding to one's word's enough. The hardest thing to do is hold one's tongue.

Director: You're saying silence is the essence of the lie?

Extrovert: I think it's certainly a part of it — perhaps the greatest part. It's hard to keep a secret, Director, and liars always must.

Director: The secret here's the truth.

Extrovert: That's right. But isn't that the case with every lie?

Director: Not when a liar thinks the false is true. Now, when a liar holds his tongue he may not speak another lie, but through his silence he might work deceit, correct?

Extrovert: Of course. He's lying by omission.

Director: And when one opens up one's mouth and speaks a lie one still omits the thing one really holds as true. So both the speaking and the silent liar mark themselves with absence of the truth outside their inner core. If truth is light then they surround themselves with darkness, yes?

Introvert: But if there's really truth within the liar then I'd think that it must shine, regardless of the efforts one expends to keep it covered up, and make a sort of ring of light behind or through the shadow of deceit — as when then sun's eclipsed, or when translucent objects shade a lamp. I know the metaphors are mixed, but this truth's hard to grasp. So there are different sorts of liars — those who hide what's true, and those who hide what's false — which is to say that there are those who hide their light, and those who hide their darkness.

Director: Darkness hides itself (and others, too) without our efforts, Introvert. But getting to your point about the mastery of words, it's true that someone knowing how to use a thing will also know when it's not good for something, right?

Introvert: That's right.

Director: And if he doesn't know the proper way to use a thing he will not know exactly when that thing will do no good. So those who lie, if ever they would lie with words, must be articulate, regardless if they choose to speak or not, in order that they'll know the proper time for words and recognize when rests are written on the score. To link these words with what I've said before, consider that transparent paper marked with dark and heavy ink becomes opaque. So when a liar uses words to work deceit what skill, exactly, is employed? It can't just be articulation or command of language, can it, Introvert? Why, every writer or great speaker then would be a master of the lie. That isn't what you think, now, is it?

Introvert: No, since I don't know what else to say.

Director: I thought that you would say beyond command of language and articulation one must have sophistication. One sophisticates by complicating simple things and recognizing simple things made complicated. Liars and deceivers have to hide the truth, but also hide the thing they do in hiding truth — they have to hide their art. They seek to cover up their tracks. Sophistication seems to let them do exactly this.

Extrovert: But how can they obscure their art through complication when to complicate unduly is exactly what will give them up, will make them seem unduly complicated — make them seem to lie? That makes no sense.

Director: It seems they have to make the complications seem as though they're natural. But let me ask you if it's true that everything that's complicated is that way because it is the object of an art?

Extrovert: Why, no, some things are simply complicated.

Director: Making complicated things seem simple also is a way of lying or deceiving, no?

Extrovert: That's true.

Director: It seems the skill is really making something seem to be quite different than it truly is, and not just complicating it. Are there not times when liars use not subtle but more brazen lies?

Extrovert: There are.

Director: And do those make the complicated things seem simple?

Extrovert: Sometimes. But they also may be used to say that something simple is another sort of simple thing it's not.

Director: And isn't that exactly what the subtle lies must do? For what's a thing that's complicated if it's not comprised of many simple things?

Extrovert: But how do you describe the difference that there is between a subtle and a brazen lie?

Director: I think it's got to be how soon the liar wants to be found out.

Extrovert: To be found out?

Director: Of course! Or did you think that any lie will ever hide itself forever, Extrovert?

Extrovert: I think that every lie must always come to light.

Director: Well, what's the sort of lie that comes to light the fastest?

Extrovert: Brazen lies will always be found out much quicker than the subtle ones.

Director: So subtle lies are used by those who want their lies to last.

Extrovert: And brazen liars want to be found out?

Director: It seems they must, assuming that they lie with skill. There may be those, you know, who do not like to lie (perhaps as is the case with tyrants) but decide they must. Regretting that they have to lie they come to hope that all their lies will one day come to light as such, revealing truth for what it was and is, while showing what their reasons were for telling lies. A brazen lie might be employed for just this reason — so the lie will come to light. But I don't know. I'm only guessing, Extrovert. Oh, I suppose that one might offer other reasons for a brazen lie. A subtle lie is most precise, correct?

Extrovert: It is.

Director: Precision takes a knowledge of detail?

Extrovert: It does.

Director: And if we lack that knowledge subtle lying can't be done.

Extrovert: That's true.

Director: So when's it likely that we'll lack detail? When situations are complex?

Extrovert: Of course. The subtle lie's a scalpel that can't rive a hardened knot — it takes an axe.

Director: So liars have to know which lie is best to suit the situation, then they have to choose the one that works their chosen end.

Introvert: And that takes judgment, Director.

Director: It certainly requires that they know the situation well.

Introvert: But then it's clear to them what sort of lie is best?

Director: Well, that depends on what they want, now, doesn't it?

Introvert: Suppose that someone's not so sure.

Director: Then I would say it's best for him to hold his tongue.

Introvert: But what if he must speak or seem to be perverse?

Director: Well, what about the truth?

Introvert: Suppose the truth won't work.

Director: You mean because the truth will lead to harm?

Introvert: That's right.

Director: Then one must have some nerve and make an educated guess — and be resolved to try one's luck, it seems.

Extrovert: You make it sound as if the liar must have courage.

Director: Some say that's the moral aspect to the lie.

Extrovert: The moral aspect to the lie? And do you think they're right?

Director: Oh no — I think they're very wrong. It takes great courage if you wish to persevere in doing what you know is right. But those who say the brave are those who take a stand and hold their ground no matter what will never care to learn when they are wrong. They're stubborn fools — afraid to think, afraid to change, afraid to own the errors of their way — but not afraid to lie to cover up their tracks. They're stubborn fools who think that they should get exactly what they think that they deserve.

II. Contempt

Persons of the Dialogue:

Persons of the Dialogue:
  Guru
  Director
  Conservative

Guru: Contempt is something that we have to overcome.

Director: But don't you have contempt for those who fail to overcome their own?

Guru: I don't, for that would indicate that I believe that what they do is wrong and what I do is right. There is no right. There is no wrong. There only is The All. The more of it one sees the less contempt one feels. Contempt is nothing but discomfort over dealing with a part of All that one would rather not.

Director: And you prefer to deal with all?

Guru: It's not a matter of one's preference, Director. The comprehension of the All makes man complete, and man complete can never feel contempt. To him all actions are explained, and when he understands he then forgives. There is no greater good than harmony with All.

Director: You do admit that isn't very likely, right?

Guru: It's very few who come to know the All.

Director: Then what about the rest? They're bound to feel contempt. And since they form the vast majority we'd better know a thing or two about the way they feel.

81

Conservative: It's fine to talk about a universal harmony, but Director is right: we need to have a fighting creed for daily life — and that includes contempt for certain sorts of acts.

Guru: Those acts are done by those you fight, correct?

Conservative: That's right.

Guru: Then do you have contempt for those you fight? I thought you'd want a worthy enemy, not one that you despise.

Conservative: Of course I want a worthy enemy.

Guru: Then you must fight an enemy whose actions you admire.

Conservative: But I would want a man like that to be my friend!

Guru: Then you don't want a worthy enemy?

Conservative: Of course I do! The more contemptible his acts, the worthier he is to fight.

Guru: Is bravery contemptible?

Conservative: Of course it's not.

Guru: Is strength contemptible?

Conservative: It is when used for vile things.

Guru: Then that is true for bravery as well?

Conservative: It is.

Guru: And is it true for every other thing?

Conservative: It is.

Guru: So it is not the man himself but what he does that makes him worthy of contempt. Is this your fighting creed?

Conservative: It is.

Guru: The man himself consists of all his traits. Do you agree?

Conservative: I do.

Guru: Now bravery and strength are traits.

Conservative: They are.

Guru: A man who's worthy of contempt, can he be brave?

Conservative: He can't.

Guru: Can he be strong?

Conservative: Why, certainly he can.

Guru: What's this? But why be strong but never brave? Suppose he knows that doing something base will draw you to a fight — and let's suppose he knows that you are strong and brave and thus an object he might fear —

yet still he works the deed for which you have contempt. What then? Is he not brave?

Conservative: Of course he's not. He's just a fool.

Guru: And that's because a man's not brave unless he serves a worthy cause?

Conservative: That's right.

Guru: But does it follow then that one's not strong unless one's strength is used to serve a worthy cause?

Conservative: It's not the same. Some evil is quite strong.

Guru: Well, let me see how far you go. A man who does a deed that's worthy of contempt cannot be brave. Can he be wise?

Conservative: Oh, no.

Guru: Can he be just?

Conservative: He can't.

Guru: Can he be any trait that's good?

Conservative: He can't.

Guru: But he can be their opposites?

Conservative: That's right.

Guru: So he is foolish and unjust and cowardly.

Conservative: That's right, I guess, by definition of the sort of deed that he has done.

Guru: So all your worthy foes are bound to be both foolish and unjust and cowardly, but maybe very strong. But must a man be wise and brave to fight a foe like that?

Conservative: If he is strong it takes both bravery and wisdom to succeed.

Guru: And if he's weak?

Conservative: Then maybe not as much, that's all.

Guru: Alright. I'd like to ask about the causes here in play. For now we limit talk to two: the worthy and the evil cause. Do you agree the worthy cause makes those who serve it brave?

Conservative: I do. As long as they are serving it they're brave.

Guru: And then the evil cause makes those who serve it cowardly.

Conservative: That's how it seems to me.

Guru: Do you agree the worthy cause makes those who serve it wise?

Conservative: It's always wise to serve a worthy cause — and those who serve an evil cause are always fools.

Guru: Is every fool the servant of an evil cause?

Conservative: Why, no. Some fools are merely harmless idiots.

Guru: And do you have contempt for them?

Conservative: I don't.

Guru: Are cowards always servants of an evil cause?

Conservative: They're not.

Guru: But do you have contempt for them?

Conservative: I do.

Guru: But why? I thought that you would say your fighting creed involves contempt for those who serve an evil cause.

Conservative: I do.

Guru: But now you say you have contempt for those who serve an evil cause and also for the cowardly.

Conservative: A man who's worthy of esteem is always brave.

Guru: By this you mean to say that either you esteem a man or hold him in contempt?

Conservative: Of course.

Guru: But what about the harmless fool?

Conservative: Alright, alright. There is a class of man I neither hold in high esteem nor scorn. A man like that's not worthy of a thought.

Guru: Well, could it be a man like that is also cowardly?

Conservative: I guess.

Guru: Your fighting creed is simply scorning those who serve an evil cause.

Conservative: It is.

Guru: Now, what's the use of scorn? Might scorn not make one underestimate the strength of those one fights? Why, surely this has happened in the past, and more than once.

Conservative: That's true.

Guru: Might healthy fear not be a better thing to feel?

Conservative: Perhaps — but only just enough.

Guru: In order not to fall to cowardice?

Conservative: That's right.

Guru: Then why not fight without contempt? It's as I've said: contempt is something that we have to overcome.

Director: But you did not discuss the fight I had in mind, the one I wished to hear you talk about. I meant the fight within. I meant the feeling that a man will have against himself. I meant the feeling of contempt for what one might well do.

Guru: It's all the same. That, too, is something that one overcomes.

Conservative: What's that? No shame for any deed? Is that the thing you preach?

Guru: You're right. Contempt and shame are closely paired. An honest man will never feel contempt for what he does.

Conservative: That may be true but that's because he feels contempt to do a deed of shame!

Guru: But why not fear?

Conservative: A coward lives like that.

Guru: And you have scorn for him?

Conservative: I do. A man must fight the urges that he feels.

Guru: And he who fails to fight is evil to your mind?

Conservative: He's worthy of contempt, though maybe he's not evil yet.

Guru: What keeps him back?

Conservative: I think it's as you said: he's too afraid to do the things he wants to do.

Guru: So neither he who fights nor he who fears will do these evil deeds. Perhaps you're fighting fear?

Conservative: I think it best to let your comment slide before I lose my cool. Now, Director, it's clear to me you see these things the way I do. I've worked with you for many years and know you hold yourself upright. I'd like to hear you state the case for why contempt is natural, is something that we need — is even something good.

Director: I'm really not the best equipped to state this case, my friend. But I would say the question has to do with fear, as Guru seems to know. If fear is all there is to check an evil deed then power is the key — the power that can make another fear. But here we've got a problem, friends. It's not so clear what role contempt will play if we assume that men are ruled by fear. Contempt exists. The question is what shape it takes by whom and when. The ones who cause the fear are strong. The ones who fear are weak. Then who will feel contempt?

Conservative: The ones who're strong will feel contempt for those who're weak.

Director: And what about the weak? Or do you think that they'll have come to see and understand the All, as Guru says?

Conservative: I guess they'll have contempt for those who're strong.

Director: Now, what could make the ones who're strong decide they do not feel contempt for those who're weak?

Conservative: I guess they might feel pity for the weak.

Director: And what could make the weak decide they do not feel contempt for those who're strong?

Conservative: They wouldn't pity them, so I don't know.

Director: Oh, Guru, do you know?

Guru: It's possible they'd feel a love for them.

Conservative: Although they rule through fear? Impossible.

Director: The weak will always feel contempt for those who're strong and rule through fear?

Conservative: I think they will, unless they're so afraid they can't.

Director: Then is this how it always has to be or is there something that will give?

Conservative: There's never anything to give except through force.

Guru: It seems to me that change must soon arise from where the force of fear derives. A handful of the ones who rule will come to feel a pity for the weak. That's always how it starts.

Director: And their contempt?

Guru: Will shift toward the ones who rule through fear and fail to feel a pity for the ruled.

Director: You mean that their contempt has not been overcome?

Guru: Oh no. Their pity and contempt must stand opposed. It's always so. You never find an ounce of pity standing by itself without contempt to back it up. And all the same you never find contempt without an ounce of pity deep inside.

Director: For whom do those who rule through fear feel pity?

Guru: Those who rule through fear. It isn't pleasant ruling thus.

Director: And why will some of them begin to feel a pity for the ruled?

Guru: They lose their pity for their fellow rulers, Director.

Director: And why is that?

Guru: They see that some of those who rule enjoy their rule. In other words, they see that some are now corrupt. They see their pity is misplaced, and then they feel contempt. But soon they'll grow confused. The ones who like their rule are bound to be quite cruel, since that's the virtue of this state. Their pleasure comes through slacking off and shooting far beyond the mark. The ones who only use sufficient force to cause the necessary fear will start to ask: why take the pains we do to be precise with fear (our form of justice in this state)? You see?

Director: So now we have the uncorrupted ones who rule through measured fear, the ones who've grown both lax and greatly cruel, the ones who're now confused and start to feel contempt for those who've grown unjust along with pity for the ruled, and those who're simply ruled. But in the latter camp are there now factions to be found?

Guru: Oh yes. A handful of the ruled may start to have a pity for the ones who pity them — because the fiercest rulers who are now unjust will surely turn on those who have a pity for the ruled. The other ruled will have contempt for those who have a pity for the ones who rule. Divisions soon on harder lines will come and battles will be fought until the cycle starts again. Yet in the course of this a very few will grasp the fact that there is no way out until contempt is overcome — and pity, too.

Conservative: What then? They sit and watch while everything goes down? It seems to me you preach a voyeuristic creed. But all of this is based upon the notion that the rule through fear is just. Suppose one rules through other means.

Guru: Alright. What means are those?

Conservative: Abilities and skills and strengths. Suppose the best will rule — an aristocracy.

Director: Aristocrats will have contempt for whom?

Conservative: For those who doubt their right to rule.

Director: It seems that this could be aristocrats themselves or those who're ruled.

Conservative: That's true.

Director: And those who doubt their right to rule will have contempt for them?

Conservative: Correct.

Director: And what about the pity corresponding to contempt?

Conservative: The rightful rulers pity other rulers for they know the difficulties that they face. Those rightly ruled have pity for the rightful rulers, too. They may not understand in full the difficulties that their rulers face but sense the rulers bear a heavy load and pity them the same.

Director: And their contempt?

Conservative: If all are rightly ruled they'll have to find another object for contempt, perhaps outside the state.

Director: Might this not be the way a war would start?

Conservative: It surely might.

Guru: So here's the fighting creed: the pity that you feel will drive you to the ones you scorn.

Conservative: That doesn't sound so good to me.

Guru: Do you recall the words you said a little while ago: we need to have a fighting creed for daily life — and that includes contempt for certain sorts of acts. I asked you if those acts are done by those you fight and you said yes. Now here you say the act is challenge to a proper rule. You are a guardian, my friend. That's clear. But guardians exist outside the state as well. Each body formed by men must have its guardians. Each body also has to have the one or ones who rule. A proper rule requires that the rulers bear great strain, and this engenders tenderness for them. Perhaps we've had it wrong. Perhaps it isn't pity that one feels for them but love. So here's your fighting creed: the love you feel will lead you to your enemy.

Conservative: That's somehow weird but much more right.

Director: Perhaps you think it's weird because the opposite of love is not contempt but hate.

Conservative: You're right. One hates one's enemy.

Guru: Well, Director, you're right of course. Contempt is just a secondary thing. Contempt derives from hate and fear. Contempt is thus impure, or blended, if you will. But hate is pure — and so is love — and so is fear. Beyond these things, these primes, emotions all, there lies biology — and that is all.

Director: And that is all? But should we be so quick to go beyond? You've said that there's no right and there's no wrong. But surely right and wrong are very real to all who fight. A guardian should fight for what is right.

Conservative: That's right.

Director: Unless you tell me that a guardian does not exist you cannot say there is no right. A guardian will fight for proper rule against improper challenge to that rule.

Guru: But that of which you speak is only "real" within his mind.

Director: Where else would right exist? But will a guardian feel love and hate and fear and nothing else, or will he also feel contempt?

Guru: He'll surely feel contempt.

Director: And this is fear and hate combined? Then why are they combined and what's the object of contempt?

Guru: It's all the same. A handful of the guardians will start to feel a pity for the ones who lack ability and then contempt for those who shove them down, as always must occur in aristocracies.

Director: I thought you said contempt is nothing but discomfort over dealing with a part of All that one would rather not. What part is that? It can't be pity, eh?

Guru: It surely is.

Director: By dealing with you mean to come to understanding, no?

Guru: I do.

Director: You've said contempt is hate and fear combined. Are we to think that pity's something similar?

Guru: It is. It's love and fear combined. A guardian might feel a love for one kept down and be afraid of what a love like that might mean. It's thus that pity's born — a love that's watered down by fear. And so contempt is just a hate that's watered down by fear.

Conservative: I'm not so sure that's right.

Guru: Well, how do you define these things?

Conservative: To me the two involve a looking down. You cannot feel contempt unless you think yourself above the object of your scorn, and anyone who pities feels himself above the one for whom he's sorry, right? A man in love looks up. A man who hates? A man who fears? I'm not so sure. But we are speaking of contempt. Contempt involves a high opinion of oneself, in moral or in social terms. The object of contempt is seen as standing low in moral or in social terms. There need not be a bit of fear in one who scorns, as anyone can see.

Guru: But one who scorns declines to act against the object of contempt. Now, why is that?

Conservative: That isn't always true. There is a risk, as you have said, that one who scorns will make mistakes and underestimate a foe. But those one scorns aren't always foes. One simply values them quite low. To overcome contempt one levels everything. With neither high nor low contempt is now impossible — and so is pity, too — and so is love.

Guru: You think that equals cannot love?

Conservative: That isn't love. It's just respect.

Guru: And do you think that equals cannot pity one another's fate?

Conservative: That's more like sympathy.

Director: So on this leveled field we find some sympathy and some respect. But what of fear and hate? Are they reserved for foes?

Conservative: They are.

Director: Do foes exist on leveled ground?

Conservative: Of course they do.

Director: What sort of foe are they?

Conservative: I think that there are only two kinds possible: a natural opponent or an enemy by choice.

Director: And on a leveled field there's no contempt for them.

Conservative: That's right.

Director: Just hate and fear.

Conservative: Exactly so.

Director: And bravery is possible because of fear.

Conservative: That's true.

Director: And clemency is possible because of hate.

Conservative: You're right.

Director: And what is possible because of sympathy? Or should I ask what makes it possible itself?

Conservative: We've said that it's equality that makes for sympathy, which makes for generosity.

Director: And what is possible because we have respect? But should I also ask what makes it possible itself?

Conservative: Equality is what we said is also necessary for respect, which makes for admiration and a leaving well enough alone.

Director: A leaving well enough alone? You mean respect cannot be had for enemies, assuming that we do not leave our enemies alone.

Conservative: That's right.

Director: Our enemies are not our equals then?

Conservative: Correct.

Director: And yet we don't look up or down on them.

Conservative: Of course we do. We must look down on enemies less powerful. But as for enemies more powerful than us we must look up in one respect but down when thinking of the matter in dispute, the moral cause.

Director: So that's the limit of our leveled field. As soon as one has enemies the third dimension's there, the Z coordinate — and then we have contempt. But wait! As for the types of enemies you've said that there are only two: the natural and that by choice. What sort is this that makes us have contempt — or is it both?

Conservative: It's that by choice. An enemy by nature doesn't choose to be an enemy: he simply is — and thus there's no contempt. But he who is an enemy by choice is worthy of contempt.

Director: And that's because his choice runs counter to the moral cause?

Conservative: That's right.

Guru: And so without the moral cause there is no enemy and no contempt.

Conservative: We cannot live without the moral cause, though what you say in empty argument is strictly true.

Director: But that still leaves the enemy by nature, right?

Conservative: It does.

Director: This sort of enemy is like the wolf who hunts the rabbit, right?

Conservative: That's right.

Director: But rabbits don't look up to wolves.

Conservative: That's true.

Director: And wolves most likely don't look down on rabbits, eh?

Conservative: I think that's true.

Director: And there is nothing moral in the difference in the power from the rabbit to the wolf?

Conservative: Oh no. The wolf is stronger, that is all.

Director: Now let us take two human beings, one who's strong and one who's weak.

Guru: But strong and weak in what?

Director: I thought you'd ask. Well, let's suppose their strength is in their limbs. Will one look up and one look down?

Conservative: Perhaps, depending on the sort of men they are.

Director: You mean depending on their moral choice? In other words, depending on their choice to make an enemy.

Conservative: I think you're right.

Director: From this shall we infer that differences in strength do not provide the grounds for being enemies by nature?

Conservative: Yes.

Director: And what about the rabbit and the wolf?

Conservative: It's different for the animals. Their species differ, Director.

Director: But man and man by nature will not fight? If wolf fights wolf is that because of moral choice?

Conservative: Of course it's not.

Director: If man fights man it's always due to moral choice?

Conservative: If they are not to be like animals it is.

Director: So moral choice is how we separate the animals from men.

Conservative: It is.

Director: And what about contempt? An enemy by choice, we've said, is worthy of contempt.

Conservative: That's right.

Director: Contempt is thus a fundamental feeling for a fighting moral man.

Guru: That's nicely done. You've left it open that a moral man who doesn't fight won't feel contempt.

Conservative: You read too closely into what he says. A moral choice, once made, necessitates that one will be prepared to fight. A man who's not prepared to fight has failed to make a choice.

Guru: Prepared to fight? For what?

Conservative: For what one's chosen as the right. You say that there's no right — at least no right that you uphold. I say that you have failed to choose.

Guru: You think that I am not a moral man?

Conservative: That's right. I do.

Guru: You're right. I'm not. I live beyond both right and wrong — and I have peace.

Conservative: I think that you have nothing but a voyeuristic view of life.

Guru: And do you have contempt for me?

Conservative: The truth? I do.

Guru: And your contempt is based upon a choice you've made?

Conservative: It is.

Guru: A choice to be a moral man?

Conservative: That's right.

Guru: But don't you see how empty such a choice must be? Why, you and I have nothing in dispute.

Conservative: Not so. A man must choose or else he can't be worthy of one's trust. Your view of life as understanding "All" precludes the sort of choice a moral man must make.

Guru: What sort of choice is that? To choose to fight?

Conservative: To choose to serve a cause that might require that you fight.

Guru: And do you have contempt for those who fail to choose to serve a cause like that?

Conservative: I do.

Guru: And so you have contempt for me.

Conservative: That's right.

Guru: But I don't have contempt for you.

Conservative: But don't you think you're somehow better than I am?

Guru: I think I take the broader view.

Conservative: And what's so good about a broader view? You seem to think that
seeing is the simple good.

Guru: It is — as long as one is dealing with the things one sees.

Conservative: So that's your cause: to see. But what is that? You say that you have
peace. I'd like to know the cost. You do not fight the evil that exists. You
claim to see and know and understand. But can you know the meaning of
a sacrifice for right?

III. ARCHITECT

Persons of the Dialogue:

Director

Architect

Engineer

Artist

Director: Now, Engineer, Architect and his friends maintain that memory and intelligence and all such things are what is best in life; while my friends and I maintain that what is most enduring and also most difficult to render enduring is what is best in life, and this we say is trusting human relationships. Is that correct, Architect?

Architect: Yes, the matter appears to stand as depicted.

Director: Then it is up to you, Engineer, to decide what it is that you maintain. If after taking in what it is that I and my friends maintain you feel that it is not to your liking you must argue against it; or if it is to your liking join us in its maintenance.

Engineer: Indeed, Director, things stand as you say. And I will begin by asking you something that has troubled me about your doctrine for some time now. You state that the most enduring is best: yet what do you say of something beautiful such as a rose? The beauty of a rose is a good, as I am sure you would admit, yet it is exceedingly fleeting. Your doctrine would seem to say that a stone is better than a rose, and on this ground alone I have serious doubts as to the authenticity of your teaching.

Director: Well, and in your opinion, what is more intelligent a thing, the stone or the rose?

Engineer: The rose, certainly.

Director: And what is it that makes the rose more intelligent, if we are sound in applying such a term to a plant?

Engineer: The rose grows and then blooms while the stone remains unchanged.

Director: Then do you admit that there is such a thing as momentum?

Engineer: Of course.

Director: And momentum, is this not the opposite of intelligence in the sense that once gained it continues on without change or any modification appropriate to circumstances?

Engineer: Yes.

Director: And may we not consider momentum as similar to the river ever flowing in the same course that digs the depths of the Grand Canyon over time?

Engineer: I suppose.

Director: Then would you admit that there are different types of growth, and not just growth simply; or if you assert that there is such a thing as growth simply and in all cases then will you be so good as to tell us what it is you take this be?

Engineer: I do indeed believe that there is only one type of growth, and it is simply increase.

Director: But if all growth is nothing more than increase, how do you account for the man, now in sound physical form, yet who was at a younger age of greater weight than he is now? You would admit that such cases do occur?

Engineer: Of course they do.

Director: Well, how is it? Did he grow, and if so, in what sense did he grow?

Engineer: For one, he grew in stature.

Director: Agreed, quite. Yet while growing we may also say he did the opposite?

Engineer: Yes.

Director: And if the opposite it may not be maintained that he grew simply. Rather, might one not assert that there was a certain cancellation of forces, as it were?

Engineer: I suppose one might maintain this.

Director: And if this were so, how is it that this man grown fit differs from the stone, which has neither grown nor shrunk, relatively speaking?

Engineer: Here, Director, it appears quite clearly why your teaching is unsound: for if you cannot see the difference between a man and a stone there really is no point in my arguing with you any longer, and I will side with Architect and adopt and maintain his teaching.

Director: Yet in what sense does the rose have any more intelligence than the stone? Does it in some way manage its growth intelligently, or is it not rather like the case of the river that it flows on, as it were, in its growing until it blooms and then begins to fade? Tell me: does the rose have a say in the manner of its growth?

Engineer: No, it does not.

Director: Nor does the rock have a say in its seeming to remain the same?

Engineer: No.

Director: Yet the man, he does indeed have some say in the character of his growth?

Engineer: Decidedly so.

Director: Then in respect to the type of intelligence we are discussing that of the man differs qualitatively from that of the rose or the stone or any other inanimate object for that matter?

Engineer: It follows from what we have admitted.

Director: Now this man clearly must not take growth for its own sake as what is best?

Engineer: On your own admissions he has used his intelligence to regulate his growth, and we see that intelligence is the controlling factor, the thing that is best.

Director: But do you say then that intelligence regulates growth so as to make it intelligent growth?

Engineer: Yes, that is what I say — and that only goes to show that intelligence is better than endurance.

Director: And in your opinion all regulation of a process or thing is done with an end in view? For instance, when the flow of the river is regulated by the Hoover Dam is this not done, at least in part, for the sake of the generation of electrical power?

Engineer: Yes, it is.

Director: In this case the dam regulates flow in order to produce power. And how is it with the case of intelligence regulating the flow of growth? For the production of what does intelligence regulate growth?

Engineer: For the sake of health.

Director: Then you must believe that health, not intelligence, is what is best in life. Indeed, this would seem to hold from your views of other matters as well. Take your profession, engineering: for what purpose do we design and manufacture goods by means of technology if not for the sake of human health and well being?

Engineer: Indeed, Director, that is the reason for my profession — and it is a noble profession, serving mankind as it does.

Director: Thus, in your hands, intelligence is not the end but rather the means to the end of health and well being for all mankind.

Engineer: That is so.

Director: Then all engineers are doctors or psychologists?

Architect: Really, Director, I do not follow you here.

Director: No, nor would I expect you to. But let me attempt to explain. And if I am not successful in making clear my meaning to you perhaps it will become so with one of the others here present.

Architect: Yes.

Director: Engineer has just affirmed that engineering exists for the sake of the production of the health and well being of mankind. Now would you agree one produces only that which one knows how to produce?

Engineer: Of course, Director. What do you think: that we engineers simply churn things out without considering their use?

Director: No, indeed, Engineer — I do not accuse you of that. Yet I simply say that you must be both doctors and psychologists, or some other named profession that understands what health and well-being are and how to go about producing them. And I have one further question for you, since you are eager to answer: do the same things produce health and well being in all men?

Engineer: Of course not.

Director: So for some men one diet is best while another for others?

Engineer: That is correct, Director.

Director: Well, Engineer, it follows from this then that those of your profession engineer some things for some men and other things for other men, no?

Engineer: We most certainly do.

Director: And is it intelligence which you use to determine what things to manufacture for whom or is it some other regulative principle?

Engineer: You ask as if you did not fully well know that it is the market which regulates what we produce.

Director: Then the market takes the place of intelligence here? For in the case of the good doctor or psychologist do they not use their intelligence to judge what treatment if proper for what patient?

Engineer: Are you implying that what we do is done without intelligence?

Director: Far from it. But what I doubt is whether intelligence is not, even in your own view, that which is best in life. For if it were, I believe you would determine what to manufacture not by means of the market — which I take it you would say is unintelligent, at least in the same sense as we agreed that the rose is unintelligent — but rather by means of intelligence, in order to render all that you create intelligent, or in the likeness of intelligence. Yet I say that you do not actually take intelligence to be the best thing by virtue of your deference to the market. For it is quite clear that engineers as a whole are some of the most able men in the world. Yet they regulate themselves by means of the market. Now, what is the market that engineers put such trust in it to order their business? It seems to me in this light that the market may be a mechanism created by humans for the sake of maintaining sound human relationships. Now since I am not at all certain about this I ask you and all others I meet who chance to discourse upon such topics, what they hold: what is the function of the market?

Engineer: The market is indeed what you have said, a means created by humans for controlling conduct and interaction.

Director: Then the end for which the market exists is control of conduct and interaction?

Engineer: Yes.

Director: And does the market admit of any higher regulation than that of the market itself? In other words, what regulates or limits the market?

Engineer: Here, Director, you touch upon a topic that is much contested, as you must be well aware.

Director: Indeed, I have heard arguments about this very subject — but it is your opinion that I am interested in here: what do you say about this?

Engineer: Well, certainly governments interfere with the markets.

Director: And in your view is this as it should be?

Engineer: I cannot say. I have gone over this very issue over and over again without coming to certainty one way or the other.

Director: But perhaps our difficulty, Engineer, is not as great as it might at first appear: for we were interested in the market as an institution created by human beings for the sake of human relationships. Now regardless of whether your or my opinion is that the market ought to be the highest form of regulation of those relationships or whether there ought be one yet higher, such as government, now seems to me to be a matter of little or no consequence.

Engineer: How so?

Director: Really, have you not followed? Both the market and government, in our sense here, are about the same thing: regulating the creation of goods by means of technology for the sake of human relationships. Or do you think that government operates for some other purpose?

Engineer: No, I would agree that it is the task of government — not very often fulfilled — of regulating human conduct for the sake of relationships between individuals.

Director: Yet I fear that we will have to deepen our inquiry in order to determine whether you will join with me and my friends or Architect and his. Now it was once thought that the end of government was the good of man. Were this the general view today you and I would proceed to debate whether the end of government ought to be intelligence and such or formation of trusting human relationships, yes?

Engineer: Yes.

Director: But we today hold that government is distinct from society, but together they make up the nation. Do you agree?

Engineer: Of course.

Director: Then let us consider: is there anything that regulates the nation or is the nation unregulated? For if there is something that regulates the nation we must then turn our inquiry in that direction, or is it that there is nothing that regulates the nation?

Engineer: Director, I think there is indeed something, but I confess that I do not know what.

Director: In that case ought we not consider what there is in common between government and society in order to see if we may trace what is shared to something regulative?

Engineer: I see no other way.

Director: Then let us consider: government is according to law in liberal democracies, is it not?

Engineer: Yes, it is.

Director: And society has no law?

Engineer: I do not think this is so clear, for culture and tradition may play the role of laws.

Director: Certainly they may, Engineer, but do they today in the states of which we speak?

Engineer: I do not know, Director. Have not anthropologists shown us that there are unwritten rules obeyed by different societies?

Director: That is what they profess to have demonstrated. But if they are correct that there are such rules, then they must have been created by someone or others at some time or other?

Engineer: But many of the anthropologists maintain that these rules have simply evolved, that they were not consciously or deliberately created by anyone.

Director: This seems to me to open up to another rather long discussion. But let us consider what we are about here. If we say that these societal 'rules' were deliberately created they must have been done so for the sake of some end. If not deliberately created, then not for the sake of some end or according to an end not chosen by or of man. Yet in the case of governments we agree that they, at least the liberal democracies, were clearly founded for the sake of some end of man?

Engineer: Certainly.

Director: Then there is the end of government and there may be an end of society. If it turns out that there are two ends we must then determine whether they are actually one and the same or whether they are different, and if different, complimentary or in competition with one another, no?

Engineer: Yes.

Director: So, are there one or two ends?

Engineer: I say there is only one: that of government.

Director: And can you say what that end is?

Engineer: Yes, the end of government is to provide the framework for the flowering of the individual within society.

Director: Why, Architect, do you hear what this amazing man says?

Architect: Yes, I do, Director, and I must say that it seems to me to have been well put.

Director: Yet do you not wonder about this seemingly small addition "within society"?

Architect: Will you tell us what it is that makes it seem otherwise to you, Director?

Director: Indeed, it is now incumbent upon me to carry things forward having brought us to this point. Are we all agreed that in this manner we best proceed?

Engineer: That is how it seems to me and I believe Architect agrees.

Director: Then we proceed. We began by considering whether intelligence or enduring relations is best. We then considered the difference between a stone, a rose, and a man. This led us to consideration of both growth and momentum. It was then said that there is only one type of growth but that growth may be regulated by intelligence. We then considered whether growth was regulated for the sake of intelligence itself or for health, and it was the latter which appeared to be the end. We next considered human health and well being as the ends of engineering, but that as with medicine or psychology, different things are needed for different people, and that it is the market which in this case regulates what things are to be produced by engineering. We next took up the character of the market and its usefulness for humans and considered whether the market is the highest regulative institution, and if so to what end it regulates. This led us to a discussion of government and the difference between it, the nation, and society, and the ends of these different three. Now in considering these three at this time we are looking to see if they exist for the sake of intelligence or if they are established to provide support for the flourishing of trusting human relationships. There was agreement that our liberal democracies have been founded with an end in view, but there was some discussion as to whether our societies had been founded or evolved of their own accord. Now at this point it seemed that we had to choose one path or another, whether the ends of government and society were mutually supportive, one and the same, or contradictory. It is at this point that our good man here, Engineer, affirmed that there is only one end, that of government, and that the end is to provide within society the framework for the flowering of the individual.

Architect: Director, it seemed to me that you were offering an excellent summary of our discussion so far — at least until the very end: for you have moved that little phrase, as you put it, to a place in which it renders or suggests a meaning quite different than that which I believe our good man, Engineer, intended.

Director: Well, and what do you say is the import of this difference?

Architect: It seems to me best for you to take this up with Engineer.

Engineer: I am ready.

Director: I take it you think you understand that to which Architect refers?

Engineer: I believe so.

Director: And do you think it a matter of small moment?

Engineer: No, not in my view.

Director: Then it is a question of whether the 'open range' still exists, as it were.

Engineer: In a sense.

Director: But by this 'in a sense' you have said practically nothing. Surely you aspire to obtain to more certainty on a matter of such importance as this?

Engineer: I admit, Director, that I find it hard to follow you in all this and how it relates to our initial question: whether intelligence or endurance is best.

Director: But this is not such a difficult thing, is it? For surely you would agree that it may be useful for a man to reason by analogy in difficult cases?

Engineer: Of course.

Director: And in this case we are discussing a most important issue — whether enduring, trusting human relationships are better than memory and intelligence and the like. Yet in our discussion the argument led us naturally enough to consideration of human institutions. And as we consider the ends of these institutions we may imagine ourselves, may we not, as being able to found them and determine the end toward which they are to aim?

Engineer: Yes, we may certainly imagine if we are not able to actually do.

Director: Yes, good enough. So, tell me, if you were granted the power to found the institutions we have named, and any others you may see fit, toward what end would you point them?

Engineer: Toward the end of human happiness.

Director: Then in your view happiness and intelligence are the same?

Engineer: Yes, they are.

Director: Then, in your view, are all of those with high intellectual abilities necessarily happy?

Engineer: They have the potential to be.

Director: Yes, for you engineers hold that 'anything is possible given enough money'. But they are not always so?

Engineer: No, certainly not.

Director: And what is the cause of this, a failing in their intelligence?

Engineer: That may very well be the case.

Director: Granted. But is it not something more often like, for example, inability to please someone for whom they have a high regard or even love — a parent, a sibling, a friend, a spouse?

Engineer: That is the case often enough, as it seems to me.

Director: And is pleasing another a matter strictly of intelligence?

Engineer: If it were things would stand quite differently.

Director: And are there not other reasons why a man of high intelligence might not be happy? Shall we proceed to name them one by one, or do you agree?

Engineer: No, I am quite agreed.

Director: You have saved us time. Then we are agreed that intelligence and happiness are not the same?

Engineer: Yes.

Director: Yet you still maintain that intelligence and the like are what is best in life?

Engineer: I do.

Director: Then will you not consider with me what it would mean to found institutions the end of which are the promotion of intelligence and the like? For surely if you believe that intelligence is what is best you would wish to found institutions dedicated to this end?

Engineer: There seems to be no other way but to agree.

Director: Then how shall we begin? There is the market, the state, the society, the nation, and any other of various institutions both real and imagined.

Engineer: But Director, you cannot found a market — markets are just a natural phenomenon of human commerce.

Director: Then markets have always existed?

Engineer: No, of course not in the sense we understand them today.

Director: But really, Engineer, are you telling me that as long as there have been humans there have been markets, in each and every civilization and spot on the globe, as seems likely to me?

Engineer: No, Director, I am not fool enough to make that assertion: for anthropologists and natural historians have showed us that there have been and still are societies in which no market exists. But it seems to me that this is because there are things impeding the natural flow of goods and services from one to another. Take away these barriers and a market naturally arises. But this seems to me, along with society, to be the more difficult case.

Director: Then does the state seem the easiest place for us to begin?

Engineer: Yes, it does.

Director: Then shall we imagine that we have been charged with the founding of such a state and that we will dedicate it to the proposition that cultivation of intelligence is the highest end of human endeavor; and then we will see if we can determine whether in practice intelligence is truly the best thing in life and worthy of this dedication?

Engineer: That seems to me an excellent idea; and in the process we may also examine your proposition that enduring human relationships are what is best in life.

Director: Alright, upon what grounds shall we build — for we must select a plot of land, as it were, before laying the foundation?

Engineer: Of course.

Director: Well, since we have the freedom of speech let us discuss what grounds would be most favorable for such a state.

Engineer: Why not say that it is a colony on a newly discovered planet?

Director: And shall we set aside the issues of technology and the concomitant expenses, assuming that all of this is economically viable?

Engineer: Yes, let us set that discussion aside.

Director: And this colony, is it to be large or small?

Engineer: Small, I should say.

Director: Then it is all the more important, is it not, for us to select carefully how it will be populated?

Engineer: Yes.

Director: And how shall we populate our colony, which is to form a state dedicated to intelligence?

Engineer: I confess, Director, that I am somewhat at a loss on this question.

Director: Come now, Engineer, and do not get shy on me at this early stage in our work. Would it make sense to select as highly intelligent a population as possible for our colony?

Engineer: I suppose.

Director: And how do we go about selecting such a population, by IQ or some other such standardized test measuring intelligence?

Engineer: I suppose some sort of standardized test would be good, sort of like the governmental exams.

Director: But are those exams not designed to measure proficiency at a particular function as opposed to general intelligence?

Engineer: Yes.

Director: And it is conceivable that those who are best at a particular function may not be most generally intelligent?

Artist: It is more than conceivable; I should say it is rather likely.

Director: Do you have any objection, Engineer, to my proceeding with your brother for a while, as it may prove useful to our discussion?

Engineer: Not at all.

Director: Then tell me, Artist, do you object to a high degree of specialization, or what?

Artist: Yes, I do, Director. For unlike my brother I am not willing to limit myself to dry, technical topics.

Director: Then with what topics do you concern yourself?

Artist: I am concerned with humanity, Director.

Director: And in this, how is it that you differ from the rest of us — for are we all not concerned with humanity?

Artist: Of course we are: but I am concerned with the depiction of humanity.

Director: And I take it that in your opinion one must have knowledge of what it is one would depict, at least if one is to do an adequate job?

Artist: Of course.

Director: And if there were a builder about to construct a home, would he have to know the plans before he would be able to do a proper job?

Artist: Yes.

Director: And if a man were a pilot, would he have to know the flight path or whatever navigational information might be required in order to be successful in his calling?

Artist: Certainly.

Director: And in both cases, is intelligence required?

Artist: A degree of intelligence, of course.

Director: A degree, yes — but I take it that it is your opinion that it is not a great degree of intelligence?

Artist: That is correct.

Director: And in your opinion, is intelligence a thing admitting of degree, or quantity, or is it best judged by quality.

Engineer: Quantity, Director — there is no doubt of that.

Director: And if quantity, would the man with the greater quantity of intelligence be better able to perform the job?

Engineer: Yes.

Director: So that the more intelligent pilot is the better pilot and the more intelligent builder is the better builder.

Engineer: Truly, not in all cases in fact, but all other things being equal, yes.

Director: And by this 'all other things being equal', why, whatever is it to which you refer?

Engineer: You know what I mean: circumstances.

Director: So by circumstances do you mean whether the builder comes from a prominent family with many connections?

Engineer: That is one type of circumstance.

Director: Or could you also mean that market conditions will determine whether he is successful or not?

Engineer: That, too, is a relevant circumstance.

Director: Then what is it about that builder that makes him better than another? Is it the number of houses he builds or the margin of profit he earns?

Artist: No, it is most definitely not that: it is the quality of the houses he builds.

Director: And if the quality, as seems only proper, the more intelligent builds the better quality house?

Engineer: The plans have something to do with it as well.

Director: Then must we have both an intelligent builder as well as intelligent plans, or does it suffice to have intelligent plans?

Engineer: Both are required in my opinion.

Director: And if both, is the construction of a sound house guaranteed?

Engineer: I would say so.

Director: But of course the builder must follow the plans?

Engineer: Indeed.

Director: And is following the same as intelligence in your view?

Engineer: Of course not.

Artist: Here I am in full agreement with my brother.

Director: No doubt. Then faithful execution of the plan is required over and above intelligence?

Engineer: Yes.

Director: And if we assume that one knows how to read a plan, is intelligence still required in order to execute it?

Engineer: Yes.

Director: A lesser degree of intelligence to follow than to develop?

Engineer: Yes.

Director: And faithful execution, is that something best judged by degree or by quality?

Engineer: By quality — either the plans are faithfully executed or not.

Director: Now the plans, are they always perfect so that if faithfully executed a sound house results?

Engineer: Of course not.

Director: So faithful execution alone by the builder does not guarantee the sound house. Is it ever the case that a builder gets plans that are faulty yet comes out in the end with a sound house?

Engineer: That is certainly possible and does indeed happen on occasion.

Director: How does this happen?

Engineer: The experienced builder recognizes when there are faults in the plan and compensates for them.

Director: So it is experience that allows him to avoid disaster?

Engineer: Yes.

Director: And are experience and intelligence the same?

Engineer: No, they are not.

Director: Then when we choose our colonists, is it not apparent that experience is of more import than intelligence? For in the case of the colony our colonists will be more like the builder than the designer?

Engineer: They most certainly will.

Director: Then let it be said that in the colony dedicated to intelligence, experience is more important to the population than intelligence.

Engineer: But you assume that our plan will be flawed.

Director: And what of that? Do you expect we will come up with a perfect plan?

Engineer: That is the intent.

Director: And if the plan is perfect then is intelligence of more import than experience for the colonists?

Engineer: That is my opinion.

Director: So when we design the legal system and seek to fill the posts in the courts, for example, are we to select judges without regard to experience?

Engineer: No, experience is certainly valuable in a judge.

Director: And in the engineering corps, shall we choose the highly intelligent student right out of school over the less brilliant but experienced man?

Engineer: There is no more certain recipe for disaster than entrusting a project to an inexperienced engineer with a high opinion of himself. Much rather we should choose the experienced man.

Director: Then again, we see that experience takes precedent even in the state dedicated to intelligence. And so I ask you, Engineer, of what does the experience consist? Are the cases that come before a judge that much more complicated than those students study in the schools?

Engineer: No, I believe they study the most complicated of cases in school, and I have heard that the actual cases are usually much less interesting.

Director: And in engineering, are the jobs in practice much more complex and demanding than those worked through hypothetically by students?

Engineer: The student certainly works on more glamorous hypothetical projects, but I cannot say that they are more demanding than those of the practicing engineer.

Director: And what is it about the practice as opposed to the theory that makes it more demanding?

Engineer: Without doubt it is dealing with the people involved.

Director: So when we say that one gains experience in an area, it is not further experience in the theory of the profession but rather experience in making the theory effectual, and the difference lies in human interactions and relationships?

Engineer: Yes.

Director: And would you call this practical knowledge as opposed to theoretical knowledge?

Engineer: Indeed, I would, Director — but I also feel that the knowledge of the science of engineering is also eminently practical.

Director: But if we are not able to give effect to the knowledge and plans of engineering then does that knowledge remain practical or is it not then simply theoretical in your opinion?

Engineer: If engineering is not able to render any practical effect it most definitely remains theoretical.

Director: Then I take it that all engineering and architecture is dependent upon science in your view?

Engineer: Of course it is.

Director: And this is because science discloses the truth about nature and builders, architects, and engineers simply plan and act based upon the truths disclosed by the scientific method?

Engineer: Yes.

Director: And the scientific method itself, is this not a sort of plan or blueprint for the proceedings of the scientists, who may be likened to the builders?

Artist: Yes, Director, what you say is excellent.

Director: And do you affirm, Artist, that if the scientific method is like a blueprint that there must have been one who created that blueprint?

Artist: That would seem to follow from what we are saying.

Director: And will you tell us who is this designer of the blueprint for scientists?

Artist: I can tell you that it is definitely not God.

Director: Then if not God, was it some man who set down this scientific blueprint?

Artist: Not some man, Director, but a certain set of men: the capitalists. And I will say further that you could not have chosen a better manner of carrying on the discussion than your idea of founding a colony. For that is exactly how these men conceived of the New World. To them it was nothing more than a natural resource to be exploited for their own selfish ends.

Engineer: That is absurd, Artist. Do you really think that the generations of poor scientists who have spent their lives toiling in laboratories have done so in order to further the greedy designs of the rich?

Director: Architect, our young friends are growing quite heated in disputing this matter. Does it not seem best to you if you and I carry the discussion forward ourselves in hopes of preventing a break between brothers?

Architect: This does seem best. Yet perhaps we should also set ourselves the task for the sake of the memories of those scientists referred to just now?

Director: Your point is well made and taken. So we begin again with the question of whether intelligence is what is best in life, which is what you and your friends maintain. Now I have been arguing that intelligence cannot be what is best in life for when we found institutions to regulate our lives we do not dedicate them to intelligence. Rather it seems to me that we dedicate them to the fostering of trusting human relationships. And such relationships seem to me to be both most difficult to render enduring as well as most enduring once rendered. But I suppose, Architect, that you would object that there cannot be such a thing as well-placed trust without intelligence?

Architect: That is so.

Director: And that in a community of the intelligent trust would be well placed?

Architect: Yes.

Director: But what of that which we shall take to be the opposite case, a community of those with enduring, trusting relationships all around? Will not trust there be well placed as well?

Architect: That is not an easy question to answer, Director — for it depends on a good many things.

Director: Even so, would you say that trust is well placed when there are grounds for trusting?

Architect: Yes.

Director: And if there are grounds for trusting, the relationship of trust will endure if the parties continue to so desire?

Architect: That is certain.

Director: And you, too, agree that the builder, or he in analogous position, requires both experience and intelligence in order to complete the plans successfully?

Architect: Quite right.

Director: And must a community of those with enduring, trusting relationships be planned?

Architect: Absolutely, if it is to endure.

Director: Then in the community of the intelligent, could it, too, endure if there were no grounds for trust among the members — in other words can we say that a community exists without trust?

Architect: No, we may not.

Director: And do you agree that community is required for human life?

Architect: I do.

Director: Then on the one hand human life is impossible with intelligence but no trusting relationships; and on the other hand human life is equally impossible with trusting relationships but no intelligence.

Architect: Quite subtly put, and I cannot not agree with you further.

Director: So some combination of trusting relationships and intelligence is required for life. And if this is so, then the way to resolve our argument is to determine which of the two is higher.

Architect: Having gotten this far together, Director, and seeing that both our friends, the brothers, have let off preparing to attack one another, it is time to hand over my place to them.

Director: Who shall take Architect's place in the argument?

Artist: I will, Director, for what you and Architect have been saying is quite satisfying.

Director: Then tell us, Artist, in your opinion which holds the higher place?

Artist: Trusting relationships, of course — and I believe the reason for this is rather obvious as well: one may be intelligent without trust but one may not trust without intelligence, as you have just shown.

Director: But, you remarkable man, I must see if Engineer agrees with what has been said; for I sense that he is not pleased.

Engineer: No, how could I be when such foolishness is allowed to stand?

Director: And do you think it foolish to affirm that there is not trust without intelligence?

Engineer: Not that, Director, but that it is possible to be intelligent without trust. With that I do not agree. But I fear that I cannot explain why this is so.

Director: Then shall we consider this matter and see whether this is always the case or only sometimes, and in the process determine whether we may understand how to explain why there may not be intelligence without trust?

Engineer: I would like that very much.

Director: Then let us first consider what seems to me to be the most difficult question: whether it is possible for intelligence to exist without trust. For would you say that a thing which requires other things in order to exist is stronger or weaker than that which does not require the support of some other thing or things?

Engineer: That which requires no support is clearly stronger.

Director: So if we were to convince everyone that it is possible for intelligence to exist without trust we would be certain that intelligence takes the prize?

Engineer: I suppose.

Director: Is the function of intelligence, in your opinion, similar to that of a microprocessor?

Engineer: Indeed, Director, it has occurred to both me and many others that this is so.

Director: And microprocessors are valued according to their speed?

Engineer: Yes.

Director: And the speed of the microprocessor, why is this important?

Engineer: The faster the chip the more data it can process.

Director: And that which can process more data is more powerful?

Engineer: Yes.

Director: And power, do you not define that as the time rate of doing work or delivering energy?

Engineer: I do.

Director: So it follows that work or energy equals power times time?

Engineer: Yes.

Director: And it also follows that time equals work or energy divided by power?

Engineer: It does.

Director: And if these simple formulas hold for all things does it then not become clear that we may view the world as governed by a coefficient of power? In other words, consider the famous formula of Einstein. If work and energy are the same, then work equals mass times the speed of light squared.

Engineer: I agree.

Director: But there are also different types of energy, kinetic and potential?

Engineer: Surely.

Director: Then we may say there are also different types of work?

Engineer: That would follow.

Director: And is there not another view, which is perhaps the same in essence, which says that power may be measured by quanta of heat in relation to time; for energy, they say, is a matter of heat.

Engineer: Yes.

Director: And if it were possible to measure all the heat in the universe, we would be able to determine the sum total of power?

Engineer: Not without considering time.

Director: And that is where speed comes into play?

Engineer: Precisely.

Director: So as the quantum of power approaches infinity so too will time decrease?

Engineer: I suppose.

Director: But then what of our little silicon chips — how powerful could they be? But perhaps it is not very much work at all that they truly perform?

Engineer: But how can you say that when they are able to do in five minutes what all the scientists and engineers in the world that have ever been could not do in the amount of years of their total lifespan?

Director: That, Engineer, seems to me to be an excellent question for you to consider in all seriousness. And I would be willing to take this question up with you, but it must be at another time — for we still have not finished our discussion of whether intelligence or trust is higher.

Engineer: Yes, we ought to finish what we have set out to accomplish.

Director: And in order to do this we must decide whether intelligence may stand alone without trust?

Engineer: Right.

Director: And when the computer performs a calculation for you which you rely upon in building a bridge, must you not trust the result that appears?

Engineer: In a sense, yes — but I would hardly consider that this is the sort of trust we are talking about.

Director: But why not? The computer, in order to produce the desired result, must have been manufactured properly?

Engineer: Of course.

Director: And in order to be manufactured properly the designs must have been sound?

Engineer: Yes.

Director: And for the designs to be sound, the designers must have had a sound grounding in electrical engineering or some such similar science?

Engineer: Yes.

Director: And moreover, when you are operating under a construction deadline you will be unable to produce the design of the bridge unless power is supplied to the computer?

Engineer: Of course, Director. But I fail to see why you are wasting our time with all of this.

Director: What seems to you to be so obvious, Engineer, seems to me to be an incredibly complicated system of trusting human relationships that culminates in the calculations performed by your microprocessor. For the workers at the power plant must trust that their employer will pay them for their labor. And the people who manufacture the computers must trust that the credit of their customers is sound. And you, Engineer, must trust that the mathematical instructions programmed into the computer square with your own mathematical understanding. All of this, my good man, seems to me to require a great deal of trust.

Engineer: That may be, Director, but what you have described is what is necessary for any society to function, whether cannibals in the jungle or Americans in Silicon Valley. That does not tell us whether intelligence itself requires trust.

Director: So you affirm that the work — of whatever quantity or quality that may be — performed by the microprocessor does not constitute intelligence?

Engineer: It most definitely does not.

Director: You would not say that the microprocessor trusts in any sense, would you?

Engineer: Of course not.

Director: And the microprocessor is unintelligent?

Engineer: Yes.

Director: And we seek to determine whether intelligence and memory or trusting relationships are best?

Engineer: Yes.

Director: And we are, to that end, considering whether intelligence may exist without trust. Yet, oh, Engineer, we seem to me to have been proceeding as though without intelligence — for we have not yet said what it is we take intelligence to be.

Engineer: No, we have not.

Director: Well then, intelligence is not 'number crunching'?

Engineer: No, not all of itself.

Director: Then intelligence is 'number crunching' plus some other element?

Engineer: Yes.

Director: Then intelligence is a sort of whole comprised of parts?

Engineer: It certainly seems that way to me.

Artist: But this is ridiculous! How can you say that intelligence is composed of parts, as if you were building a machine called Intelligence?

Director: Then intelligence is an isolated whole? But if it seems this way in your view, Artist, tell me how it is that you maintain that trusting relationships are higher than intelligence, but that intelligence may exist without trust but not trusting relationships without intelligence? Or is it that you would maintain some sort of distinction between trust and trusting relationships?

Artist: Yes, I would — and with very good reason, Director.

Director: And is it, in your view, the case that intelligence as isolated whole may exist because trust is somehow isolated along with it, within and as a part of this whole, yet without having external, as it were, trusting relationships?

Artist: It seems to me, Director, that you know exactly what I am talking about.

Director: Then surely, Artist, you would be able to tell us what it is that constitutes this internal and integrated trust? For all trust must surely have an object, must it not?

Artist: Yes.

Director: And if there are no external trusting relationships in an isolated intelligence then the object of the trust must be internal? And if it is internal, then surely the intelligence must have knowledge of that which is within its domain? And if so, one might articulate that which is the object of this internal trust. Then tell us, Artist, what is this object?

Artist: One trusts oneself, Director, as you of all people know quite well.

Director: Yet I have never made this claim, Artist; nor do I know what you claim to know that I do. But perhaps I will learn what it is you say I know. Would you be willing to help me?

Artist: Yes, but I think you are fooling with us now.

Director: No, Artist, you could not be more mistaken. You have heard of Odysseus?

Artist: Of course.

Director: And you would say he was an intelligent man?

Artist: A most intelligent man, Director.

Director: And did he, in your view, possess this isolated intelligence?

Artist: One might say he is the archetype.

Director: Very good. And I presume you recall the story of his sailing past the sirens?

Artist: Yes.

Director: And would you say he trusted himself in having his crew bind him to the mast?

Artist: This is not what I am talking about.

Director: Or perhaps when he sat day after day crying his eyes out along the sea shore, longing for home. Did he, in your view, show trust in himself then?

Artist: Director, you twist what I am saying.

Director: To the contrary, Artist, I untangle. Or perhaps you prefer the method of Alexander?

Artist: It seems to me that you follow that method quite well enough as it is while professing the opposite, Director.

Director: But this field through which we now walk, gentle Artist, does it appear to you to be fertile?

Artist: Oh, Director, quite the opposite. I have spent many a night turning the question we are now discussing over and over again in my mind, tossing and turning. For this seems to me to be a bleak and terrible and yet inescapable truth. I know of no more barren desert than this.

Director: But would you believe me if I told you that to me none appears more fecund?

Artist: How could that be?

Director: Though you are not a farmer, would you agree that the clods of Earth must be broken and tilled thoroughly before planting?

Artist: Of course.

Director: And is it best to plant in a soil that is rich?

Artist: Certainly.

Director: Then Artist we have a fair prospect before us! For does not our very discussion presuppose a most rich soil?

Artist: With that I most definitely agree.

Director: And are we not tilling the ground by means of our very conversation?

Artist: I feel what you say to be true.

Director: Now, was there not a time when colonies were said to be planted?

Artist: Indeed, Director, they were even referred to as plantations.

Director: Then ought we not consider the seed?

Artist: That is of the utmost importance.

Director: Well, and this seed, what is it? Shall we say it is trust and see where that leads us?

Artist: Yes.

Director: And shall we distinguish between trust and trusting relationships, or turn to that only later as a refinement of the broader concern?

Artist: We will discuss this later, you and I.

Director: That is if we do not forget. Seeds require nourishment in order to grow?

Artist: Yes, they do.

Director: And a seed typically requires water and sunlight?

Artist: Yes.

Director: Then what are the analogs with the seed of trust?

Artist: It seems to me that the most important thing is keeping promises.

Director: And when both parties keep their promises a relationship of trust obtains?

Artist: Yes.

Director: Is this trust binary, which is to say it exists or it does not, on or off; or does it admit of degrees so that one trusts some more than others?

Artist: It certainly is a thing that admits of degree.

Director: Our seedling, then, in order to set its roots well and grow into a deeper trust requires more than the simple keeping of promises? Or does it suffice to go on keeping promises and by means of this alone a deeper trust results over time.

Artist: It depends upon the types of promises being made.

Director: So the more significant the promise, it being kept, the greater the trust?

Artist: That is how it seems to me.

Director: And would you say that the more significant promises have to do with the more important things, and the most important promise has to do with the most important thing?

Artist: That follows from what we have said.

Director: Do you think that the most important things and the best things are the same?

Artist: Yes, of course.

Director: Very good. Then let us review where we stand. We are considering whether intelligence or trust is best, and if best most important. We further considered the nature of intelligence, what it is and whether it may stand alone. We have compared our discussion to tilling the Earth and say that planting ought follow. In order to test whether trust is best we are considering it as a seed and tracing its growth to see just what sort of plant or flower or what it will produce. We say that keeping promises of an increasingly important nature serves as the water and light for the growth of the seedling. We then said that the most important things are the best things. And all of this is another way of looking at the same thing which we have considered as the building of a house or the founding of a colony or state. Then just as a plant cannot grow without sunlight and water, trust cannot grow without the keeping of promises of importance. But this plant of ours, grown from the seed of trust, Artist, is it like the rose we spoke of earlier?

Artist: In what way?

Director: In that it does not regulate its own growth. In other words, as promises are kept of an increasingly important nature the trust continues to grow almost, as we might say, as according to a law of nature.

Engineer: That is very well put, Director.

Director: But what do we learn from this?

Engineer: According to what we said before, this shows that trust is not best because the plant we refer to does not in any way control its own fate — for what intelligence does it take to go on trusting someone who always fulfills promises? It is as you said, Director, just a law of nature to go on trusting in such fashion, and requires no intelligence whatsoever.

Director: Engineer, you have said many remarkable things. But do you know what is most striking? You have shown that trust is actually stronger than intelligence.

Engineer: You must be joking!

Architect: No, Engineer, Director appears to me to be on solid ground here.

Director: Have you forgotten already, Engineer, that we have affirmed that a thing capable of standing on its own is stronger than that which requires support?

Engineer: Of course not.

Director: But have we not just shown that trust requires no intelligence?

Artist: That, Manger, is because you have assumed that the promises kept must be of an increasingly important nature.

Director: But did you not agree with this proposition?

Artist: Only for the sake of argument. Everyone, knows, Director, that trust does not keep on increasing like this, as if it did nothing but go on growing.

Director: So you do not think that our analogy of the seed of trust was appropriate to the discussion?

Artist: No, I do not.

Director: Yet you would still affirm, whether seriously or not, that trust admits of degree?

Artist: Yes, I do.

Director: And you still would affirm that it is the importance of the thing promised and delivered that controls or at least influences the degree of trust?

Artist: I do.

Director: And do you hold that the stronger is always the better? What do you say, or would you like to quibble about what I am asking?

Artist: It seems to me that you, Director, are the expert in quibbling. No, I agree with what you have said: the stronger is indeed the better.

Director: You seem to me, Artist, to be quite adept at quibbling yourself. You neglected to include 'always'. How is it? Always or no?

Artist: Yes, you impossible man — the stronger is always the better.

Director: And you, as an artist, are, of course, a man of taste?

Artist: What are you suggesting?

Director: Not suggesting, Artist, but attempting to firm something up in my own understanding. Would you say that with taste the stronger is the better, or is this case an exception?

Artist: What does strength have to do with taste?

Director: I am not sure, but they say that there are on the one hand those with strong tastes and on the other those with more delicate or refined tastes. Would you agree?

Artist: Certainly.

Director: And who are those with strong tastes?

Artist: The indelicate and unrefined, as you know yourself.

Director: Then are the indelicate and unrefined better than their opposite parts?

Artist: Hah! Far from it indeed. It is the exact opposite of what you are bold enough to assert.

Director: Then, Artist, I do not see how it is — though you may think I am not speaking seriously — that you can maintain that the stronger is always better. For every time you, or anyone else for that matter, make this assertion there is always an example readily at hand to show that it is not as you say. But here I think it high time to remember what I feared we would forget — namely, the distinction between trust and trusting relationships.

Engineer: Why does that matter now?

Director: We have seen that trust is stronger than intelligence, because we have seen that trust may stand alone, unassisted by intelligence. But we have yet to determine whether intelligence may stand alone. You suspect that it may not. Do you still maintain that intelligence is more than 'number crunching'?

Engineer: I do.

Director: And that intelligence is comprised of parts, rather than being a whole in and of itself?

Engineer: Yes.

Director: And one of those parts is processing?

Engineer: Yes.

Director: What other parts are there?

Engineer: There must be as part of intelligence some way of choosing what is worthwhile.

Director: Judgment, or discernment, or some other such thing?

Engineer: Exactly.

Director: And what about trust? Shall we say this, too, is part of intelligence?

Engineer: I am not sure. This seems to me to be a very difficult question.

Director: But it is really not so hard, is it? Did we not say that in order for an engineer to build a bridge using a computer he must trust that the computer is programmed according to the same understanding of mathematics that he has? Or that the program he uses to convert between meters and feet uses the same conversion ratios?

Engineer: Of course.

Director: And could we not show quite easily that in all cases where intelligence is exercised there is a ground of trust upon which it must stand in order to operate? For instance, when a doctor performs a procedure he trusts that the anesthesia will not wear off too soon — if he did not, could he have the state of mind required in order to perform the surgery?

Engineer: No, no one can perform an operation requiring intelligence when his mind is preoccupied with such worries.

Director: And trust dispels or allays these worries?

Engineer: Yes.

Director: Then trust is a necessary part intelligence? Or would you argue that intelligence is a thing which can exist apart from the activity of thinking or exercising of intelligence.

Engineer: No, I would not argue that.

Director: Then since you and I, Engineer, are in full agreement that there is no exercise of intelligence without trust at some level, we shall affirm that trust is a part of intelligence, and thus we must admit that intelligence cannot stand alone and is therefore weaker, if that which stands unsupported is stronger, than trust. And now can you see why the distinction between trust and trusting relationships is of the utmost importance?

Engineer: No, I am afraid I cannot, Director — though I very much would like to understand what you are saying.

Director: You and I, my friend, maintain that trust is part of intelligence. Yet I still maintain that what is most enduring and also most difficult to render enduring is what is best in life, and this I say, along with my friends, is trusting, human relationships.

Architect: You say much, Director.

Director: But does Engineer agree with me?

Engineer: I am beginning to feel that I should like to, Director. But something holds me back. I still feel that intelligence is what is best.

Director: We have come, Engineer, to a rather narrow pass. It seems to me of the utmost importance whether we proceed through it one after the other, or one of us turns back and each go our separate way here.

Engineer: What is the nature of this pass?

Director: Would you say that the best thing in the world is something that exists without plan, without effort, by chance or luck, as it were?

Engineer: Of course not.

Director: And intelligence, my friend, is this a thing that is obtained by striving or is it more as a gift?

Engineer: Indeed, Director, it is more like a gift — we even call the highly intelligent the gifted.

Director: Then by your own admission, intelligence is not what is best in life. You have affirmed that intelligence admits of degree?

Engineer: Yes, and I still do.

Director: And this degree, does it ever change during the course of one's life?

Engineer: No, it remains the same.

Director: But there are things which influence its development? Proper nutrition and the like?

Engineer: Of course.

Director: Then if intelligence is a gift, and not the given but rather that obtained or achieved is what is best, do you agree that intelligence cannot be what is best in life?

Engineer: I do. But I cannot say what is best.

Director: Perhaps you will, but let us trust in the argument for now. While we deny intelligence the highest place in life, we certainly do not accord it a lowly place.

Engineer: Absolutely not.

Director: No, in fact I know of no other more important 'gift' one might receive.

Engineer: Nor do I.

Director: Then what are we to do with this most precious of gifts, my dear friend? Or ought the gift remain within its box, unused?

Engineer: That would be a crime.

Director: Further, have we not said that intelligence is not a thing that may exist without being in use, that an idle intelligence is in fact nothing at all?

Architect: Are you following, Engineer?

Director: But, Architect, he seems to me to be listening most attentively.

Engineer: Yes, Director, I hear you. An idle intelligence is nothing.

Director: Then we say that intelligence has a purpose, a use, an end?

Engineer: Yes, it most certainly does.

Director: The intelligent man is not without purpose?

Engineer: No.

Director: And may his intelligence be taken away?

Engineer: Not unless he himself is the criminal or some other deprives him of his life.

Director: Then intelligence is enduring for life, unless destroyed by one's own hand, whether wittingly or no is of no matter.

Artist: What are you saying, Director?

Director: What? Is this conversation not to your taste, Artist?

Artist: It seems to me most foul.

Architect: We are all here of our own accord.

Director: I repeat: intelligence endures. But I also say that what is most enduring as well as most difficult to render enduring is what is best in life. And we have agreed, Engineer, that it is not difficult to render intelligence enduing?

Engineer: No, Director, it is only as difficult as it is to preserve one's life and not harm oneself.

Director: Does that seem very difficult to you?

Engineer: I can see how it might be; but, no, I confess it does not seem so to me.

Director: Very good, my excellent friend. But why do you cast your eyes downward? Be of good cheer! Have we not every reason? Come, let us carry on as before our interruption. Is it not ten times easier to destroy than to create?

Engineer: I should say more than ten times.

Director: Infinitely more?

Engineer: Infinitely.

Director: Then you would agree that those who are able to render enduring a thing most delicate and easily destroyed are worthy of the highest praise?

Engineer: Yes.

Director: And this thing which is most delicate and most easily destroyed we should call that which is best in life?

Engineer: Yes.

Director: Then I shall continue to say that trusting, human relationships are what is best in life. For trust well placed between men seems to me to be not only most excellent but also most delicate a thing and requiring the highest intelligence and discernment and vigilance in order to maintain truly.

Engineer: Director, I am convinced. I join with you in saying that trusting relationships between men are what is best in life, and that it is not just any trust but trust well placed, intelligent trust. And I will guard against those who would destroy such a rare thing, those who are evil.

IV. BRILLIANCE

Persons of the Dialogue:
Author
Director
Student

Cities

Author: Athens was more brilliant than Sparta.

Director: Why are you frowning, Student? Do you doubt?

Student: No, I'm frowning because I think Author is right.

Director: You feel that Sparta should be regarded as more brilliant?

Student: I feel that brilliance might be overrated.

Director: What is it about Sparta that makes you feel Athens was overrated?

Student: Its courage, its honor — its brotherhood!

Director: And none of those is brilliant?

Author: Not unless brilliance means nothing more than goodness or excellence.

Director: What does brilliance mean, Student?

Student: At its worst it's flash over substance.

Director: And at its best?

Student: It's the virtue of the mind.

Director: As opposed to the virtue of the heart?

Student: Yes.

Virtue

Director: Cheer up! Is it so clear that the two are divorced?

Author: The character of the virtue of the heart changes when the virtue of the mind begins to flourish.

Director: How?

Author: It attaches more to the individual than the group.

Director: Is this how you see it, Student?

Student: Yes. Brilliance undermines the order that sustains it.

Director: Hmm. But does the order sustain brilliance or stifle it?

Author: True — brilliance struggles against order in order to free itself.

Director: Because that order does not sustain its heart?

Student: Yes!

Author: No. Because the development of the virtue of mind is the highest end of man and worthwhile for its own sake. It's not some sort of second-best compensation.

Director: But is virtue of the mind possible without virtue of the heart? What? No answer, Author?

Student: I think it is. It's evil genius.

Director: Let's take a step back. Suppose the virtue of one's heart is fully developed — one is a Spartan, through and through, fully attached to one's people, one's state. Does one feel the need to develop the virtue of the mind?

Student: No, one is content.

Author: Really, now! It is my turn to be surprised. Did the Spartans not develop the art of generalship, to say nothing of politics, to the highest degree? And did this not take the virtue of the mind?

Student: Of course, but it didn't take brilliance — just hard competence.

Director: And this is because brilliance is more flash than substance.

Student: Precisely.

Director: Author, I recall having read an article about your latest book which declares you brilliant. Now, please, don't show false modesty when you answer. Do you think your work shows more flash than substance?

Author: I think my work shows a considerable bit of substance.

Director: More substance than flash?

Author: There is not all that much substance in this world, Director, that it can predominate easily over the flash. But that substance is worth more by itself than all the flash there ever was, or will be, put together.

Director: And the articulation of this substance is the work of hard competence.

Author: Of course it is.

Director: And is your heart in your work or are you, forgive me, an evil genius who writes with a completely cold head?

Author: You know better, Director. A clear head is a cold head — but it is sustained by a warm, if not hot, heart.

Director: So the evil genius that Student mentioned is a cold head coupled with a cold heart.

Author: I think that's a fair description.

Director: Then is that our definition of brilliance, the effect of which is a work that more resembles a diamond than a portrait?

Nature

Student: I think you're onto something, Director. It seems it's the difference between organic and non-organic, or natural and artificial.

Author: Diamonds are nature under great pressure, friend.

Student: Fair enough, but it's something about the difference between life and death.

Author: The Athenians weren't alive?

Student: No, not that. I can't explain it.

Director: Well, if the Spartans were at least equally alive as the Athenians, were they not under greater pressure than them? Didn't they spend their whole lives training for and exercising military virtue? Didn't they live surrounded by conquered peoples who were given to periodic revolts? Didn't they take the virtue of all Greece upon their shoulders? I ask this because I'm not sure that brilliance is more flash than substance. It seems possible brilliance must be pure, unalloyed, ruthlessly uncompromised virtue — and there is little doubt the Spartans had this, unless we twist the meaning of virtue out of all natural recognition. And if this is so about brilliance, then the politic wisdom in the Spartan's laconic wit renders it even more awesome.

Student: I agree! But that's not how most people would see it. They would see the Spartans as dull, uncultivated, uncultured.

Director: Maybe that's because they mistake brilliance for virtue when brilliance is actually the gleam of virtue brought to its sharpest edge. Brilliance crowns virtue. True, the Spartans were not known for their literary or technological abilities — their state was organized according to principles different than our own. But because we excel in these endeavors and acclaim great works, such as Author's, brilliant, we ought not assume that all brilliance attaches to the virtues particular to our own people. Wouldn't you agree, Author?

Author: Yes, but that doesn't change the fact that the Athenians were more brilliant than the Spartans. The Spartans gave their whole lives to military training and the Athenians, who did not, would have beaten them in the war had they not reached too far and invaded Syracuse. So one may say that the Athenians were, if not more brilliant than the Spartans in military virtue, at least equally so — and they had so many more brilliant virtues beyond. Trade, poetry, drama, philosophy, history, geometry, science. Athens was more brilliant than Sparta because she honed more virtues to a high degree than did Sparta.

Student: But were the Athenians happier in their heart of hearts than the Spartans?

Author: That is a question for individual Athenians and individual Spartans. Some were happy; others were not.

Director: What about Americans?

Progress

Author: America is a mixed regime.

Director: And in this mixed regime, what attaches the virtues of the American mind to the heart?

Author: The belief in progress.

Director: And so is brilliance spectacular progress?

Author: Not necessarily.

Director: You mean something might appear to be progress but really isn't? Are your brilliant works progress?

Author: They are for me, personally, and perhaps for a few of my readers and friends. But in general? No. In fact, I tend to think of them as a sort of return.

Student: To what?

Author: Truth.

Student: But is there no truth to progress?

Author: Yes, but it is quite limited. And we mustn't forget that going backward is progress, too — if that's where you want to go.

Director: A brilliant retreat.

Author: Yes.

Director: But while in retreat do you, like an army in good order, attempt to show yourself to be stronger that you really are in order to discourage pursuit?

Author: Not necessarily. Besides, a return may require the form of an attack.

Director: I see. A re-conquest of lost ground. Well, the ground we set out to win was that which would give us a clear view of what brilliance is — and it seems no one argument has been able to drive the others from the field.

Grace

Author: Look, no one will deny that brilliance is the grace of virtue — of whatever virtue. A brilliant soldier, a brilliant engineer, and brilliant financier, a brilliant author — what do they all have in common? They achieve their effect with grace.

Director: By that do you mean by some divine gift?

Author: Why, yes.

Student: You can't be serious.

Author: Why not? Consider Mozart. Would you agree that he was brilliant? Well, what exactly made him brilliant? Was it the technical arrangement of notes? Was it the facility with which he composed? Was it his memory? His ability to learn quickly? His IQ? His diligence? His training? His circumstances? Experience? Luck? What?

Student: I think it was all of those things.

Author: And what brings all of those things together other than grace? Virtue alone makes for virtuous and — even virtuoso — music. But it doesn't make for true brilliance. That is something else entirely.

Director: While I prefer baroque music to that of Mozart, I take your point and suspect it may be applied equally to my favorite composers. Yet when we answer the question what is virtue by saying it is grace we're really no closer to our goal unless we consider what you were suggesting — that brilliance is no one thing but a happy combination of things. But we don't understand what it is, exactly, that brings those things into harmony.

Student: Maybe we should consider further what brilliance is not in order to bring it into higher relief.

Director: Well, if brilliance is a happy sort of harmony, wouldn't it seem that the brilliant work is marked more by a sense of effortlessness than intensity?

Student: That's exactly the case with Mozart.

Director: Shall we consider other cases? What of famous people of all sorts: Pericles, Alcibiades, Brutus, Constantine, Lorenzo de Medici, Machiavelli, Queen Elizabeth, Shakespeare, Bacon, King James, Hobbes, Locke,

LaRochefoucauld, Washington, Hamilton, Jefferson, Adams, Paine, Bach, Telemann, Vivaldi? Or how about Jimi Hendrix? Keith Moon? Neil Peart? And what about O. J. Simpson, Dolph Lundgren, Bruce Lee, Jackie Chan? And Tolkien, Ayn Rand, Tom Clancy, Dan Brown, Houellebecq, Dostoevsky, Bakhtin?

Author: That's quite a mix. But in the case of Dostoevsky alone I would say that you've demonstrated that intensity does not preclude brilliance.

Director: Then perhaps happy sort of harmony is not the right way to describe brilliance — unless from a certain perspective it becomes clear that Dostoevsky was able to portray intensity itself effortlessly.

Student: But don't we know too much about his life to believe that?

Director: Far be it for me to say that brilliant men are not familiar with intense suffering. Maybe it's exactly that suffering and the intense effort to overcome it that leads to that happy sort of harmony, however fleeting it may be.

Student: So brilliance takes perseverance. But what about a brilliant fop or wit, the sort that sparkles with irony?

Director: If I know the character you're thinking of, I know that what shines there is more sarcasm than irony — and it's a sort of fool's gold.

Author: What's the difference?

Director: Sincerity.

Author: Is that then for you a requirement for brilliance?

Director: Is divine grace possible in any other way?

Author: I agree. But what shall we say of someone who solves a great puzzle faster and better than anyone else? Does sincerity matter there?

Director: If he wasn't sincere in trying to solve the puzzle, I don't see how he could, except by dumb luck — unless it wasn't really a puzzle after all. But why do you speak of puzzles, Author?

Author: I thought I would help account for the political actors in your curious list of examples. After all, isn't politics the working out of a great puzzle? And don't some actors do this brilliantly while others —

Student: Only appear brilliant.

Author: So who's to say? I, for my part, consider it necessary to study each case discretely before pronouncing.

Director: No doubt good advice. But I suppose in addition to the divine sort of grace you also mean the human sort — finesse, touch, savoir faire, urbanity. Why should these traits be so necessary to political brilliance? Isn't politics a hard-headed game?

Author: Of course, but it periodically requires new ways of doing things. A brilliant politician learns all the rules and then proceeds to break them. Things go better if he doesn't draw attention to the fact.

Director: What? So grace and therefore brilliance require a sort of deceit?

Author: New things are never allowed by the established authorities unless they resemble the old. In the case of any art, one must demonstrate a mastery of existing techniques before one's new methods are given consideration.

Student: Otherwise one seems crazy.

Vision

Director: But are we going to say that grace allows for brilliant new ways without saying what leads one to those ways?

Author: Necessity.

Director: Alright, but if necessity drives one, with what does he steer?

Author: Discernment.

Director: I see.

Student: Do you know what comes to mind? The character Paul Atreides from *Dune.* He was brilliant. He was able to see the various possibilities and ways of the future.

Director: Was this from some sort of extravagant dreaming on his part?

Student: Oh, no. It was very much a necessity — and a torment.

Director: So, was he a prudent leader?

Student: What do you mean?

Director: I mean, wouldn't a prudent leader, one who sees the ways and possibilities of the future, lead his people to safety?

Student: He led his people to victory.

Director: Isn't the greatest safety in victory?

Student: Yes, but it involves great risk.

Author: Which is precisely what brilliance involves.

Director: As a matter of choice? What, silent again, Author? But what are we saying — that it's dangerous to see, to know?

Author: Of course.

Director: So brilliance is knowledge and knowledge is dangerous.

Author: A little knowledge is dangerous — a lot of knowledge brings you grace.

Director: So grace is prudence.

Student: But what if being prudent won't get you what you want?

Director: Isn't prudence taking care to do what will get you what you want?

Student: Yes, but brilliant men don't want safety.

Author: Oh yes, they do, my young friend — they just want other things more. And that is why brilliant men have a duty to learn patience. They must not try to force things. They must allow things to unfold naturally.

Student: Natural in the sense of "that which does not kill you makes you stronger"? I mean, that's what we're talking about here, isn't it? The brilliant man has hard luck.

Author: No, the brilliant man rises above hard luck. He garners strength through hard work to articulate his unique perspective on the world.

Perspective

Student: Are you talking about a perspective above luck, beyond fortune?

Author: It's more than that. The point beyond chance is at the top of a pyramid whose base is seen by many, whose middle is seen by few, and whose upper portion very few see. The brilliant man takes this all in. At first it comes to him at once, in a flash. This makes him aware of something, something that haunts him. This is what artists mean when they describe themselves as possessed. Their minds contain the negatives of images they feel they must print. But how? The brilliant man knows he doesn't really understand — and yet he sees! Thus his labors begin with vision and seek perspective, the knowledge that relates the high and the low. For it is perspective alone that will enable him to articulate what he sees. And when he does, the low will understand the low and the high the high, while both will recognize the other — and all will sense the touch of brilliance.

Student: And it's more than that, too, isn't it? This is how a team of men must be organized in order to be brilliant — everyone in his place, and led by a brilliant man. All social organizations are hierarchical, no matter what we might call them. The people are on top in a democracy just as a king's on top in a monarchy. Only in a democracy, the question is which people are on top.

Director: So led properly a people can be brilliant? Perhaps the Athenians and the Spartans were equally brilliant for a time.

Student: Yes! But the arrogance of the Athenians spoiled their brilliance. Arrogance is always a sign that one only thinks oneself brilliant. While the arrogant might have great ability, it's not being put to good use.

Author: Because they lack perspective.

Director: Why do they lack perspective? Is it because they haven't done the necessary work?

Student: I think they are seduced by what they think their ability can gain them and don't bother with it.

Author: To know one has important work to perform, one must first have vision, and — for whatever reason — the arrogant never have that vision. It's not something you can disregard once you've had it. It becomes necessity.

Director: Then perhaps the Athenians lost their brilliant leader when they decided to go to Syracuse.

Student: They were led by Alcibiades, but he was recalled.

Author: Yes, it's a complicated question. He fought for the Spartans when the Athenians wouldn't let him lead. And then when he and the Spartans had had enough of each other he went back to Athens. He is perhaps the most brilliant man of infamy of all time.

Student: But I think he may have been misunderstood. I don't think brilliant men ever deserve infamy, and there is no doubt Alcibiades was brilliant. Some say he may have been brilliant in abilities but a demagogue in politics — but then how could he have succeeded so well at Sparta? No, I think he had the true perspective not only of Athens, or of Sparta — but of Greece, of all Greeks. His vision went beyond that of nearly all of his contemporaries. But there was no Greek nation to lead so he had to deal with individual cities, and he was more brilliant than they could allow.

Seduction

Director: An able defense, Student. I wonder, though, if both the Athenians and the Spartans were seduced by Alcibiades' brilliance and sought to make it their own. Author tells us the truly brilliant man's vision guards against seduction into arrogance, but what of those with whom the brilliant deal? Aren't they subjected to a sort of seduction?

Author: An excellent question, Director, and one which reminds me of another, related, question. There is a debate among my friends as to whether women can be brilliant.

Student: Of course they can!

Director: Why Student, one might think you've encountered a brilliant seductress!

Student: You're right to laugh, Director. But the question annoys me. Of course women are brilliant — anyone can be brilliant in his or her proper sphere. Goya was a brilliant painter but not a brilliant mathematician. So what? Was he less brilliant on that account?

Author: But isn't this neat reduction of the question one of the seductions of the modern age? Everyone is brilliant. Everyone is special in his or her own very special way. Do you believe that?

Student: To a limited degree, yes.

Author: Well then, the limit you place on this is precisely the point of interest. What is that limit?

Student: To the degree to which they don't encroach on the rights of others.

Author: So, for you, it comes down to rights, the obverse side of the coin of neat reduction — for we all have equal rights, do we not?

Student: In theory, yes.

Author: Only in theory? I thought it was also in law. That's quite a difference and not merely one of degree.

Student: What's your point?

Author: The brilliant are never seduced by facile arguments, false likenesses, and meaningless distinctions. The brilliant know how to think.

Director: What's this, Author? Does the brilliant pastry chef think his way through the kitchen?

Author: Yes, he does — to the extent that he is a brilliant pastry chef.

Director: And what about the brilliant drunk? Does he think his way through the bottle?

Author: Thank you, Director. You've very neatly shown the problem with the argument that anyone can be brilliant as long as he is in his proper element.

Misfits

Director: Well, I was wondering when we would discuss in more detail the notion that the brilliant are always misfits.

Student: Except when they are in their proper element.

Director: Could it be that the brilliant are absolute misfits everywhere except in their proper element?

Student: That seems likely to me, and it may be why they are brilliant.

Director: Why they are brilliant? I thought we agreed they are brilliant because of their vision and perspective.

Student: Maybe gaining perspective involves finding one's sphere.

Director: So what of the brilliant man born into his proper sphere?

Student: I would call him happy, Director.

Director: But without perspective.

Author: Perhaps it's best to say he has a limited perspective.

Horizon

Director: Now, Author, really! Weren't you the one to warn us against false distinctions? And don't beg off that this only goes to show you're not brilliant — we're not having it! Wouldn't all the brilliant have perspectives limited to their own proper spheres? Or do you believe there are two levels of brilliance — limited and unlimited? It wasn't clear to me if that point at the top of your pyramid was attached or floating.

Author: You are right to ask. There are two types of brilliance — the brilliance that exists within spheres and the brilliance that exists amongst them.

Student: I don't understand. Then wouldn't that just be the same thing except its sphere is some form of communication?

Author: Yes, but the difference here has to do with ideas. One type of brilliance exists within an idea or combination of ideas, the other exists without.

Student: So the brilliance of a brilliant wrestler differs from the brilliance of a brilliant author?

Author: That depends.

Student: On what? Can the wrestler really be brilliant if he doesn't have a vision of and perspective on wrestling?

Author: No.

Student: And doesn't the very word "wrestling" express an idea of what sort of physical activity that is?

Author: It does. But I don't see what you're driving at, Student. It seems to me that there are two types of brilliance. The first is as you describe for wrestling.

Student: But an author writes, and the very word "writing" also expresses an idea of what sort of mental activity this is.

Author: Very true. But writing is also as physical as wrestling — perhaps not as vigorous — but physical nonetheless. The point is not the type of activity. All types derive from ideas by definition. The difference is in whether that which typifies determines or is determined by virtue of the exercise of the activity in question. You've heard talk of living language? A brilliant author keeps language alive, just as a brilliant wrestler keeps the sport alive.

Student: But now I'm confused. If there are two types of brilliance, one of which makes language come alive — are you saying that there are brilliant authors whose language is dead?

Author: Ah, I'm guilty of confusing the misuse of the adjective brilliance with its true meaning. I've confused the common use of the term with what we have agreed on here. Given how often this happens, I suppose one might be inclined to forgive me if I show good behavior from here on out!

Director: Don't fret, Student. It seems that Author is in good earnest with us, and that he unwittingly confused the meaning. But how opportune a mistake! He showed us how easily it is to allow language to die.

Author: Thank you for putting my failing to use, Director, and breathing life back into the word.

Director: Even Homer nods, as they say — and how many authors through the ages have assented to nonsense by falling asleep as they write!

Student: Is this why you asked whether the point above the pyramid was floating or attached, because of the question whether one is determined by or determines the idea?

Director: Yes, but in the same breath I confess that I don't understand what this means. I suspect, my young friend, that you are wondering whether one must rule or be ruled by ideas — use or be used by them.

Student: Yes. But things don't seem to be adding up. Author said that there is the brilliance that exists within spheres and the brilliance that exists among them. I'm not sure if he still thinks that's true.

Author: I think we should move beyond this troubling point and refocus our question. We want to understand what brilliance is.

Student: Then don't we have to know if there is one type of brilliance or more than one?

Author: Think of colors. They are nouns in and of themselves but also adjectives. I hold up this coin and say it is silver. But I might also have a gold, or a bronze, or a seemingly infinite number of other colored coins. Is each of these colored coins a type of coin? Yes, in a sense — but it does not mean that, in essence, a coin isn't one thing. Similarly with brilliance. We have said what brilliance is, much as we might define a coin as a portable, fungible object designating value and used for exchange.

Student: Then maybe if we talk about the use of brilliance it will help me understand.

Living, Dead

Director: Haven't we already intimated what that use is? Brilliance breathes life into things. So brilliance is the articulation of a vision by means of perspective in order to give life.

Student: Shouldn't we say a true vision?

Director: We certainly might, to put on both belt and suspenders — but I'd taken vision to refer to actually seeing something, which means to perceive the truth. But it won't hurt to add the qualifier true.

Student: I guess that goes to show just how brilliant I am.

Director: Don't be sarcastic, Student. You do yourself injustice. A noble sentiment led you to say what you did. Don't ever be ashamed of that. It's the most precious commodity on earth. Besides, you've given us an excellent example just now of how language begins to perish. It's stifled by shame.

Student: Are brilliant men shameless?

Director: No, but we'd have to get into the same sort of discussion about shame that we're having now about brilliance in order to know what that means. Perhaps another time, if we have the chance.

Student: I hope we do.

Director: But now we speak of the living and the dead. And I suspect you're wondering what happens when a writer of dead language reads the words of a brilliant author.

Student: I'm not being sarcastic when I say that I fear I know.

Director: Are you referring to yourself?

Student: I am. I know I am not a brilliant writer, but when I read Author's works, or those of any other brilliant writer, I feel as though wind filled my sails, as though the ice of winter were melting into spring.

Author: Perhaps you are then a brilliant reader.

Student: I'd like to believe that, very much.

Author: You must be, you know. There is no other way you would have the feeling you just described.

Student: Yes, but if you asked me to repeat to you now what I'd read last night, I would have a very hard time.

Author: Then either you must not have a brilliant memory or you must not be a brilliant speaker.

Student: True on both counts!

Author: I will tell you again, without your being a brilliant reader — one who has a vision of what it means to read and has gained perspective enough to appreciate brilliant writing, really appreciate it and not just parrot praise heard spoken by others — it is not possible for you to feel what you do.

Student: Am I really brilliant by virtue of a feeling? Is all brilliance derived from a feeling?

Author: Yes, and this involves a complicated discussion about vision or perception and feeling. But one thing I can tell you for certain: the dead feel nothing at all — and they never will again. There is a terrible warfare in life, my friend, that begins with conception and carries through until our light goes out. Many are killed from the start, as in the opening scene of *Saving Private Ryan* — the front of the landing craft opens and those entrenched on the beach open fire with machine guns. One must not only get ashore, but ascend the dunes and kill the enemy. But a number — perhaps greater, perhaps fewer — suicide in despair.

Student: And this is a metaphor, right?

Author: Yes, and this is why I spoke of brilliance within and brilliance without the sphere of ideas — or attempted to speak intelligently about it, I should say. Language is the medium of ideas, so to speak of language is the height of a perilous sort of artificiality. In this case I am speaking of brilliance in living. Now, one might argue with me about the metaphor employed, about whether one must climb, or about whether one must kill, and so on. But no one can deny that there are the walking dead among us, hollow souls. Such as these will never be brilliant readers or brilliant anything. In fact, I declare that any form of brilliance presupposes brilliance in life. There, we have our two types of brilliance — the greater and the lesser. There is no fame, no honor, no pleasure higher than the goodness of brilliance in life. And I believe that all brilliant men have their vision about their own lives, which then shows the way toward their own specific brilliance beyond that of life, not the other way round.

Authority

Student: So all brilliant men are authorities on living.

Author: Yes, but here a qualification is in order. They are authorities on living — their own lives.

Student: But can't they help other people — people who haven't yet died inside — live their lives? I mean, if they can't, what's the point of producing brilliant works?

Author: One can only hope one's own example inspires others.

Student: That's all?

Author: That's all.

Student: But the brilliant do command respect.

Author: Yes, they do. But have you considered who it is that respects them? Their counterparts in life. Brilliant readers admire — and I prefer this word to respect — brilliant authors. They are counterparts to one another.

Brilliant authors admire brilliant readers. Counterparts. As for the rest, they merely pay lip service. But we need to be careful to distinguish the two types of brilliance. You just spoke of brilliant works, and you were right to ask what's the point of producing them. I don't believe in art for art's sake — and I don't believe in art for the sake of others, whatever the altruistic justification. I'm not just speaking of art, of course. I'm talking about anything that one might do, any action by which one becomes distinguished. Is this selfish? The concept of selfishness doesn't make any sense to me here. Is it selfish to want to live your life? Who would make this assertion, and why?

Student: They'd say you're being disingenuous, that it's much more than mere life you want.

Author: Yes, it's true that under certain circumstances mere life is not worth living. But we're not talking about mere life, Student. We're talking about the life that has that feeling you described. Do you think it takes very much for that?

Student: No, I don't. In fact, I think it requires more the absence of something than anything else: interference from others, people telling you how to live. And this is where I'm having the most trouble with what you're saying. Who tells you how to live? Well, the authorities do — parents, teachers, priests, politicians, police, bosses, insurers, and experts of every type. But above all of this is the notion of public opinion. This is a democracy, after all, so everyone appeals to this. Now, what's a brilliant citizen? First, by our definition, it's someone who knows how to live his life and does indeed live it. That makes him happy, or if not quite happy he is at least proud and wants nothing from anyone in respect to himself and the way he lives. What he wants most is to be left alone to live his life. If the majority of citizens are brilliant in this sense, the democracy is healthy and the right form of government for the people. In this case, a brilliant politician — or statesman, even, to use a more exalted word — will seek to ensure that the citizens are interfered with as little as possible. Thus they are natural counterparts. But what happens if the people become corrupt? What happens if more and more people — for whatever reason — do not live brilliant lives? I can picture to myself a map of the country growing darker and darker. And I have to ask myself, what then? What makes for a brilliant citizen? What makes for a brilliant statesman?

Praise

Director: Before we tackle that great big question, Student, let's take on a few smaller ones. You seem to be asking about the political principles of brilliance, irrespective of the character of the regime or the state of its people. In other words, you have divined that brilliance is trans-political.

Student: Yes!

Director: And you wish to have, so to speak, a sort of compass that always points toward brilliance. It occurs to me, of course, that people often speak of their moral compasses, and that we could make the case that brilliance and morality are one, since both morality and brilliance in the primary sense are concerned with how one lives one's life.

Student: Exactly, and that's why I'm concerned with what happens to public opinion as people grow increasingly corrupt.

Director: Yes. Hmm. I see. This is a problem, indeed. You're talking about the political importance of praise. This has to do with freedom. How does the old argument go? A free man gives law to himself and is free to the extent he obeys.

Student: Yes, but democracy is a churning melting pot. Anyone that gives a law to himself that differs from the norm comes under scrutiny.

Director: What is it that people praise most?

Student: Different people praise different things. But there is a general tendency toward the worship of what is called flexibility, going with the flow.

Director: By flexibility I take it you mean absence of principle.

Student: Yes. People no longer know what it means to give law to themselves. They don't practice it and I'm starting to fear that they can't understand why anyone would want to, anyway.

Director: I take it you are concerned with this because you sense it is having or will have an impact on your own ability to live brilliantly. I also take it that you recognize this praise of flexibility as, in fact, nothing more than the abject worship of power in which the brilliant pairing of citizen and statesman degenerates into the dark interactions of master and slave. What is it about masters and slaves? I suspect we would do well to examine the manner in which these two praise one another.

Student: A citizen praises a statesman for managing things in a way that allows him to continue to live his life in the way we've been discussing. A statesman praises a citizen for doing exactly that. But a master can never praise his slaves sincerely. He uses a different standard for himself and those he considers equals. If he praises a slave for being intelligent, it is either a warning or a lie. If he praises him for being hard working, he inwardly laughs that he would never work so hard himself. I think it comes down to that: whether the praise is genuine, true. There are counterparts of brilliance and of darkness, of life and of death. One type of praise is honest admiration while another is deceitful and manipulative. I think this extends to all types of counterparts. A dark author's counterpart is a dark reader. They don't deal honestly with each other. They never have the good feeling that the brilliant have. They have perversity. They have wicked delight in secrets and things gotten away with. They delight in sarcasm and mockery, not irony and gentle teasing. Each thinks he is playing the other, and both are right.

Director: So have you got your compass?

Student: Yes, but it's more like a Pentagon-grade GPS.

Others

Author: Let's take this further. If the brilliant admire one another and make for good citizens together, what is it that makes the brilliant society so rare? Are the brilliant so scattered and few that they seldom come together in sufficient strength? Or perhaps there is difficulty recognizing one another, and in the period of negotiation to establish mutual trust and admiration much evil befalls them? Perhaps they are easily fooled, not given to deception themselves. The dark ones surely see that it is easier to deceive a brilliant man than to become one himself. Does it all come down to laziness or some innate weakness? Do circumstances so crush the dark that they never manage to step into the light? Is that all there is to brilliance — luck? No, we've agreed wholeheartedly that great effort is required in order to achieve perspective. And as for the initial vision, who's to say it is more blessing than curse? Without perspective it is indeed a curse, as I have no doubt that all brilliant men will confirm. So maybe that's it. The dark are those who've had visions but failed in gaining the perspective to articulate them. That is why they rely on shadows and innuendo to make their questionable points. So in considering politics, we ought to allow that there are three classes of citizens: the brilliant, the dark, and the others. We might even liken them to protons, neutrons, and electrons. The protons and neutrons join together to form the heart, while the negative particles orbit the core. But following this atomic metaphor we can see how politics can be so explosive. Tremendous energy is involved in changing the posture of the subatomic particles. Clearly, a brilliant citizen and statesman must recognize the danger.

Student: Yes, and thank you for bringing things back around to my initial concern. Are you suggesting that the brilliant must make allies of the others against the dark? Must the allies attack the dark, and would that be only in reactive self-defense or in pre-emptive self-defense? But I understand that there's a problem about the dark. Will they always be dark? Can they be encouraged to complete their effort to obtain perspective and thus become brilliant themselves? And what about the others; might they not someday have a vision themselves? Do they then become dark until they've struggled their way through to brilliance? Or do we have to just take courage and be resolved to act with what knowledge we have when it is time to act?

Director: Isn't that all one can do, Student? But I am impressed by your compassion. The brilliant always wish to find more of their kind.

Author: Unlike the dark, Director — or the others, for that matter?

Director: One might think the dark would be given to keeping their numbers small. As for the others, I would have assumed they were indifferent.

Student: Masters always want more slaves and fewer rivals. The dark strive toward infamy, not brilliant fame — if they strive toward anything at all other than power. In fact, they don't even understand the difference between infamy and fame. They think the brilliant are naïve, the dupes of the others — when they are not convulsed in paranoid doubt that the brilliant are, in fact, darker than they. After all, they don't have the perspective to know. And what's worse, they think they do. They think that power is all, and they deny that brilliance belongs to any but the powerful. They see all power as ultimately derived from individual ability or strength, while political power is nothing but the accumulation of individual talents.

Biochemistry

Author: So they put great store in the body and the brain.

Student: They put great store in the body. They see the brain — and the heart, and the soul, and the spirit — as nothing but body. They do, however, see the brain as the most important part of the body. To that end they are greatly interested in advances in neuro-psychology and psycho-pharmacology and all genetic engineering as it relates to the mind. And while we might say that none of this means anything unless they know how to live, the fact is that they will devise never-dreamed-of tools of tyranny. It may one day become impossible for a brilliant man to survive. It may become clear that the vision we've been talking about is due solely to the predominance of a certain endorphin or hormone or chemical relationship we've yet to grasp. What if they make such a relationship impossible? What if they outlaw it? What if they breed man in such a way that its chance of occurrence drops to nil? What if they develop tools to detect it, to "correct" it?

Author: Why not turn it around, Student? Why not ask whether we might not make it possible for everyone to be brilliant?

Student: I don't know. I just don't know. I mean, what if brilliance is a function of one's relationship to others, one's position in a configuration? Suppose, for instance, that each person has a number, and there are only a hundred numbers. Every time someone gets number seventeen — bingo! Brilliance.

Author: And by leveling the field, one way or another, we preclude the possibility of one occupying a certain position in a certain social configuration? I see what you're saying, but have you really abandoned the idea we had of vision and effort to obtain perspective?

Student: No! But what if it's only number seventeen that has the vision? What if statistics and genetic databases tell us that, on average, only one in a hundred has this ineffable thing we're calling vision? And what if they see it as a sickness to be cured? We will have arrived at an absolute and final tyranny. Mankind may as well never have existed. It all would have been for nothing.

Author: This is why you're so concerned with democracy and public opinion — because of science and technology?

Student: We all know that most "science" isn't science in the sense of free philosophic inquiry. It's technology — for a price. The market drives the direction of research because it promises the rewards. Do the brilliant outnumber the dark and indifferent? I don't think so. Will technology likely develop in favor of brilliance? You tell me.

Author: You suggest a change of regime?

Student: I suggest nothing. We have a problem. Something must be done.

Author: You seem very quick to abandon our allies, the others. Shouldn't we give more attention to this before we consider more radical approaches? Can't it be that we have mutual interest in preventing the perversion of science? Besides, if we can't agree on a national health care bill, how are we going to agree on a eugenics program?

Student: In both cases, just because we can't agree doesn't mean something won't be passed. And who wields more underhanded influence in Washington, the brilliant or the dark? What's most likely is some Frankenstein of legislation that will wreck this country.

Director: Have you considered running for office?

Student: Who would vote for me? Should I start the Brilliant Party? Can you imagine what sorts of attacks I'd be subject to, with almost no prospect of success?

Director: I have some idea, as I'm certain does Author. But why not focus on the alliance? Spend some time finding out where there are points of agreement. Inspire others with the spirit of mutual interest. Is there a better way of fighting the spreading darkness?

Student: I don't know. It seems impossible.

Director: Are you afraid you will lose your private brilliance in the course of the fight?

Student: No, especially with friends like you. But, frankly, it seems like I'll be opening myself up to a lot of pain for no good reason.

Director: You don't think ensuring the future of brilliance is a good cause?

Student: No! It seems like no good reason because I honestly don't know what good I can do.

Director: Why don't you spend some time trying to figure out what good there is to be done, then honestly ask yourself what you can do. If you can find something you really think you can do in furtherance of a good cause, even though it opens you up to pains, would you rather not? I know you better than that, Student. The question now is what can be done, and that's not something we can resolve today. It's something that will take a considerable amount of attention over an extended period of time. Only then will you be in a position to come back to your trusted friends and discuss what presents itself to be done. And I promise you that I will never advise you to undertake what amounts to a suicide mission. After all, if what we've been saying today proves true, I have every interest in preserving you as an effective allied fighter in our cause. Your mere existence as a brilliant man does more for me than whatever brilliance you might obtain in the political sphere. You should only move into the realm if it is in keeping with your personal brilliance.

Student: But I doubt that I really am brilliant.

Director: Are you accusing Author and me of being dark?

Student: No, but friendship might be clouding your judgment.

Director: I don't know what's worse, frankly — having cloudy judgment or being dark! Regardless, mustn't courage support brilliance?

Student: I have no doubt of that, and I think you are both very courageous.

Director: Perhaps we must always work to develop our perspective. We may have been wrong to suggest that once one climbs the mountain, that is all. There are other mountains in the range, and other ranges may come into view. It may be that having climbed one summit, Student, you have seen another, one that promises a breathtaking view. Will you make the effort?

Student: How can I do anything but smile and nod, Director. You have a way of encouraging me.

Director: And you have a way of encouraging me, Student. Counterparts.

Depth

Student: I can't imagine how.

Director: Each of us struggles to live a true life, a life imbued with the delightfully ineffable light of brilliance. As I see you fighting manfully to articulate your vision, it inspires me all the more toward mine.

Author: A sublime description, Director.

Student: The dark scoffers gloat, in their more confident moments, that brilliance is nothing more than sublimated sexual energy.

Author: Well, there's truth in that, isn't there? The dark scoffers I'm acquainted with don't hesitate to spread their seed in or upon whatever objects strike their perverted taste. Do they hold true and save themselves for meaningful intercourse? They don't even hold true to their avowed principles of sex as a meaninglessly natural urge. How can they, when their very core is suffused with the mélange of power-based sex. One with a healthy sexuality shudders at the lurid details the imagination presents when contemplating the mingling of power and sex. Sublimated sexual energy? This is merely to say that one places a value on sex beyond the animal act. Yes, this means that animal urges are redirected to nobler objects. But what is the animal urge? If we say it is toward reproduction and the continuation of the species, then is it so bad to focus some of that energy on ensuring the brilliance of the future? Or would these scoffers like nothing better than to articulate, exactly, in biochemical terms, what it is that makes for sexual urge and attraction? Good luck to them, I say. They are heading down the rabbit hole and may well have no intention of ever coming back. How's that for sublimation? Have you ever heard, Student, that there is only one level of sublimation possible — surface or depth, and no other possibility? This happens when all depths are equal. There is still infatuation with secrets, and the writing and figuring of secrets, cryptography — which is, essentially, no different than spending one's life mastering chess or any other intellectual game. But we're not playing games, are we, my friends? We are engaged in the most real and noble of fights — the fight for life.

Student: As you were speaking of the scoffers it occurred to me that I have nothing but contempt for them. And it further occurred to me that this contempt can serve as a fuel for my struggle to obtain perspective. If I ever do work beyond the living of my life, I will use this energy to polish my work until it gleams as an example in the night. But if I think about the heavy lifting required to articulate the vision, I think of the fundamental emotions — love and hate. These provide the power drive, while cold contempt sustains the effort through the finishing touches.

Director: What of pride, my friends? Does that not sustain? Is pride not the counterpart of contempt? Would not my pride in my friendship with you prevent me from having anything but contempt for those dark ones who would offer me a false coin by the same name? And what of my pride? Would they say that it, too, is the result of some sort of sublimation?

Student: Just let them, Director! They expect us to wear our hearts on our sleeves so that they might slip poison into them at every pass. Our pride is indeed beneath the surface — of necessity. In fact, I don't know if we would even have any pride at all, were we not forced to fight their machinations at every turn. They may be the very reason why we have to fight to gain perspective in order to articulate our vision. I don't even know if one can be brilliant without having a problem along these lines, without some sort of opposition. And yet sometimes I ask myself, in earnest: why would anyone want to oppose, prevent, or destroy brilliance? The only thing I can think is that the dark ones, for whatever reason, gave up before they achieved it. They therefore believe it impossible for anyone to achieve pure brilliance. And if they start to suspect that anyone has, they're hell bent on proving them some sort of fraud, no better than themselves. But when they start to suspect that the brilliant man is true, they at first fly into an impotent rage. Over time this develops into a cold and profound hatred fueled by jealousy and self-loathing, the nature of which they dare not understand even themselves. It's precisely this hatred that the brilliant man must meet with contempt. Once someone has gotten to this point of hatred, I don't think there is any way back, short of a complete breakdown and starting again from scratch. But that seems all but impossible. By now the evil man has set too many things in motion ever to be free of them enough to have the time to gain his full perspective. He's spent too much time trying to persuade others that the brilliant are radically selfish, that they are dangerous, that they are antisocial, wild animals at heart, dangerous to society and their fellow men in every way. He's told them that they need to be broken, harnessed, and tamed. He's tried every negative argument to see what will stick and then focused his attack there. Can such a man have a profound change of heart? Can such a man undo all he has done? Imagine how much harder this solitary task of recovery will be if this man has made a name for himself and become famous for his attacks!

Surface

Author: What of those who've made a name for themselves but haven't made clear their antipathy to the brilliant?

Student: They're even more dangerous because the others aren't put on their guard when dealing with them — if they're inclined to be just to the brilliant, that is.

Author: I suppose it's worse still if they are reputed to be brilliant in the public sense while not having become brilliant in the private sense.

Student: Yes, I think this happens often with actors. The public sees a dazzling performance and assumes there must be a brilliant man behind it. Even if lots of people know better, there are more who are fooled than ought to be. As for the dark, I have no doubt they only care about the surface performance. But the battle for public opinion is fought among the others.

Director: This surface — the performance or the product of whatever art — this is the only thing people see, isn't it, if they know nothing of the private man. If there's a difference between brilliant and dazzling public displays, the latter being the product of the dark — how is one to know which is which if one doesn't know whether the private man himself is brilliant?

Student: I think there are signs in the work that are clear enough.

Director: That may be, but clear to whom? The brilliant reader? The brilliant listener? The brilliant viewer? I don't ask because I want to upset everything we've said and agreed on. When talking with you today I feel confident that I know what brilliance is, that I know what it means to live, that I know what it means to work and produce meaningful results. We three know that brilliance does not equate with fame. We three know that brilliance is more often quiet and reserved than not, and that the famous of the brilliant become that way more by virtue of accident than will. But a little voice whispers to me: if it takes one to know one, how do you know you are one yourself and not just like all the others as you spin out elaborate justifications for the ways of you and your friends?

Student: But, Director, we've said that the brilliant artist truly appreciates those who truly appreciate him. You can tell! There's an honesty in the work. There's a confidence among friends. There's mutual respect. A brilliant author doesn't deny his weaknesses but he doesn't dwell on them either. Similarly, he doesn't deny that his reader has weaknesses but demonstrates that he doesn't condemn the man for them either. There's a humanity in the work. There is justice. Can we like the work but not the man? I can't. Why? My sense of justice won't allow it. That's why I distinguish between dazzling and brilliant. I don't want to be dazzled. I don't want art to do nothing more than make me forget my troubles. I want art to speak to me as a human being. I want art to be firm, to be strong. I want it to be just. I want it to ring true like a clear bell across the land, not explode in a shower of sparks. And if I'm looking for pyrotechnics I want it to be exactly that and nothing more, not some allegory. I can appreciate the virtuosity of a master pianist, but I don't want him to interpret the music he plays as some allegory for the oppression of the poor by the rich, or some other nonsense outside his sphere of expertise. The brilliant pianist, unless he is also a brilliant composer, plays the music of another. I admire the pianist who plays and leaves it at that. I admire brilliant jugglers, for that matter, provided they understand that their competence is limited to juggling.

Justice

Director: So justice consists in knowing one's sphere and keeping within it.

Student: Yes! This is what is wrong with the dark. They have not even defined their own spheres properly and they busy themselves in encroaching upon those of others. I was concerned when Author was talking about the brilliance that exists between the spheres because I think this is exactly how the dark think of themselves: masters of the interstices. They scorn those who stay within their own spheres as simpletons, as limited. Well, I ask: who is he that has no limits? Who? The dark believe, in their heart of hearts, that humans have no limits, that this is the nature of humanity. And they believe that political society requires us to have limits, to have functions, to have roles. They love to think of themselves as master playwrights, as puppet masters who make others dance upon the stage of life. Why limit yourself to writing plays when you can think of your plays as channels for political engineering? This is what obsession with public opinion brings us! We believe we use our minds for progress, but all of this progress is contained or made possible within our political structure, and therefore it is to political engineering we must turn. Ha! The dark don't even believe in this, yet they play this game because they think it's the only one going. They don't believe in progress. Their belief is that of those who make their living in arbitrage on the currency markets: that change is good because it allows them to shave off the difference in the exchange to pocket for themselves. They are middlemen, and nothing more — but they have pretensions to some sort of wisdom beyond, and they can't resist in meddling in others' affairs.

Author: Allow me, Student, to put the final nail in the coffin. There are those who are as you describe, who believe that they deserve a more exalted place in the order of society, one that allows their talents more natural play. Their belief in what they deserve is their only belief. They wish to sacrifice the beliefs of all others at their own altar, and they set out on a dark mission to destroy everything that everyone else believes, through whatever means possible, in the hope that their own unfailing belief in themselves will ultimately allow them to prevail.

Student: So they burn Rome down in order to possess it the better. The works of men like this are exactly what people mistake for brilliance. They dazzle their audience with contradictory arguments that are intended to leave us questioning everything except the prowess of the author. The one lesson is that power is all. And there are always those ready to convert to this religion. Director, isn't it clear how different the works of such men must be from those of the brilliant?

Contrast

Director: Yes, the contrast is clear to me. It seems that the brilliant can depict lava flowing beside a blooming rose, while the dark must engulf the flower and burn it up. Something along those lines, no?

Student: Yes, and if he doesn't come right out and show the lava burning the flower he will set things up in way that the viewer feels he has no choice but to believe it inevitable. The dazzler destroys contrast. He reduces everything to power. He can't maintain the differences between things since he believes they are all conventional.

Director: Does he limit it to things?

Student: No, he believes people are things, biochemical blobs of power of varying degrees. He laughs at the idea of virtue because he sees it as just so much channeling of power through political means. He even laughs at knowledge for the same reason. He'd rather not trouble himself with learning anything but would be all too happy to control a mass of thinking slaves. He'd be perfectly happy as the head of science in the Third Reich. He sees political society as nothing more than an elaborate extension of control. The only real contrast he sees is that between control and being controlled, between master and slave.

Author: But really, Student, aren't such people to be laughed at rather than feared? Imagine we went walking through a meadow on a beautiful summer day. At noon we come upon a man with a long grizzled beard wearing rags. He's lying on his back and staring directly into the sun. We realize at once he is blind, and wonder whether he was born that way or had done it to himself. He hears us approach and says: "You are my slaves. You believe in flowers and grass and hills and streams, when there is only darkness and light." Would we be afraid of him? Perhaps we'd feel sorry for him. But suppose he had in his right hand a great walking stick. He flails out suddenly and strikes you in the shin. What would you do?

Director: I think I'd take up a handful of grass and sprinkle it over his face, then stick a flower behind one of his ears and be on my way.

Madness

Author: The blindness is, of course, a metaphor. But for what? For making oneself mad by means of prolonged monomaniacal reflections. There is nothing so sure to lead to madness in this world than the systematic reduction of all phenomena to one cause. Student, you've surely heard that the brilliant are mad. Well, I think this is the propaganda of the dark. They can't believe that the brilliant think any way other than the way they think themselves. I suspect that when the dark give up on gaining perspective they fall back on their one insight, the one that flatters them the most, and they work it up into a system, one which they believe to describe all of reality, ineluctably. But the brilliant fight to maintain their sanity. They don't give in to such dark temptation. They maintain the difference between phenomena and struggle to make sense of them. Does this drive them to the brink of madness? Yes, I believe it does. Necessarily? I don't know, but in my own experience I can say that it was (and may again be) so.

Student: What was it that kept you from going over the edge?

Author: The feeling you spoke of. When I doubted everything else, I looked back at that feeling and realized that, no matter what the cause, the feeling itself was real — very real, and good. So I asked myself how to get back to that feeling and set out, one foot in front of the other, in that direction, though it seemed so very far off to me at that time. I got there, and here I am. I walk with this feeling always. Yes, I feel unease at the question Director raised. Are we a self-selecting lot that spin justifications for the way we feel? Well, I don't know that it is different for any other way of life. And is it so bad to defend oneself when attacked? Am I going around telling everyone that they have to learn to feel the way we feel? No. In fact, I don't wish the struggle I've gone through on anyone. But why should I lie about it? Why should I pretend it didn't happen? Why should I think of myself as bad, or ugly, or evil? Am I? Well, if I am can that be said of my works? And if not, is it so bad if the works justify the man? Yes, I'm aware that might seem to cut counter to what we've been saying about private brilliance being required before the public. But what if it's true that it takes one to know one? Can the others ever really know the brilliant? And if they can't, isn't it the works of brilliance that attempt to build that bridge? And is this not a means toward enlightening the public? I don't know. But I do know that I won't let these doubts make me give up. I have more perspective to gain.

Student: Does it ever stop?

Author: It can stop, and does for many.

Heights

Student: How can you know if you've gone far enough? Is it just something you can feel?

Author: Yes. Sometimes I think it best to describe it like the pressure you feel when ascending or descending quickly. Then again it seems to me like a sort of vertigo. I used to wonder if it weren't best to get down to sea level, or even below it in some hidden valley, and stay there. But storms and their great waves come to the shore and no valley is so hidden as to keep out all predators.

Student: Man is the only natural enemy of man.

Author: I doubt whether the animosity is natural, but I take your point. When pursued we sometimes must take to the heights. But we have to take care not to get dizzy and fall.

Student: Madness.

Author: Yes, and we would be equally mad to forget that we once dwelled quite happily beneath. The view from atop a solitary mount, once one has become accustomed to it, can seduce the best of men to an exaggerated belief in their knowledge and power. To view the valleys below is not to know them and command them. Some of the dark ones never made their way down the mountain.

Student: Just as some of them never climbed it.

Author: Indeed, and they therefore lack perspective.

Student: The brilliant must be sure footed.

Author: Yes, and don't let anyone tell you that they spend their time contemplating their navels. They contemplate the ground, my friend, in order to determine where best to plant their feet. Do you think they'd listen for a moment to someone who'd never left the peak telling them how best to descend? Or how about the opposite — someone who'd never left the shore describing in great detail how the rocks and sand are the same? Or worse — that the mountains are all made of sand and that there is no such thing as rock?

Student: This sort of thing happens all the time.

Author: So the brilliant are wont to gain repute as being deaf, eh? You laugh! That's good. It is funny. Goodness knows a brilliant man born on a prairie will hear told countless tales of the dangers and uselessness of life on high. And the brilliant man born on a peak will hear the same of life below. And maybe both would hear much worse, eh? Moral failings, arrogance, ignorance, corruption, vice, inferiority in every respect. What is one to make of it all? Well, the brilliant man first finds his feet and then his ground and then begins to walk. But you know, Student, that this is all a metaphor. One might live in the same house one's whole life, traveling absolutely nowhere, geographically speaking, and still be quite brilliant.

Student: Why then is there such profound importance attached to the adjective high? Why is there high and low culture? Why do we speak of high end and low end goods? Why is the best liquor on the top shelf?

Author: I don't know, Student. I've been in Chinese liquor stores where they keep the best on the bottom. But I know what you mean. Director?

Director: It seems to me some sort of historical accident. But maybe there's more to it than that. Consider a lighthouse. What is it? A beacon placed on high to guide captains to port. Maybe the kernel of the idea is in this.

Student: Well, even in the jungle they build huts on stilts.

Director: Yes, and in cities the most expensive commercial real estate is the highest up. In the case you mention there's sound practical reason. But downtown? It's a status symbol and nothing more.

Student: Maybe they think of themselves as beacons to others, communicating from peak to peak.

Director: I'm sure some of them do, and I'm also sure that in some cases it's true.

Student: So it's more than a historical accident. There's something to it.

Director: Something brilliant?

Student: Well, I suppose if someone can occupy a contested height and serve as a beacon to others — yes, there may well be something brilliant in that.

Director: But would a brilliant man storm a defended height merely in order to occupy it and show others that he has?

Student: I don't know. Would he?

Director: No, he wouldn't. What would that make him? A brilliant stormer? I suppose we should consider that. Storming for the sake of storming seems nothing more than barbaric. Wouldn't you agree? But what if the object were not the storming but the throwing down of someone making ill use of the height? What would such a man be?

Student: A philosopher?

Director: Ha! Now it's my turn to laugh. And what about someone making ill use of the low lying lands? Whose concern is that?

Student: Everyman's.

Immortality

Author: Ah, this raises such questions! Student, your answer serves to reinforce the idea that the heights are the preserve of the few. What is it about the heights that seduces those few who count themselves worthy? Why, when one strives to the heights — or to be a beacon to others, or any other similar aspiration — is one hoping for anything less than immortality?

Student: I think you're onto something, Author.

Author: What has immortality to do with brilliance? Do we all long for immortality?

Director: You know full well, Author, that a brilliant man might long to burn out like a sun, leaving his light to traverse the universe for centuries after he is gone. Is that immortality? No. The light eventually fades. And the light is nothing more than that. It is not immortality. No, I say. A brilliant man who aspires to leave something beyond himself only wishes to leave behind some light — and that is all. Don't tell me that the man lives on in his light. He doesn't, any more than does wood consumed in a fire. Yes, he is the cause — or one of the causes — of this light. But that light belongs to him as much as it does to any other who perceives it. Once he is gone it is his no more. It belongs to those who see by it.

Student: What light do philosophers leave behind?

Director: If all a philosopher does is dislodge imposters from the heights, what sort of light do you think is that?

Student: A bright and pure light, Director.

Director: Is that so? Philosophy is love of wisdom, is it not? Or was Socrates sarcastic?

Student: Why are you getting upset?

Director: Am I? I really want to know what you think. Is philosophy the love of wisdom, or were those words spoken sarcastically? Does the philosopher think that wisdom, all wisdom, is a sham? Is wisdom nothing more than the justification of interest?

Student: Of course not!

Director: Really? Then what is it, Student?

Student: Why are you doing this to me?

Director: What is it I'm doing? Asking you questions you can't answer? Do you think my questions are insincere? Do you think I really don't want to know what you think? Would a brilliant man ask rhetorical questions? Does a brilliant man employ rhetoric? Eh? At a loss for words? What is wisdom?

Student: I think it's the same as what we've been saying about brilliance.

Director: Oh? And what have we been saying? That brilliance comes down to nothing more than some ineffable feeling?

Student: Yes, and I don't understand why you are so upset!

Director: Then what is wisdom other than knowing how to live in such a way as to keep this feeling alive?

Student: Nothing!

Director: Then do heights matter?

Student: No!

Director: Then does immortality matter?

Student: No!

Isolation

Director: Then knowing how to keep the feeling alive is all that matters. Do you have to know how to do this on your own?

Student: What do you mean?

Director: Are brilliant men available to other potentially brilliant men whenever they need them?

Student: Well, they leave behind books and other works as examples.

Director: And who teaches the potentially brilliant how to read? Brilliant men? Can a brilliant book teach someone how to be a brilliant reader?

Student: I think it's possible.

Director: Possible. Mmm. Quite a lot rides on that possibility, my friend. Do you know what happens to the brilliant who live in isolation? The madness Author described can't even touch upon the torments of soul that await such men. It's bad enough if they are surrounded by the indifferent. But do you know what happens when they are surrounded by the dark? They don't even approach the frontiers of madness. They burn in the living fires of hell, keeping close to the conventional because they can see no other way.

Student: I have some idea what that means.

Director: Then do you know how important it is to catch a glimpse of another way? Do you see what it really means to be a beacon in the night? Does any other concern but life enter into the mind of one who has broken through to daylight? Do you think such a one wishes to make a reputation toppling the arrogant perched on high? Is that what this is all about?

Student: No!

Director: What happens to potential brilliance in isolation? Rot. Decay. Degeneration. Insanity. Suicide — and that's no metaphor.

Student: I didn't think it was, Director.

Communion

Author: Director seems to suggest that communication — nay, communion — is the goal of brilliant life. After all, the very word brilliant implies light and the sharing it makes possible.

Student: Sharing or liberation?

Director: Why not liberation by means of sharing? And liberation from what? From prejudice? There's no liberation from that — unless the brilliant rule.

Student: And why shouldn't they?

Director: Maybe they should. But who's to choose? The self-professedly brilliant? Do I seem bitter here? That would be rather ironic. Showing emotion precisely here might seem to obfuscate rather than clarify.

Student: Why would you obfuscate?

Director: Why don't you wear your heart on your sleeve in front of the dark?

Student: I see.

Director: Do you? I wonder. What sort of communion is possible in a world of feints and thrusts? Are the brilliant pure? Is that what you think? Do they dine on honeydew and drink the sweet milk of paradise? Let me tell you: they are often bitter. But they are not bitter to the core, and they certainly don't grow bitter pining away for something useless.

Student: I know that, Director. If you had no bitterness I would wonder whether you had ever really struggled.

Director: So how do we rise above our idiosyncratic bitterness? Communion? Sharing? What is it we share? Our light. Yes, I say this in truth. Our light. Of what is light made? Burning. Destruction. Depending on what's consigned to the flames, I suppose we see brilliant and dark or evil light.

Student: Does it have to be thought of as burning something up, Director? Nuclear physics shows that fusion — combination — also makes for the release of energy and light.

Director: Is fusion not destruction? Things once distinct exist no more, regardless how they are combined into new matter. Still, is that the sort of communion you want? Reduction of the brilliant into some fused state? Well, fusion depends on the heaviness of the elements involved. But both fission and fusion release energy. So which are the brilliant, Student? The products of both? We've come full circle to Athens and Sparta. Are the Spartans — those fused into their regime — weightier than the Athenians? Perhaps we ought consider, my friend, whether we've placed an idea of brilliance upon the heights that we must now throw down.

Individuals

Student: It may well be that being a brilliant individual requires being part of a greater whole. He requires fusion. He requires love beyond himself.

Director: What whole is that? Do you mean some voluntarily constituted whole? Is the city fully voluntary? Why not just fuse with individuals you love, Student? Or is that something different?

Student: It certainly is something different! Have you given up on the possibility of this sort of larger fusion into a whole?

Director: You must be talking about a political whole. Just me and my closest three hundred million Americans fused into one big happy family?

Student: No! Oneness with those who uphold our political ideals — the ones who live our ideals.

Director: The brilliant citizens and statesmen who promote the brilliant life?

Student: Yes, exactly.

Director: Do you doubt that I admire such people?

Student: No, but I doubt that you'll ever take that next step.

Director: Which is?

Student: Forming lasting bonds.

Director: Are you talking about secret societies?

Student: What? What are you talking about? Of course not!

Director: Well then, I confess I am at a loss as to what sort of bonds you mean. It seems to me that no bond is more meaningful or lasting than that of unfeigned, natural admiration of one man for another. Do you have in mind some sort of contractual relation? Or perhaps we've come back around again to the notion of a political party. I would vote for you, Student, as long as you held true to what we've agreed on today.

Student: I don't want your vote.

Director: What is it you want?

Education

Student: I don't want to feel like it's just a handful of brilliant people fighting against all odds. I want to find ways to encourage brilliance. I want to find a way to bring the brilliant together. I want a society suffused with brilliance. I don't care if the surrounding nations consist of the dark and indifferent. I'm not fool enough to think that states can exist without war. But I'd rather die in the service of those I admire — those I love — than live in hiding amongst the indifferent and dark. Why not wear my heart on my sleeve? Why does my pride have to remain beneath the surface? Why shouldn't I be able to speak openly about the dark and indifferent? They would have us believe that brilliance harms society. Ha! Brilliance is the very basis of society! It's what society is meant to foster and protect!

Director: So then the task is to study the contemporary scene and find what incremental changes can be made —

Student: Incremental? Where will that get us? We're constantly scraping to get by and escape their persecution as it is! We need more. No, I'm not talking about open revolution. I'm talking about winning hearts and minds. I'm talking about educating the young. Of what would this education consist? Teaching them how to think on their own. There's no magic formula to memorize, no political catechism.

Director: Then you're talking about a loose federation of independent powers, of individuals. So who conducts the education? The brilliant, I must suppose. And you've already described them as a hunted minority. How likely is it that the dark will entrust their children to such teachers? Not very likely. And how likely the indifferent? It seems to me that here is the battle. But what if they have their own teachers? Wouldn't they entrust their children's education to their own? And wouldn't the dark set up schools? Wouldn't they offer more allure than your simple brilliant teachers?

Student: Why are you trying to discourage me?

Director: I'm just asking you to think through what you're saying. And it's not that I think what you're saying is bad or wrong or even naïve. To the contrary. Education toward life is noble. But you seem to want something more and I can't understand what it is.

Revenge

Author: It seems obvious to me, Director. He wants revenge.

Student: Is there anything wrong with that?

Author: I think that depends on the cost. Are you willing to provoke a backlash against the brilliant that will result in their annihilation? Suppose you set up your nation of the brilliant. Won't we be surrounded? Won't we be outgunned?

Student: I wouldn't count on our being outgunned.

Author: Okay. But unless you think we should rule the others, there's always the chance that we'll be overrun, and if overrun perhaps we'll be wiped out. Is it wise to concentrate the brilliant such? Shouldn't they disperse themselves throughout the world in the face of systematic risk?

Student: Maybe we should rule them.

Author: How, by substituting tyranny for statesmanship? Won't brilliant rule, of necessity, degenerate without its natural counterpart in brilliant citizens? Maybe we'd do better just to kill them all. And whom should we kill, do you think — only the dark? Well, setting aside the difficulty in determining just who the dark are, given their skills in dissembling and deceit — are we to deny them the chance to struggle through and gain their own perspective and brilliance? We're forgetting something implicit to what we've been saying, Student. The brilliant were once dark themselves. But suppose we resolve this difficulty. Shall we slaughter the others? Even if they mean us no harm, they are not brilliant and therefore cannot participate as full citizens in our brilliant state. Or shall we exert great energy in maintaining a balance of power favorable to the others above the dark in all our neighboring states? But then we have the same problem: lacking brilliant counterparts, what sort of task is such diplomacy?

Student: So while you're every bit as bitter as Director, and want me to become the same, you would deny me the outlet of revenge. Brilliant.

Author: I don't want you to become bitter. Sure, I'm bitter about some things — but I don't let that set the tone of my life. And I'm not bitter when I ask you the kinds of questions I'm asking now.

Student: Maybe all brilliant men have to dedicate a portion of their lives to the unpleasant business of dealing with the others and the dark.

Author: Maybe? Ha, ha, ha! Maybe. Oh, I'd say that's a certainty, my friend — as certain as taxes and death. And I'll also say that there will be times when you'll get your wish. Revenge. And it's much sweeter when it happens through a logic of its own in the course of events rather than by being forced by an act of will.

Example

Director: Indeed. And what sort of example would it set for the youth if their elders were bent on revenge, the object of which they could not possibly have the experience to understand? But perhaps these children are already dark and do understand quite well what it is their parents attack. Then again, they may merely be indifferent. In that case all examples are lost on them.

Student: Maybe we were wrong to say that the brilliant must struggle in the dark as they gain perspective. In fact, I don't know how we even agreed to that. Why can't the brilliant be those who are born into the light — which is why they have their vision — and struggle to remain in it while they work out their perspective in the full light of day?

Director: Alright, let's suppose that's the case.

Student: Why suppose? Doesn't that seem how it has to be?

Director: I don't know, Student. It might be. So let's suppose that brilliance is merely a matter of luck.

Student: Why luck?

Director: Well, aren't you saying that one is either born into the light or not? And if so, what happens with those who don't work out the necessary perspective in order to articulate their vision through their manner of living? Do they become dark? Irretrievably so? Do we then cast them out so that their example doesn't corrupt the youth? So only the successfully brilliant remain and influence the young. But who is to judge whether a youth has gone dark? Do the youths receive warnings if they begin to enter the gray? Who says where day ends and twilight begins? Who says where twilight ends and eternal darkness begins? Or perhaps we should merely quarantine those who have gone into night, keeping them away from the children and youths, until their sun rises once again the following day. But are the quarantined prisoners or simply students? Who will teach or guard them? Who is the natural counterpart to such people? It seems to me likely that all the brilliant will have to dedicate time to non-brilliant tasks such as these if there is any hope of reclaiming what seems lost. Then again, perhaps the brilliant youths need the example of the gray and the dark in order to understand the importance of staying in the light. One might think that they need no negative example to teach them, since staying in the light will come natural to them. But then why are the dark and the gray the gray and the dark? If we're not going to reduce it to mere luck or circular argument, we have to consider that one has meaningful choice in the matter. After all, if that weren't the case then there would be no point in worrying about examples one way or the other. If brilliance can't be taught then there would be no hope of setting up a republic of brilliance or any other more permanent group or society, more permanent meaning to exist across generations — unless there were means guaranteed to reach the brilliant, and only the brilliant, across the generations. Why, we've come full around again to Author's description of the brilliant pyramid that extends from the low to the high! Except this time it seems the brilliant are the high while the dark would occupy the middle and the indifferent the base. Perhaps the brilliant man must be able to speak polyphonically — at once sounding notes in the high, middle, and low registers.

Audience

Author: Of course, that assumes the brilliant man wishes to speak to all people at once. If we don't live entirely within the society of the brilliant, it's inevitable that a brilliant man will have to speak to brilliant, dark, and other men. But will the brilliant man always speak brilliantly? Will he speak brilliantly with the brilliant, darkly with the dark, and in another, rather indifferent manner with the others?

Student: He can do that in private but not when speaking in public.

Author: Well! Won't the brilliance of what he says be lost on the dark and indifferent?

Student: They might not appreciate it, but I don't think they'll fail to recognize it. The dark will resent it and attempt to persuade the others that what the brilliant man is saying is pernicious. It's as we've said before.

Author: But if the dark think the brilliant man speaks darkly, will they attack? Do the dark attack one another?

Student: Of course they do. They've no reason not to.

Author: So speaking darkly doesn't help. But what of speaking otherwise, or rather, indifferently? Wouldn't the others see nothing but themselves in the speech, while the dark would be stymied in attempting to turn the others against the brilliant speaker — speech here being metaphorical, and representative of any form of public communication? Why, the others would think the dark mad and begin to suspect them for what they are.

Student: Then what would make such speech brilliant and not merely indifferent?

Author: Suppose a man known to a certainty to possess great knowledge addresses a general audience and speaks indifferently about things falling within his knowledge. Wouldn't those knowledgeable about these things be compelled to wonder why he had done so? Yes, they certainly would. Would the others, the indifferent? Why, they'd have no reason to wonder at anything. All would seem proper. Now, given the heightened state of attention thus brought about among the knowing, wouldn't a brilliant man recognize this situation and play to it? How? He would leave hints, suggestions. He might even argue by enthymeme, by means of syllogisms dependent upon suppressed premises — premises known to the brilliant, and perhaps also by some of the dark. What would the dark do? Would they cry out that a dirty trick was in play? That would certainly do them no good and would diminish their standing long before they might gain the perspective they lack.

Student: That sort of speech would require incredible grace under pressure. So we have to read between the lines. But how can we know for certain that we're not just imagining something to be there that isn't?

Author: A brilliant speaker will know how to make it sufficiently clear. But he understands that reading between the lines presents the difficulty you raise, and he accepts that his speaking may serve as nothing more than an invitation for us to undertake our own investigation of the matter. Heaven knows he doesn't want to be taken simply on faith! His rhetoric consists of addressing both the brilliant and the others or indifferent through the language of the indifferent or others while keeping the dark at bay with devices that, at best, spur them to work to gain perspective on both the method of the address as well as the address itself. Substance and style are of a piece.

Director: And what of the laconic style of our Spartan friends?

Author: Socrates said that there were more philosophers in Sparta than any other Greek city. This is generally considered to have been a joke — and I concur. But I think the joke was ironic.

V. AMBITION

Persons of the Dialogue:

Old Man

Director

Clown

Young Man

Old Man: Ambition that is left unchecked is bad for all society. Ambitious men will tear the fabric of our common lives in two while they go chasing after what they want, whatever that may be. Ambitious men must be rebuked. Their spirits must be curbed and trained towards useful ends. And this is good for them. Unchecked ambition is a curse upon the one in whom it grows. It is a viper in the breast that causes agony with every bite, a pain that drives a man insane. It causes men to waste the best years of their lives on fantasies of what they think they can achieve. Remorse is never greater than when visiting a man who broke upon ambition's rack. Ambition serving proper ends provides the drive a man must have to grow up straight and strong so that he'll play his proper part in life.

Clown: But who's to say what ends ambition serves? The old?

Old Man: The ones who've seen and know!

Clown: The ones who only know the past? The ones whose eyes no longer see?

Old Man: The ones who're wise because they have experience!

Clown: Experience of how their own ambitions took their shapes from those yet older and much wiser still? You'd have us steer ahead by looking back

---

into the mists of time where foggy heads and hazy dreams will always feel at home!

Young Man: The Clown is harsh yet wise. The old desire the young to re-enact the past. That's simply how it always is. If they succeed entirely in their desire the world grows stagnant like a swamp. There must be change. Ambition is the key that opens up the gate to let the fresher waters in. Ambitious youths take pride in throwing off the shackles of the older times. They spend their strength in seeking out the bold and newer ways. Where one of them will fail another comes and pushes further on. It's thus a path is cleared. It's thus we find our way to greater things. But only few of us experience this call, this drive — and of this few the greater part are curbed and tied to older ways before they have a chance to prove their worth. And that's, in part, because ambition doesn't get its due. It's seen as bad. It's seen as something that must be restrained. But once restrained ambition dies, and we are poorer with this loss.

Clown: Well, Director, it comes to you to speak your mind.

Director: I think our friends have said enough.

Old Man: But, Director, you cannot let the matter stand like this! The Young Man's way destroys the moorings of society! You can't agree to this. I know you don't. So speak against his foolish pride.

Director: I'll only note you both agree ambition is a good. One thinks it's good when free. One thinks it's good when trained.

Old Man: But that's the point, my friend. We need to show this younger man ambition can't be free!

Director: But first I need to have the answer to the questions what is free and what is trained.

Clown: "What is?" you ask! "What is?" you always want to know! What is, what is, what is! This is your artful dodge! This is the way you hide!

Director: The way I hide from what?

Clown: The question, Director!

Director: I see. I'm sure that you won't mind repeating what that question is?

Clown: The question is whose side you're on!

Director: I tend to side with beauty, good, and truth.

Clown: Of course you do! But which is that, you would-be fool?

Old Man: Have peace, you Clown!

Young Man: Well, Director, I'd like to hear the way you judge and find out where you stand. The Clown, again, makes sense, although he's rather rude.

Director: I really mean it when I say we can't proceed together to the answer that we want unless we're all agreed on what ambition is.

Young Man: That's easy, Director. Ambition is the noble soul unfolding to its fullest size and left to sail, to soar, to ride in freedom on the wind, to breathe in deep the freshest air, to live each day with zest, to thrive, to reach one's furthest ends, to take in ever more experience and then give light as though one were a star, to feel the warmth of earth beneath the feet and stretch to reach the sky above, to sow then reap the sweetest fruits, to clear the way to build great dwellings for a godlike race of men. Ambition that's fulfilled will give the greatest sense of satisfaction, self-esteem, and all-around well-being that there is. It is a tonic to a sick and weary soul. It cures unease within the heart and mind. And even when ambition's hopes are dashed — until the very final fall — the striving that one undertakes will give the face a ruddy glow of health. Ambition should be given its full reign and left to ride its course.

Old Man: That's nonsense, boy. Ambition is the love of praise. Unchecked, a man will always seek the grand applause. The more his lust for this is left unchecked, the more a slave to it he must become. He's like a drunk who lives from high to high. To check ambition gives this man a chance to sober up and gain his independence from the clapper-clawing mob. The man must learn to favor praise from those who know and not just anyone. But I must note that this is something best learned as a boy. Indeed, I have great doubt that one full grown can ever learn. Instead, it seems to me, he must be forced to stop his reckless course before he trounces on the things that other patient souls have built and love.

Director: The Old Man gives a definition that is very short: the love of praise. Can you, Young Man, be equally concise?

Young Man: Of course I can. Ambition is the love of life and all it takes to live it to the full.

Old Man: To live it to the full? You mean to live in great excess, to have excitement as your god, to be a prodigal who ends his run with nothing left to show!

Clown: So how now, Director? Are you in favor or opposed?

Director: To what?

Clown: To what? To what's been said!

Director: About ambition, Clown?

Clown: Of course!

Director: I'm not sure what it is.

Clown: Of course you are!

Director: But we are not agreed, and I have got no definition of my own. Have you?

Clown: The question still remains! Ambition's either free or checked!

Director: The question still remains exactly what ambition is. Ambition is the love of life and all it takes to live it to the full? Then is the taking of our daily bread an object of ambition's sting? We have to eat to live, in full or part it matters not. Ambition is the love of praise? Is this to say the boy who wants to please his father by the proper doing of a task is thus ambitious in his heart? It's that we really mean? You see, my friends, I'm really at a loss.

Clown: You're not! It's just a trick!

Old Man: But, Director, it doesn't do to try to be precise with things like this. They're simply things one knows, that's all.

Director: They're things that come much easier to you than me. One day I might believe I know the truth about a thing and then the next it seems I've lost the knowledge that I had. It's always so, and been that way for all my life. I'll try and try to find the truth about these simple things and then the wind will blow and scatter all I've learned and here I am with nothing left to show.

Young Man: That's ludicrous! Your reputation stands intact. You're known to be a man who thinks before he speaks and offers prudent counsel to his friends.

Director: But still I cannot say exactly what ambition is.

Old Man: But there's no need to say exactly what ambition is! You'll know a man's ambitious by the things he does.

Director: You mean, for instance, if he runs for offices?

Old Man: Of course. Exactly that.

Director: I guess you do not mean the office of the chairman of the library?

Old Man: Well, no, not quite.

Director: You surely mean an office that is high.

Old Man: That's right.

Director: How high, my friend?

Old Man: The sort for which a man would truly have to fight.

Director: But what about our friend the chief librarian? Might he, as well, have had to fight?

Old Man: Well, I don't know...

Clown: Ah ha! The Old Man's not so wise! Ha, ha!

Old Man: Be silent, Clown! I'm simply trying to help my friend. It's not so easy helping others understand.

Clown: Oh ho! The blind will teach the eagle how to see! Ha, ha!

Director: I am no eagle, Clown.

Clown: To speak like that is wise. I stand corrected: you are but a snake.

Director: At times I feel as though I were a turkey in a tree. But getting to the point: we said ambition has to do with offices and fights. "How high? How hard?" I ask. The answers needn't be precise as long as they ring true. Perhaps the answer simply is too high, too hard. Perhaps ambition is too much.

Old Man: Oh yes! That's it! You've hit it right upon the head! You see? I knew you knew.

Young Man: Ambition is too much? To take a trick from Director: is that to say the man who eats too much is overly ambitious, eh?

Old Man: We said, Young Man, it has to do with offices. It has to do with reaching out beyond one's proper scope.

Clown: One's "proper" scope, oh ho! And who's to say what "proper" is? The old?

Old Man: The ones who know.

Clown: Regardless of their age?

Old Man: Experience is necessary if one is to learn. This only comes with age.

Clown: And what about the old who haven't got experience?

Old Man: It isn't possible to live without acquiring experience, you Clown.

Clown: Then all the old are wise?

Old Man: Of course not all the old are wise, but there are more among the old than young — and that's for sure.

Young Man: But how do we expand upon the things we know if we are always kept within our proper bounds — however they are drawn? Ambition takes a man beyond the proper limits set to where he sees and learns new things and then returns to share what he has come to know.

Director: And do you really think they'll want to learn?

Young Man: The old are hard, if not impossible, to teach. They've spent their lives adhering to a certain rule and when you try to show that there's another way they all but lose their minds. They excommunicate and sometimes even banish those who cross the lines they've set. They never learn because they will not hear the things the ones they've exiled say. They keep their narrow ways until rigidity exacts its fee. Disaster comes at last and then the knowledge won by those ambitious few is seen for what it's truly worth, is seen to be the thing that could have saved them all. But that is just the old. The young might hear these daring ones and try to understand the things they teach. By listening and learning they become much wiser than they were and rise in challenge to the old. They seek to change the rule that set the limits thus. And this is what the old will always fear, this challenge to their settled rule. And this is why they wish to rein ambition in.

Old Man: What rot we have to hear you talk! The young are always last to learn — and even from their own mistakes. They think they know it all. They think that everything is obvious and that the old are fools because they always want to take a second look before deciding on a thing. The young are always in a rush and that is not the state of mind one needs to learn. Besides, what knowledge do you think you'll have to teach? What wisdom are you bringing back? It's you yourself who need to learn. You have to see the cost of your ambition run amuck. It's you who'll pay the price, as well as those who're caught up in your wake. But I'll allow that you may serve a purpose yet. Examples help the young to learn, and those disasters that you're bound to cause yourself, because you take so very lightly all the wise restraints we old would use to guide your course to safer and more happy shores, may serve to warn the young of what must come when they exceed the proper bounds.

Clown: A scarecrow to the young is what you hope ambitious men become! But crows don't scare so easily! They'll perch atop your scarecrow's head and caw and mock all day!

Old Man: It's only bitter clowns who'd waste their time like that. The young have hope and want to learn the proper way to nurture it. They want to learn to plow and plant and reap. And while they do, it's those like me who'll chase you wicked crows away. And we will teach the young to be aware of how ambitious men would rob them of their crop. For after all, ambitious men desire to have much more than what their proper share should be — and they won't hesitate to steal. It's this, at bottom, that ambitious men do best. They're thieves! The Young Man speaks of crossing bounds, as if the old do not allow his traveling about. The bounds, in truth, he means to cross are none but moral bounds. What else could he be speaking of? What other railing would ambition jump to get ahead? For shame! He speaks as though he were a hero to the human race when really he is just a petty crook! He speaks of others picking up where he leaves off when it is infamy that he will leave to light the darkened way his followers will tread.

Young Man: Indeed! I think that that's enough. It's you, the old, who rob the young of what is theirs by right. The young have strength and energy that their ambition would employ in searching out the means to best provide for all their wants — and even leave a surplus, too! Yet you, the old, would stifle them and harness them to ends that serve your own desires. You speak of breaking moral law? Well, let us take a look at what you really mean. You say ambition is the love of praise and you would use your praise to train the young to serve your ends. The things that tend to serve your ends are good, while those that don't are bad. With time, your praise becomes the moral law. The highest thing that you would want the young aspiring to is nothing more than being good, according to your view. If anyone begins to question whether what you praise is truly good you shout him down with insults to his character, and you are backed by all your young and barking dogs. For what are they but dogs who lap up all your calculated praise? It seems to me this praise is poison to a young and open heart. And sure enough, in time you see the hearts of those who drink it down grow closed and cold — a sign of wisdom, you might say! But I will charge you with a greater crime than theft, Old Man. I say you are a murderer of those who drink yet fight to keep an open heart. They cannot understand why they grow ill while on they go imbibing from your cup. Your wine is sickly sweet but also bitter, too, at times. One word of blame from you to one who has an open heart will bite down deeply in his soul. He doesn't know that you cannot be trusted to distribute praise and blame without an eye to your own selfish ends. The only antidote for him is knowledge of this fact. Once armed with this he shuts his ears against your wicked words and opens up his eyes as wide as they can go to see exactly how you act.

Old Man: A murderer with praise? You really go too far when you're emotional like that. As if it weren't a simple thing to praise or blame from nothing but the truth! A boy performs a task. He does it well or ill. That's all! There's no agenda secretly at work. There's no conspiracy to close his heart, as you would say. As long as praise, or blame, is given strictly in accordance with the truth the rearing of the young goes well. It's when a youth is lavished with excessive praise ambition starts to rise within his breast beyond its proper bound. His head begins to swell and soon he's dreaming of the things he'll do. These things, of course, are well beyond his means. So he begins to scheme. He thinks up ways of getting more than he deserves, of fooling men to think he's better than he is. And how he promises! He gives to others expectations that they'll benefit from all he'll do. So they grow lax in their affairs in expectation of the gains from him. And so it goes. It's best to praise and blame in firm accordance with the truth. This serves to limit all ambition to its proper sphere. When praise and blame are justly meted out they give to all a knowledge of their limits and their strengths, a knowledge that they'll act upon with good success.

Clown: But what about the other case, Old Man? The case where blame predominates?

Old Man: When blame is just it should be freely offered up.

Clown: But don't you see that this will also give ambition rise?

Old Man: Discouragement give rise to one's ambition, Clown? It's clear you aren't a student of the human heart. Discouragement is meant to keep one's hopes in check — and nothing ever comes without a healthy dose of hope.

Clown: But what if someone else is offering this hope?

Old Man: Then that is just the case of too much praise. To offer hope to one who shouldn't have that hope at all is tantamount to praise. It has the same effect, and it is wrong. It leads us, once again, to our ambitious men. But now they may be even worse because they have a vengeance in their hearts. They wish to show that they are better than they are. Indeed, they wish to show that they are better than the rest. It's thus they think they'll have revenge. You see, they think that they are something that they're not and they would have the rest of us agree. They wish to prove us wrong and thereby countermand the blame.

Young Man: But such are not ambitious men. They have become perverted in their hearts. The hearts of all ambitious men are pure. They want to do their best and strive with all their might to reach their goals. If praise is given for their deeds, so much the better then! But that is not the reason for their acts. The doing of the things they want — nay, love — to do is all. No harm is done to anyone when men are thus employed.

Clown: It seems that Director is keeping very still.

Director: I'm listening.

Clown: Well, on and on they'll go. The question is which one is right. And where does Director come down on this?

Director: I'd like to say if that were possible for me. The answer isn't obvious.

Clown: It isn't obvious? I thought you said ambition is too much! Then you must think it must be checked!

Director: I'm not so sure ambition is too much. I still don't claim to know exactly what it is.

Old Man: You can't be neutral on this, Director!

Young Man: I can't believe you'd side with him!

Clown: A coward would refuse to choose! Ha, ha! A yellow-bellied sneak!

Old Man: And where do you come down?

Clown: Why, don't you know? A clown will always go to where the laughter is. Ambitious men who've failed present a somber lot. But as they rise — oh ho! They laugh and laugh no end! It makes no difference if they're young or old. The old can have ambitions, too, you know — and it's the same with them. They laugh or frown depending on success. It's all the same to me if one succeeds or fails. I simply find another rising man. I form no lasting bond with those for whom I clown. And can you think this wrong of me? I only wish they all could rise! Ha, ha! So where do I come down? I don't! I cling to those who rise and trust ambitious men will never be in short supply. Oh, let them strive to rise as high as they would like! It doesn't matter anyway. They all must fall, in time. To hold them back will only make them want to rise much more. So let us laugh and have ambitious men be free!

Director: I wonder how you feel, Young Man, about this sentiment.

Young Man: He can't be serious. He is a clown, you know. But he is wrong to think ambition is a matter just of rising up in rank. This may occur, but only as an incident to what I've said before: pursuing what you love. At times this makes you rise; at times you might descend into the darkest valley known to man — where you will never find a clown.

Old Man: But clowns aside, you peg your argument upon that word forever spoken of by those who think that wisdom is for dried up fools. The tempered meaning of that verb to love is far from clear to those whose passions rule their minds. They think that love is everything, the argument that trumps them all. And so I'm not surprised to hear ambition coming down to love, as far as you're concerned. You simply want to give your passions reign and let them lead you where they may! Why, love is such a sacred thing each scoundrel vies to claim its name for what he does. This trick is old as dirt. It's only bitter men and hypocrites who'd dare to stand opposed, you'll say. Well, I, for one, am one who loves but doesn't let his love affect the judgments that he makes. Ambition also takes a second seat to judgment in my soul. I am no hypocrite. I practice what I preach, and this has left me far from bitter as you all can see. Ungoverned men — and not the prudent, tempered souls — are those who come to drink the bitter cup.

Young Man: But you would say that love takes faith and perseverance, no?

Old Man: Of course! But don't you say that you will persevere in your ambitious quest!

Young Man: I will! I will! And that's the prudence of my way! And that's the way my soul will take its fully tempered shape! I'll shape my iron with the fire of love!

Old Man: You'll only take your final shape when you've been cast out in the cold because you ventured much too far! And that's the truth, my friend, and that's the bitter truth!

Young Man: But you assume my love will fail!

Old Man: I pity you and wish that you would come to open up your eyes. The passions cool as one grows old. You do not see this now. But time will come when what you think will always be a mighty torch will barely give off any heat at all. The old contrive to curb the young from burning up their fuel too soon. It's true they try to stop the young from running wild and tearing up the land. But they have got no hidden plan to steal the talents of the young, as you believe. They rein them in with hope the young will learn to reign themselves. That's all. But your ambitious men, left free to chase their dreams — or love, or what you will — will never learn to rule their passions with the sober judgment of their minds. They run like mad until their ruling passion fails and then they're lost.

Young Man: You try to scare me into giving up. I won't. You're wrong. As long as there is life there's hope, and that is all I need. The means present themselves to those who try. There are no guarantees. Of course it's possible I'll fail. But such is life.

Director: It's possible you'll fail at what?

Young Man: At my ambition, Director.

Director: I thought that your ambition is pursuing what you love. Or is it doing what you love? Before I thought you meant ambition leads to living life in full, or something that amounts to that. I guess you mean to do the thing you love amounts to living life in full?

Young Man: That's right.

Director: Well, what's the thing you love to do?

Young Man: Well, that can be so many things depending on the one you ask.

Director: I'm asking you.

Young Man: The thing I love to do?

Clown: Why, what's so hard, Young Man? Are you ashamed of what you love to do? Ha, ha!

Young Man: It isn't that. It's just... It's just... It's just that I'm not sure exactly what it is.

Clown: You don't know what you love! And everybody says that I'm the fool! Ha, ha!

Old Man: Be silent, Clown! He's speaking from the heart.

Director: Perhaps there's some variety to what you love to do.

Young Man: In one sense, yes; but in another, no. The things I love to do all have in common something that I can't explain.

Director: Well, what's a thing you love to do?

Young Man: I love to help my friends.

Director: And what's another thing you love to do?

Young Man: I love to stand up for what's right.

Director: You feel the same when doing both these things?

Young Man: I do.

Director: And how do you describe the way you feel?

Young Man: I feel quite good.

Director: When doing other things you also love to do you also feel quite good?

Young Man: I do.

Director: Then that's the thing they have in common, right?

Young Man: I guess it is. Of course.

Clown: Ha, ha! He loves to feel quite good! He loves to feel quite good! The great ambitious man!

Old Man: Be quiet, Clown, or I will give you reason not to laugh!

Director: Well, it would seem ambition means to strive to find the means to do the things you love.

Clown: Ah ha! We have your definition, Director. Should it be checked or free? But I won't listen to a word you say! Ha, ha!

Director: Regardless if you hear or not, it seems to me that nature has provided us with checks. It's fair to say we love to do the things we truly want, correct? If someone wants or loves to eat he'll only eat until he's full. If someone wants or loves to drink he'll only drink when he has thirst. If someone wants or loves to sleep he only sleeps when he is tired. I think you get the point.

Clown: The point! The point! But you should draw the inferences that follow from this point!

Director: The point remains the same no matter how complex ambitions get. We only ever truly want enough — not more, not less. Of course, it's likely that I still don't understand exactly what ambition is although it seems I do.

Old Man: But those who want applause are never satisfied.

Director: Then either they don't really have ambition for applause — there's something else that's lacking here instead — or what I've said is wrong. In either case, if what you say is true, then they are doomed to suffer pangs of want.

Clown: Should their ambition be left free?

Director: That all depends, my sometimes friend the Clown. They'll only do the things that win applause. So if we do not want them acting in a certain way we mustn't clap — or laugh, as far as you're concerned. Is such ambition free?

Old Man: But, Director, we mustn't let applause determine how ambitious men will act! The demagogues will rise in such a state and wreck the land! There has to be another way to check these men. I take your point, of course. They are not free. But that is all the worse. If they gain power from the clapping crowd then we are subject to the worst of rule. For men who are not free can only make the people slaves.

Young Man: You give the people little credit, sir. They know the charlatans and demagogues for what they are. Indeed, there's much more wisdom in the crowd than one might think. And, Director, I think you've got it somehow wrong. A man who wants to eat will eat, but only eat enough. A man who wants to drink will drink, but only drink enough. But men who love to eat will eat beyond the point where they are full. And men who love to drink will drink beyond the point where they have thirst. Ambition has to do with love, not want. A want is satisfied, but never love. Now men who love to eat and drink are base, and will expend their greatest energies in finding ways to eat and drink. And men who merely love applause are fatuous and worthy of contempt. But there are worthy objects for one's love. I'll never have enough of helping out my friends. I'll never have enough of standing up for right. Ambition aims at things like this, as far as I'm concerned.

Clown: You love to help your friends? To what? To loot? You love to stand up for the right? Whose right? Your friends and yours? Your right to what? To loot! To loot! And how you talk! I love to hear you talk! "The noble soul unfolding to its fullest size." Oh my! The noble bank accounts expanding to the max is more the thing. Your money makes you feel "quite good" — especially when it's not earned! But you must lie to keep a decent cover on your acts and means. And that's alright, my friend! It's fascinating watching how you strive to justify yourself. You've only told us two of many things you love to do. I'll guess the rest myself, if they don't come to light. Eventually they will, you know! Ha, ha! They will! And Director is right, of course (since we are talking candidly). I am not free. And you're not free. You're just a slave to feeling good. But Director would seem to have ambition to be free. Well, that's his lie! He isn't free at all! He's just a slave like you or me — only he hides it very well! Ha, ha!

Young Man: I wouldn't even dignify his nonsense with response. But do you see my point?

Director: About ambition being love? I think I do. But then is love ambition, too? Is that the way it seems to you?

Old Man: Why take so long to answer, boy?

Young Man: Because that sounds obscene.

Old Man: Of course it sounds obscene! If you had listened to me arguing against your crazy views you'd know that everything you've said about ambition is equally obscene because it goes against the grain of proper sense! I guess it's no surprise that love would finally trip you up. The young are always hot and heavy when it comes to love.

Young Man: But you're the one who said ambition is the love of praise.

Old Man: So what?

Young Man: Well, you're the one who got us started thinking that ambition is a type of love.

Old Man: It is: the love of praise. And greed is the love of gain. So what?

Young Man: But if... But if we say ambition is a type of love....

VI. Anarchy

Friend: You and Student were talking for a long time last night. What were you talking about?

Director: A book.

Friend: What book?

Director: The book Anarchist wrote about political theory.

Friend: Even with all the smoke and noise, I could see Student's face as he walked into the pub last night. He looked hurt when he saw you there.

Director: I hadn't told him I was back in The City.

Friend: Why was he so upset? You'd think he thought you two are supposed to have some sort of understanding.

Director: There's a lot on his mind.

Friend: He must have figured you'd be a good one to talk to. What was he thinking about?

Director: It would take a long time to explain.

Friend: Well, it is a long flight...

Director: True. He had society on his mind.

Friend: What about it?

Director: Whether it is essentially natural or contrived, a good thing or a necessary evil.

Friend: But what did Student think about it? He must have had an opinion.

Director: He was not sure what to think: he could not make up his mind. It seems this is what had him upset.

Friend: He was upset about not knowing what to think about society? Forgive me, but that sounds crazy.

Director: Maybe that is how it sounds. But you must know that having knowledge of justice is a matter of the highest concern.

Friend: You mean he doesn't know what the law is? If he doesn't already know I'll be he finds out pretty fast...

Director: Oh, I am certain he knows the law well enough. It is really moral knowledge that concerns him, Friend, not the positive law. He was thinking about what Anarchist had to say about society and what it does to natural man.

Friend: What does Anarchist say it does?

Director: I really could not tell you all he says, Friend. I do not understand everything he says. But what I understand appears to me great and noble, and I believe that those things of which he writes, those things the understanding of which is his theme, which I do not understand, are also great and noble.

Friend: Well, what do you understand?

Director: Anarchist says that positive laws fly in the face of laws natural or necessity. In the course of his argument he demonstrates profound insight and great penetration into things having the greatest bearing upon the human race.

Friend: I am always amazed that you can say that even though you say you do not support the conclusions that follow from his arguments. But why do you think that the things he writes about that you don't understand are also praiseworthy?

Director: It's not quite what you think, Friend. It is very difficult to evaluate the arguments on their own account, to say nothing of contesting the conclusions drawn there from. Does it not only seem proper to assume that if an author brings to light things of the highest importance he is also not only capable of bringing to light things of a lesser — or the least, or potentially or absolutely no — importance, but that he will also necessarily have done so in the course of his ensuring that light is shed upon those things of the greatest import? (But I must note: it is, no doubt, absolutely critical that things of the greatest import or the weightiest things be made to shed light of their own. They are matters of the utmost seriousness and therefore demand to be made the objects of careful and considerate or intransigent study. Intransigent studies bear fruit only when they are made of matters of the utmost seriousness. Their light is strong commensurate to the degree to which one is made of them. The degree to which one such study sheds light depends upon the seriousness of the student and the choice of the subject. An intransigent study should suffice to raise the question of how it can be possible to understand complex things without ever having understood simple things. This should further make quite clear that if one were to appreciate simple things truly it would appear, naturally, that an understanding of complex things follows.) I see that Anarchist understands a few complex things (at least those that I understand) and that he clearly comprehends — and in such a way that we can certainly appreciate — a number of simple things. I trust I have given sufficient basis for my belief.

Friend: Fair enough. You sure take to this stuff like a duck to water. So Anarchist knows what he's talking about. What was he talking about and why did it bother Student?

Director: Student told me it was what Anarchist said about society that was bothering him. Since Anarchist says many things I asked Student to tell me exactly what Anarchist had said that bothered him. He told me that it was the argument that everybody wants to rule, and nobody wants to be ruled.

Friend: That bothered him? That's life.

Director: But he saw that if that view were true, then things are set in conflict thereby. The thing that bothered him is this coupled to the notion that the state constitutes a compromise struck to allow people to live without constant strife.

Friend: So why would that bother him?

Director: You see, Friend, he has, in my view, a desire for purity. He began to question the character of the compromise, and was not pleased with what he was afraid he saw.

Friend: What did he see?

Director: He couldn't believe that people were benefiting from the compromise. So he began to consider, seriously, Anarchist's argument that life without the state is best.

Friend: Hmph! That scrawny guy? He wouldn't last a minute in the wild.

Director: Oh, he's made of tougher stuff than you imagine, Friend. But I think he was quite aware of what you're suggesting, and it troubled him. And that wasn't all that troubled him. The idea that he had compromised himself upset him terribly. Yet I admired his dogged perseverance in turning to face the questions that he saw opening up about him.

Friend: I don't know. It sounds like it may only have been a question of his wanting to eat his cake and have it, too — like he wants to have the benefits of society without paying the price.

Director: He brought that up himself, Friend. But there was more to it than that. He's not sure whether it's desirable to rule.

Friend: To rule? What, is he descended from the Royal Family?

Director: He was considering rule in a broad sense. Women aren't the only thing on his mind, you know. It's a very real question for him. He dropped out of The Economics Institute some time ago, you know, and is now considering going to study with Political Scientist.

Friend: I heard about his dropping out. A lot of people think that's crazy.

Director: But that noble soul seems to be not so much concerned with what a lot of people think. He couldn't see what good would come from his taking up his position alongside Banker, his father.

Friend: So now he's in our line of work.

Director: That's right.

Friend: Well, I never said he wasn't intelligent...

Director: Nonetheless, he is up in the air about all this.

Friend: So did you tell him that anarchy isn't possible?

Director: We focused first on whether it's desirable. It already appeared evident to him that it is possible. He claimed that all that is needed for anarchy is no recognized rules for citizenship and no legitimate titles to rule.

Friend: But I thought he said that everyone wants to rule.

Director: He did.

Friend: So then this anarchy is nothing but brute force taking and doing what it pleases?

Director: We came to that. Do you know what I told him then?

Friend: That he's crazy?

Director: I told him that it seemed to me that the argument was beginning to substitute the desire to be feared for the desire to be recognized or famous. I wasn't at all sure about this, mind you. I don't know that things must follow in this order. But I had been considering something that Political Scientist was trying to make me understand. He was writing an essay about these things and periodically would present me with a draft and ask what I thought. He had been writing about the desire to be feared. It is, he explained, a tyrannical passion at the end of the slide or falling away from noble desires. He explained that it is apparent that there are those in whose souls a longing or a passion to rule takes hold, and that there is — if not natural to this passion, at least almost impossible to detach — the desire for recognition, for distinction, for fame. Yet when this longing is frustrated and suppressed, when it can't find its natural outlet, it seems likely, he argued, that a great spiritual ugliness — a monstrosity — may be born. And then he attempted to demonstrate that there arises the danger that one's entire personality be permeated by this passion, becoming warped and marred quite probably forever. I should mention that Political Scientist teaches that personality is accidental, while character is intentional and along these lines giving in to the ugly desires renders the development of character impossible. He is focusing on moral effort, what he calls the moral order, the bulwark against chaos. This interests him greatly. But I argue with him about the number of characters he takes into consideration, that it is not complete, that he does not consider the complete number of characters that are possible. They, they characters, are greater in number than he comprehends. Though he does accuse me of being naïve, of having too simple a view of things. What can I say? He was putting off his dinner (he said he was quite hungry) in order to teach me his doctrine. But I had grown tired from effort and decided it was time to go home and rest. He asked how tired I was and whether I couldn't stay a while longer, to hear him out, and also why I was suddenly so tired. "There is," I said, "no measure to the weariness for it is a result of infinite care, from attention to things demanding infinite subtlety and attention." He apologized and thanked me for the time I had already given to discussing his work and entreated me to take it up with him again sometime.

Friend: But what did Student say to all that talk about fear?

Director: Well, I didn't lay it all out at once, of course. I merely mentioned the bit about desire for fame or recognition transforming into desire to be feared. That seemed to make some sense to him, but I don't know exactly how or why. Whether he spoke immediately in reply or after some further discussion of tyranny I cannot recall now, but he at one point said quietly, "Only participation in the truth transcends." This seemed a clear sign to me that he wished to hear more of what Political Scientist believed and what he was teaching.

Friend: So what did you talk about then?

Director: Among the various things we discussed it at one point appeared important to the arguments concerning rule to consider the distinction often made between facts and values, or the notion that there is technical knowledge devoid of any sort of moral or substantive content — pure method, in other words — which is precisely the sort of thing that many political consultants — who are nothing more than mercenaries, really — profess.

Friend: Oh. Well, it's good you talked to him about that. Did you tell him to think about what it would be like with everyone a mercenary?

Director: Well, the mercenary, of course, does not truly care for what he is defending, promoting, or supporting. Ironically, mercenaries are, in a peculiar way, neutrals. There is nothing noble about service to a mercenary cause. But if everyone were a mercenary? Why, what cause would there be to defend? Who employs mercenaries but those who truly do care for what is to be defended?

Friend: Hmm. That's an interesting point. But people will still have things they want to defend, even in a state of anarchy.

Director: Such as what?

Friend: Why, beautiful women, for instance.

Director: Are you saying that you don't think beauty has the power to stand on its own?

Friend: What? Mountains are beautiful, aren't they?

Director: But what about human beauty?

Friend: I don't know. I just know that there will be men who will want to defend beautiful women, regardless of whether the state exists or not — and they would pay mercenaries to help them if they needed the help.

Director: So, in this state of anarchy, individuals would be free to defend or pursue whatever they understand to be worth pursuing or defending with whatever means are at their disposal, including the employment of the arms of others?

Friend: That's right.

Director: Then the only difference is that there is nothing to check them?

Friend: Nothing, absolutely nothing.

Director: And the things of interest to those people would emphatically be things of the here and now?

Friend: Why would you ask that? Of course they would be. What else could they be?

Director: I couldn't say for certain. But what of reputation, Friend? Would those people care for that? Would that be something to pursue or defend?

Friend: I suppose so. Student seems to care a great deal what you think of him, doesn't he? You could probably knock him down with only a harsh word!

Director: Yet he does not seem to care much about popular opinion, does he?

Friend: That's what he says, at least.

Director: This seems to take us back to the distinction between facts and values, and Student and I indeed discussed this, and at great length. He seemed to me to think that people were valuing something other than the fact, the significant fact, he saw himself to represent. I asked him about this. He said it is a matter of awareness, of understanding. He was seeking understanding. The fact of his worth, he did not see this valued by people, Friend.

Friend: A legend in his own mind...

Director: Self-knowledge, of course, comes into play here.

Friend: Did you tell him to go and get some?

Director: Now, you know, I always recommend seeking self-knowledge. But Student's comments appeared to be pointing toward something else and something interesting. So I asked him if his value were dependent upon the mere faith that he had in himself, and was thus truly a matter of willful self-assertion, or whether there weren't a demonstrable fact present, verifiable by third parties. So the question of to whom this demonstration must be made naturally — or by chance, as it were — arose. "Clearly," I asked, "there must not be a need to demonstrate to those to whom the truth in question is self-evident?" "No, of course not," he replied. "Then," I continued, "it is to those for whom the truth is obscure that demonstrations and proofs must be directed?" "Certainly," he replied. "But," I checked, "you're not one of those who thinks that the truth is a different matter than the facts, are you?" "No, I'm not," he said.

Friend: Now you have to tell me just how the hell the truth can be different than the facts.

Director: No one has been able to explain that to my satisfaction, Friend. But those who make this claim appear to hold that the facts represent or rather constitute nature itself while the truth represents our by necessity limited view of nature. It goes hand in hand with the notion that there is no truth with a capital T but rather many 'truths' depending upon one's point of view.

Friend: I can't see how there can be no truth. How can you have more than one truth?

Director: That really is the question, Friend. But Student indicated that he was not the type to make that sort of claim. So I asked him if his efforts in demonstrating his value to those who did not perceive it did not amount to something of an absurd effort. "Not at all," he insisted rather weakly, and not really believing it himself.

Friend: So why did he say it?

Director: "What's the use?" I asked.

Friend: Ha, ha, ha! I bet he hated that!

Director: He was certainly troubled by the question. "Look," I said, "if you really believe they are not capable of seeing the truth on their own, the best you can do is persuade them to take your word for it, right? Or do I have to demonstrate this for you?"

Friend: Ah, ha, ha, ha!

Director: He nodded after a while. I said, "You then would seem to become a sort of priest, persuading of something that you have a clearer view of than many. But still, they don't see what you see, do they?" "No, they don't." "So they necessarily have to take what is asserted as a matter of faith, that is, when they are not actively undergoing the benefits of a persuasive rhetoric or the corrective of rational, demonstrative argument." He again nodded, knowingly, it seemed to me. I continued. "Then are you beginning to see the relationship between faith and political institution or law?"

Friend: I actually think I understand what you're talking about.

Director: "You know," I said, "the man who concentrated on the distinction between facts and values and gave it its most elaborate and exhaustive articulation was expressly concerned almost exclusively with matters of faith and their bearings upon political institutions." Student had come across his works, and he acknowledged this fact. "So you are aware that societies, cultures, or regimes have their own institutionalized values, values that are not shifting like the sands of the desert, but values that are firm and strong like the foundation of a house. Now facts can be quite another matter, indeed. Assuming by facts we do not mean a natural backdrop beyond truth, but the things that are perceived, we run into all sorts of complex arguments about the characteristics of human knowledge and perception, epistemology as it is sometimes called, but the science of vision as well as theories regarding consciousness also have something to do with this. You've heard of the notion of conceptual filters, I assume?" He had. "Good. So I take it you will not be surprised if I were to say that facts and values both, to the extent they are shaped by society, the regime, or culture, are themselves quite potentially threatened by the possibility of total anarchy." He nodded knowingly once again, but this time with a touch of fear in his face. "Crazy," I went on, "as it may sound, if we follow out this line of thought we will see that true anarchy involves the risk of forever closing off the possibility of achieving what is highest in our nature, if we take it that this is knowledge and understanding and the reason associated with them." Since he was really listening now and not at all defensive as he had been at the outset, I took up the next thread which concerned the notion of chaos, inherent to so many anarchic theories. Political Scientist had explained to me that what they call 'chaos theory' itself teaches us that there will be clearly discernable order to be found in a state of complete anarchy or entropy. This is, he said, either because the order exists in nature itself, in the chaos itself, or it is because it is imposed by human will or creativity — but in either case, the end is the same. The question is whether chaos actually exists: and he asserted that the mere possibility of a being bringing order to the chaos indicates that the chaos does not in fact exist, for the very pattern stored up or incipient in the mind of the order- or law-giving individual belies the notion of true chaos, which excludes the potential of a rational order: for the notion of a rational order presupposes that upon which it is to be modeled, unless one were to continue to assert an infinitely telescoping (or microscoping) regression of chaotic impulse. This is so even if the desire (if we may refer to it so) to bring order is itself merely a function of the discharge of power: for that indicates quite clearly that man, as man, stands opposed, in the most fundamental sense, to chaos. The notion of complete chaos or anarchy, he concluded, as much excludes the possibility of creativity from the world as does the notion of the complete and universal state.

Friend: You lost me.

Director: Sorry. I forgot to mention that we had also been discussing the question of whether there can be reason without the state.

Friend: I don't see how that's a question.

Director: It's got to do with an argument about language. If language is, as a few assert, a system of oppression —

Friend: Oh, give it a rest!

Director: Yes, it can be a tiresome argument. Nonetheless, if language is a system of oppression, then language, too, must go in the state of total anarchy. But can there be reason without language, to say nothing of communication?

Friend: You had to go through all this nonsense with him?

Director: We discussed many things, more even than this. "What about the family," I asked. "Does that go, too, in a state of total anarchy? If so, how does the race continue? Who takes care of and raises the children? Do not those who do so require some sort of support? How is that to happen without some sort of organization of the work to be done, the things to be provided for?"

Friend: Hmph! I bet he didn't have anything good to say to that!

Director: Not only that, but I also asked, "How is one to choose how to live in a state of total anarchy? What is the basis for choice? Cravings? Desires? Urges? Is it all nothing but the scratching of itches?"

Friend: Ha! Scratching of itches! What did he say to that?

Director: Surprisingly he mentioned ambition.

Friend: Ambition?

Director: Yes. I asked him if he thought ambition were a natural or a political phenomenon, recalling that he had asserted that everyone wished to rule. Consistent with his earlier opinion, he said it is a natural phenomenon. "Within the state," I said, "ambition is directed toward those things honored by the state. But without the state?"

Friend: What did he say?

Director: He didn't answer.

Friend: Hmph. Not surprising.

Director: So I took it up myself. "Within the state, ambition may be described as a sort of higher desire, beyond mere sensual pleasures and needs, and may be directed to what is agreed upon as the common good. But without the state, there is no desire to obtain political office or any other position, public or private, honored by the state. But perhaps a man without the state would wish to be renowned, to obtain fame. Is this a natural desire, derived of some inherent need for recognition?" Student said he wasn't sure. "Fame differs from recognition, doesn't it, if by recognition we mean recognition for and as what one is? Fame is a blind and indiscriminate form of recognition, for one may be famous without being recognized for what one is, as is demonstrated by the unmasking of many a charlatan." He agreed.

Friend: So where did all this talk get you with him?

Director: I wasn't sure at the time and considered it best to remind him of a conversation we once had with his father, who was of the opinion that glory is only a reflection of virtue, concerning political ambition.

Friend: Banker's not interested in politics.

Director: He is, to the extent it concerns what he takes to be his interests, but said he doesn't think it a worthwhile pursuit for himself or his son. When he made this comment, I agreed that mere politicians were not the best of men, but said that he was not taking into account the statesman.

Friend: What did he say to that?

Director: He laughed, of course. But Student wasn't laughing. In fact, he was listening quite eagerly.

Friend: Student doesn't think he's statesman material, does he?

Director: Banker turned to him, with some scorn, and asked him exactly that. And do you know what he said in reply?

Friend: What?

Director: He said, and blushed as he said it, "No, father, I'm no statesman. But that doesn't mean I wouldn't admire one if he came along."

Friend: He really said that?

Director: Yes.

Friend: How did Banker react to that?

Director: He snorted in disgust.

Friend: What happened then?

Director: I asked Banker, "I take it you don't believe there's a difference between a statesman and a politician?" "Difference?" he replied. "The only difference is that what people call statesmen are only seen from a distance and surrounded by myth. That's the only difference. That and maybe some extraordinary charisma, whatever that really is."

Friend: He does have a point.

Director: I think Student was afraid he did, too. But is that what you think, that that's the only difference between a mere politician and a statesman, if there is a difference?

Friend: Essentially they're the same, but the statesman is much more successful. It's a matter of greatness.

Director: I agree with you about true greatness, but I'm not so sure that they are essentially the same.

Friend: What could be the difference if it's not only their ability? All men want the same things.

Director: I'm not so sure about that either, and it generally seems to me that exactly the opposite is true. What would you say a statesman wants?

Friend: To be famous among other things.

Director: And what about a politician?

Friend: Pretty much the same thing.

Director: And "pretty much" is good enough for our purposes?

Friend: Sure.

Director: OK. But if the difference is merely one of talents or ability, it would become pretty clear pretty quickly to the politician that the statesman had him, so to speak, outgunned, wouldn't it?

Friend: Of course.

Director: Yet he would still want to be famous.

Friend: That's right.

Director: Who would the politician think more likely to achieve fame: the statesman or himself?

Friend: Since you put it that way, I suppose he'd think the statesman more likely to become famous.

Director: So would he still seek to compete against the statesman?

Friend: He wouldn't be a politician if he didn't.

Director: But he's bound to lose out in the competition for fame, isn't he?

Friend: Not necessarily.

Director: Why is that?

Friend: You know the best man doesn't always come out on top.

Director: I believe that is the case. Why do you suppose that is?

Friend: Life's not fair.

Director: Do you mean that people will cheat in the competition for fame?

Friend: Hah! Of course they will!

Director: But it could also be something else, couldn't it?

Friend: What do you mean?

Director: Who is it that makes one famous?

Friend: People do. It's one's reputation.

Director: Do you suppose that people are always capable of discerning who is the better man?

Friend: Hardly.

Director: Why is that?

Friend: I suppose there are several reasons. For one, they're sometimes deceived.

Director: Is that what you meant about cheating?

Friend: Yeah, something like that.

Director: What else?

Friend: Well, they don't always know the whole story, let alone being deceived. In fact, they almost never know the whole story.

Director: So they can jump to conclusions on insufficient information?

Friend: That's right.

Director: So these are some of the things that the politician would depend upon in his quest for fame, if that's what he really wants.

Friend: Sounds right to me.

Director: But I suppose there could be something else, don't you?

Friend: What?

Director: I suppose the politician might not be aware that the statesman is more able or has more talents than he does. Surely you've met people who overrate their abilities?

Friend: Of course I have. I guess what you're saying makes sense.

Director: But we also have to consider what are the implications of fame only as a goal. If fame is really what is desired then it appears that it really doesn't matter what one is famous for, does it? I mean, fame is fame, right?

Friend: Sure, but they'd rather be famous for governing than for something less important.

Director: Do you think that is because the character of the fame differs in the different cases or is it because one is more likely to become famous for something that people agree is very important than for something that's not so important.

Friend: I don't know. Some rock stars are every bit as famous as Presidents.

Director: Yet don't people generally agree that being the President of the United States is more important than being a pop singer?

Friend: Of course they do, though you're bound to find some nuts who say otherwise.

Director: But isn't there also the difference between fame and infamy to consider? What's the difference there?

Friend: Some days "will live in infamy...."

Director: And others in fame?

Friend: Exactly.

Director: So does it matter to the statesman and the politician whether fame or infamy is achieved?

Friend: Sure it does.

Director: But can a politician ever be famous, or really only infamous?

Friend: I haven't thought about it like that before. I guess a politician will never be as famous as a statesman. So his only chance is infamy, but infamy that he tries to pass off as fame? This is sounding crazy but I think it's accurate.

Director: Now what about a statesman? Don't people's opinions change over time?

Friend: Of course they do.

Director: So one age might think a political actor to have been an infamous politician —

Friend: — and another could come to see him as a great statesman. Yeah, I think that's right.

Director: So when the statesman is striving for fame, it would seem he must be constantly aware that he might not, so to speak, make it to the promised land in his own lifetime.

Friend: That must haunt him.

Director: So what psychological defense does he have?

Friend: What?

Director: How can he defend himself against being debilitated by the fear that he will never be recognized for his great deeds?

Friend: He's got to believe that 'what goes around comes around' or something like that.

Director: In other words, that there's justice in the universe.

Friend: Yes.

Director: It seems that there are three ways for him to look at it, doesn't it? First, God will set things right or reward him for his deeds.

Friend: Sure.

Director: Second, that there is some sort of natural law or dynamic that will bring his true worth to light eventually.

Friend: Yes.

Director: The third view is a little different. It's a sort of faith in man, that as he continues to conquer nature through technology his power of revealing events that have taken place in the past will go on increasing ever toward the point of a perfect knowledge of what happened, a sort of perfected forensic or reconstructive science — a perfect remembrance of things past.

Friend: I'm not so sure about that.

Director: What about it?

Friend: I think that would make a lot of people uneasy.

Director: You're probably right. But a true statesman?

Friend: It might even be worse with him, wouldn't you think?

Director: Why do you say that?

Friend: I mean, he's probably got to make all sorts of difficult choices, do things that wouldn't look so good to people like you and me. Do you really think he'd take comfort in knowing that those things would all eventually come to light? Hell, statesmen pass laws that prevent people from inquiring too closely into what they've done. Do you think they do that for no reason?

Director: Friend! Are you suggesting that statesmen wish not to be known for what they were but rather for what they would appear to be, that statesmanship is some sort of personally creative act? Why, I'll have to stop and think this through!

Friend: I'm not sure why you think this is such a revelation...

Director: Hmm... Maybe the statesman and the politician are essentially the same in seeking to do this, but what differs is the quality, so to speak, of the work of art produced in the end.

Friend: Isn't that what I've been telling you?

Director: But what are the criteria for judgment of this artificial political character?

Friend: I guess it either works for what's needed or it doesn't. Image maybe.

Director: Image? Isn't it more than that? Isn't the politician blinded by how things look but the statesman concentrates on how things work, taking into account appearance as well?

Friend: Maybe.

Director: Maybe it's a matter of priority. Suppose the statesman is really more concerned with how things work but does not disdain to take advantage of appearances while the politician is more concerned with appearances and uses his knowledge of how things work for the sake of mere appearance.

Friend: Sounds pretty good, Director. But I bet you didn't go through all of this with Banker.

Director: No. We spoke, of course, about money's being an eminently political device.

Friend: Ah, ha, ha! How did Banker like that? I thought he was above politics. Ha, ha!

Director: Well, you'll laugh even harder when you hear that I told him that a pretty strong argument could be made that money is *the* fundamental political device.

Friend: I bet he wasn't laughing.

Director: No, he wasn't. He wanted to know what I meant by that.

Friend: What did you mean?

Director: Something rather simple. Money, to the extent it is made use of by a regime, represents, it appears, an agreement concerning value. So to the extent that shared values are the core of a community, money — which emphatically is nothing more than an agreement concerning value — occupies an important place, even if it is agreed — if only explicitly — that money is not of great value. But he did like the conclusion of this argument, Friend.

Friend: What conclusion was that?

Director: That key to assessing the merits of a statesman is his use of and relations with money. But this made Student uncomfortable.

Friend: Why would that make him uncomfortable?

Director: It's hard to say, but he seemed to take heart when I introduced the caveat that success as a statesman is certainly not to be measured merely by the accumulation of capital. Money is to the statesman, after all, a means, not an end. But this brought us to the question of the end of the statesman. What is that end? Fame? If so, is that end aligned with the end of the state? Answering this question required a bit of restatement. "May we say," I asked, "that the end of the state is fame?" Banker thought this ridiculous, but Student didn't, as was evident from his quiet attention. "And if so," I continued, "is the fame of the statesman in line with the furthering of the fame of the state?" Banker declared that he couldn't see what this had to do with anything. But Student asserted, quite earnestly, that this was the whole point.

Friend: So what did you tell them?

Director: I told them that I was certain there are ones for whom fame is the sole goal. But these people were not focused on what it seemed to me should be the true goal.

Friend: Which is?

Director: The ability to exercise the faculties fully. The fame is derivative. To the statesman, or so it appears to me, full, active engagement is satisfying, an end in itself. But beyond being his own end, it informs his understanding of what is the end of the state, providing him with a compass by which to steer through turbulent storms: the end of the state is to allow for the full exercise of the faculties — that is, to allow man to become whole, wholeness coming through the ascent to active engagement of all the faculties, not only the passions. It is in this engagement, I explained, that there is full interplay between the soul and the body, making the dual or divided nature of man one. From this follows happiness, as it seemed to me and as I told them. Yet we were speaking of anarchy. Is such an attainment of wholeness to be in the state of total anarchy?

Friend: You must have lost Banker by now.

Director: It would seem I did. But Student was listening seriously and following quite closely. He asked, "What are the faculties?" I told him that I don't know what they are altogether, but that it seemed that awareness or understanding is the highest, the most noble, and the most important in man, and that the state exists in part in order to promote the development of the greatest faculty. But can this faculty operate alone as though in a vacuum? Does it not require support? It was the supporting faculties of which I was not sure, I told them, and of their relation to the one in question. However, Banker said it seemed to him that I had gotten it exactly wrong, that the thing I thought was the end was actually only the support for the things I thought were the support or the means, which were to his way of thinking the ends themselves. It interested me that he conceived of it as having multiple ends whereas I had been articulating a single point upon the horizon, as it were, by which to take one's bearings. (I made a mental note to myself to go back and examine the writings of statesmen who offered multiple reasons for engaging in an action — say, an offensive war.) While I was reflecting upon this Student startled me by asking whether the state didn't actually limit one's capacity to develop awareness. I said I didn't understand how it did that, but thought it might be worthwhile to consider it from the perspective of a state of anarchy. Can the rational faculty be exercised in anarchy? He said he thought it could, and I couldn't see good reason to disagree. But, I pointed out, it seemed to me that in the exercise of the faculty or capacity the state might necessarily begin to take shape, in whatever form and under whatever name. If this were so, I explained, then to the extent that the capacity or capability is natural, so, too, is the state. Banker wanted to know how I thought this skill would manifest itself in the state of anarchy. "It orders," I said, "relations among and between individuals." Why, the cavemen even have some sort of understanding or agreement regarding how to comport themselves with one another. As these arrangements increase in scope and complexity the state begins to take shape. Yet it struck me as important, if only as an afterthought, to indicate that it had been shown that a complex state requires a great deal of preparatory study in order to be managed well. This seemed to please Banker. The argument seemed to be acquiring a life of its own so I carried forward with it. "The preparatory study of state itself," I said, "appears to require the full engagement of the political faculties." To the great statesman, the time spent in reflection may be no less demanding, exhausting, or exhilarating than the actual practice of managing the daily affairs of the nation. Student was now listening in rapt attention, but his father did not appear pleased, though I don't know that it was not something or someone he caught sight of in the mirror.

Friend: It wasn't anything he caught sight of, Director. Could his displeasure really have surprised you, saying something like that about studying political science? Did you say anything more about it?

Director: I said, "He knows that his solitary labors will or can bear fruit, perhaps not through his own taking of the reigns, but by that of others who will benefit from the true political knowledge brought forth in toil from the mines of human experience. Such a relationship is truly parental, and the heart of the reflective statesman swells in pride in anticipation of the great political deeds of his children. There is no more true love." But what do you think he fears, Friend? His fears are similar to those of all parents. Perhaps his teaching will not be taken to heart? Perhaps his children will meet untimely ends? Perhaps his line will be extinguished? Anxieties such as these whip him into a froth of rational activity, and his deep love impels him to train and discipline his energies to give them the greatest effect. No effort must be spared, no cost is too great in furtherance of his cause, his end, the cause to which his entire being is dedicated.

Friend: You said all this to Student's father?

Director: But I was addressing both Banker and Student together, Friend. I asked them, "The active life, the contemplative life: isn't it merely a matter of luck and therefore indifference to one who is capable of engaging his faculties fully?"

Friend: Banker must have choked on that.

Director: Yes, he did. But I said, "Such a man is not subject to but rather master of his circumstances, not in the sense of modifying them, but in their being overcome from within — regardless of whether or not he rules in the political sense."

Friend: I can't see how you gained any ground with Banker with that one...

Director: I was too busy following the argument to pay undue attention to that, Friend. It seemed quite clear at that point that there is an irony in the relation between the active and the contemplative. It would seem that the contemplative man wishes to see his insights put into effect, yet, as Student suggested, it is quite possible that the contemplative man has a broader scope for the full employment of his faculties, not being hampered by the drudgery inherent to the active political life. Yet I feared that we were heading too far afield and needed to return to our original concern. So I told them that we needed to consider to what extent the rational is employed in active political life. Banker didn't see how this was a question. But I told him it seemed to me that it all depends on the aim of the statesman, what he brings to bear in his function. In a liberal democracy this function is limited by law. So not all things are open to the doing. But — and this was the crux of the matter — in order to see clearly what things are possible, and further, best or most important in the here and now, the statesman's vision must be informed by knowledge of the most general nature. The object of the most general concern has always been, is, and will, I believe, be man, Friend. You see, while it is quite doubtful that a statesman can be an expert in more than one or two of the many fields of expertise, he must be an expert in mankind. And this expertise in mankind must permeate his whole being. It must be, as it were, his second nature. By this it is meant that the expertise derives not from innate knowledge (and that which is called this more often than not amounts to no more than charm) but rather from systematic rational inquiry into man, not excluding one's own self from the rigors of analysis.

A statesman is constituted by nothing short of knowledge derived from struggle and striving along these lines.

Friend: That's a pretty tall order.

Director: And the implication of this, of course, is the that true statesmanship involves action, certain action, upon knowledge of man. All other political activity is one form of charlatanism or another. Yet the most important point of that discussion was yet to be made.

Friend: What point was that?

Director: That the if the rational faculty is employed there follows the political.

Friend: I'm not sure what to say to that. Why is that the most important point?

Director: Because Banker denied that rational thought had, of necessity, to have, at the very least, a political component or elemental theme.

Friend: But why do you think politics necessarily follows rational thought?

Director: It has to do with love.

Friend: What? Love? What's that got to do with it?

Director: I suspected you'd be laughing at me if I said this, Friend.

Friend: Well, you better explain yourself, Director. You may just have backed yourself into a corner this time, you know.

Director: It has to do with reciprocity, Friend.

Friend: Go on. Explain.

Director: OK. Love isn't always fully — that is, equally — reciprocal, is it?

Friend: Of course not.

Director: Now, the lover — that is, the one loving more, at least — is operating almost entirely from feeling, right?

Friend: Sure.

Director: But what of the beloved? He's not entirely operating from feeling, is he?

Friend: No, of course not — unless you mean revulsion.

Director: So he may be thinking a bit more clearly than the lover?

Friend: Sure.

Director: And if more clearly, more rationally or with more awareness, right?

Friend: Right.

Director: So if they engage in some sort of more than fleeting relationship the non-lover must be thinking about the character of this relationship and its context, right?

Friend: I suppose.

Director: And in thinking about this he thinks of the terms and conditions, as it were, of the relationship?

Friend: Sure, you could put it that way.

Director: So from there it's not too much to say that the relationship becomes a sort of contractual relationship, in which boundaries are observed and roles and responsibilities are more or less clearly defined.

Friend: You might say that.

Director: So there may be a rational contracting involved with love?

Friend: What's the point?

Director: I'm sure you can appreciate that this is a rather delicate argument being made.

Friend: True. But what's your point?

Director: Well, this argument, if it is indeed true, can amount to the conclusion — if the beloved engages in a rational contracting, of course — that it may be the case that only when love is reciprocal — whether perfectly so or no — is there no rational contracting involved between lover and beloved.

Friend: Interesting.

Director: And it's not too hard to see, is it, how this sort of contracting can incrementally and in the aggregate lead to the establishment of the city, or the political itself?

Friend: I'm not so sure about that. Supposing, hypothetically, that what you're saying is true: how does that lead to political things?

Director: I only mean that there's a view according to which politics consists of an infinite number of small, contractual arrangements.

Friend: Oh, I see.

Director: And, among other things, these come to involve property, and responsibilities, and status.

Friend: Sure.

Director: Now what of the destruction of the political?

Friend: Destruction? What are you talking about?

Director: What? Have you forgotten already? Really, now, how do you expect to take care of yourself when you're old if you can't even remember what we're talking about here, Friend? Anarchy!

Friend: Oh, right.

Director: In every analysis of a problem it is either resolved or the problem, if it is truly a problem worthy of deep and careful consideration, ultimately leads to or causes destruction. But I told Banker — yes, I told him over and again — that destruction of the political — try, try as one might — does not — and can never, ever — result in the destruction of the rational or awareness: and under the influence of the faculty the political is ever again reconstituted.

Friend: Like the phoenix.

Director: Quite. Yet the destruction of the rational results in, first, corruption or decay, and then, the destruction of the political. I suppose, now, it was this that was in mind when it was said that the life of the law is in experience. By experience, of course, I am assuming is meant the engagement of one's environment through the use of reason. And this is of the essence of the true statesman: the mere politician is not engaged rationally in his task, and with him begins the decay.

Friend: What do you mean by "engaged rationally?"

Director: It is quite proper, in my view, for this question to be raised. Indeed, I myself have been troubled by the notion that we live in a liberal democracy ruled by law, under, of course, the sovereignty of the people, and in this liberal democracy the scope of action for the true statesman is accordingly limited, precisely as we would have it, so it can become unclear with what the statesman rationally is to engage. But do the laws define what is to be done? Typically not: laws in our tradition tend to be restrictive rather than proscriptive, though there are some important exceptions. So it is in the fields defined or left open by the laws — the interstices — that the true statesman operates. That also distinguishes him from the politician who does not have factored the weight of legal restraints into his thinking. Nature, as certainly as a thing political like any particular institution would, abhors a vacuum, so it is not only the statesman's attention that is drawn toward the interstices. Now, it is with the things he finds present here in these very openings that he must engage, wholly, the rational faculties. Here we may truly say that he steps into the breach and enters upon a titanic effort commanding all his resources and powers. Yet this difficulty remains. But let us save it for another time, Friend.

Friend: What difficulty?

Director: No, no. The weight and elevation of the subject make it very difficult to escape having to give an all but interminable argument addressing the question.

Friend: Well, at least tell me what the question is and we can discuss it some other time.

Director: Though it is to be feared that the question will seem ridiculous or worse, I make bold to declare that the question has to do with whether the statesman who has stepped into the breach, so to speak, will keep his eye on what he discovers in the interstices or on those political things to which his responsibilities attach or are directed. Saving this discussion for another time, returning our discussion to the state of anarchy, however, I will only note that at this point we are given a somewhat unique vantage point into the genesis of the tyrant, who desires to have eyes on the back of his head, as it were, so as not to confront this very basic human choice. But let us hasten to work our way back to the topic presented. Though our liberal democracy restrains the field of action of the statesman with a good, nay a great many laws, the field of political action appears to be wider than yet ever before. And yet appearances, however clearly presented to our very eyes, can be deceptive. For our liberal democracies are dependent upon public opinion and the education, broadly speaking, that goes into it. Here all the various branches of knowledge and learning are needed, and the true statesman, far from having perfected his knowledge in them all, commands them from their source in the human. The problems of, for instance, thermodynamics and biochemistry are, ultimately, only of moment as they bear upon men. The statesman, while not necessarily exploring them in detail, will have no difficulty in seeing their relation to the object of his proper or true concern and what action is required. There are those who will object that this involves a totalitarian view of the state. And were we only speaking of the state narrowly conceived this would indeed be the case. But we are speaking of this place as a whole, our regime, our entire world or world-view. And it is divided into state and society, public and private. It must never be forgotten that they inform each other. The statesman, while acting within the limits of law, still, must take his bearings from a consideration of more than just his narrow, technical function — and this must not be only a matter of charismatic self-promotion. To limit oneself too narrowly, on the other hand, is to be a technocrat. These are the things I repeated to Student last night. He was greatly interested, but quite concerned and confused, clearly. "Director," he said, "there is one thing that I cannot get beyond. There must be something of a higher rank than politics. Politics presupposes certain ends, ends which are informed by knowledge, and not just narrow political knowledge, but broad and deep knowledge of the whole. Yet politics demands nearly all of one's time, especially in a liberal democracy in which one must, if he is to be more than a mere corrupt politician, constantly educate the people, as you've indicated. And there are infinite details demanding to be mastered. So how is a statesman to have the time, the leisure necessary to pursue the truth?" I asked him whether leisure were not the preserve of the wealthy. He nodded solemnly. "But," I asked, "have there not been and are men of knowledge who have and do live in great poverty, tenthousandfold poverty?" "But they had leisure," he replied passionately. "Then it seems to be a matter of choice, does it not?" He stood silently and chewed on this for a few moments. I said, "We must understand statesmen who have come from and continued in poverty. Consider one who obtains money through his profession. In so doing is he leading a leisured and care-free life? In the time he does have to himself will he idle or choose to spend it wresting with problems of moment? Insights are to be gained deep in converse with great minds and reading will take on great significance with such a one. Money will always be a difficulty, even at the height of political power. It is a fact of our regime that money is required in order to stand upon the political stage. Surely a man of great talents or ability will find the means to obtain money enough to achieve his ends or goal. This fact should surprise nobody. But what should surprise people is when the means or method becomes the end and the man, giving up the noble quest in order to obtain dominion over an ever-increasing realm of means, stops pointing toward or producing excellence or being excellent. Currency, in other words, becomes the only end." "But that's exactly the way it is with most people, and money is exactly what most people want," Student replied. "By 'most' do you mean most of the few, those of them we may call the gentlemanly class or the ruling class? For though there may be no official class structure or class that is powerful by law certainly there is a class that dominates politics. A great statesman does not come from that class necessarily, but in order for one such statesman to be accepted wholeheartedly by this class it appears it is necessary for one to betray one's roots. Yet still there would be something missing. In this respect, a mere politician would lack nothing." Student had heard from Political Scientist that the politician's virtue is a reflection of that of the statesman. But it is not clear that this is true, that their virtues are identical to each other's.

Friend: There's a lot more than that that's not clear.

Director: Yes, it was also not clear in all this where was the ability to trust, the ability to accept on trust certain things, things which are the themes of investigation and matters of demonstration, certain most weighty things. But perhaps this will make more sense to you if I were to say that the real question, the only real question, is the end.

Friend: You mean what's the point to it all?

Director: That is what Student felt he wanted to know. But he was torn. I put forward the hypothesis that the end of life is the full employment of the faculties. But our conversation required consideration of something else: the end of the state and the end of life are not the same. It seemed to us that this was the heart of the issue. What do you think?

Friend: I'll tell you the truth, Director. Student seems harmless enough to me. But this discussion really appears to be a huge waste of time. I know you guys were out drinking and that you like this sort of thing —

Director: Oh, Friend, there you go again...

Friend: Aw, you know what I mean. But hey, I've got no problem with that. Look, you asked me what I think, right? I just think all that talk is a big waste of time. I know you don't get carried away all by yourself, but it seems like when you hang out with guys like that you just can't stop talking on and on: you just can't control yourself. What time did you guys leave, anyway? I heard that the bartender stayed talking with you two long past closing. Is that true? I would've stayed, but that kind of thing is just too damned boring to me. But like I said, whatever you want to talk about is fine with me. I just don't get it. There were some good looking girls at the after-hours club. You really should have come with us, you know. Your talent for talking would be better directed in that direction. I just can't take Student as seriously as you do.

Director: But surely you take death seriously.

Friend: What are you talking about?

Director: Why, that's what student and I were talking about around closing time.

Friend: Oh, Jesus Christ! Everyone else is off drinking, laughing, having a good time, dancing, listening to music and you're huddled away in a place that's closed talking about *death*?

Director: What can I say? Student and I hadn't finished taking in or digesting our principles or hypotheses.

Friend: Hypotheses? Christ Almighty! Do you think you're some sort of God damned scientist or what? What the hell did death have to do with your hypotheses? All this talk about exercising faculties is fine, Director, but you can't convince me that the guy you're calling a statesman is looking at anything other than how famous he can become and what goes along with that.

Director: Do you mean famous in his country or universally?

Friend: He'll take as much fame as he can get.

Director: So you don't really agree that the fame is derivative? You don't really think that the full engagement of the faculties is what satisfies, but rather the satisfaction of knowledge of one's fame? Perhaps we need to spend more time considering infamy. Didn't you say earlier that the politician's, as distinguished from the statesman's, only hope is to pass infamy off as fame? Does that no longer make sense to you?

Friend: I remember what I said. Yeah, it makes sense. But we're talking about statesmen now, Director, not politicians.

Director: So are statesmen simply those with greater talents requiring more to exercise them?

Friend: I don't know about that. There are some pretty clever politicians out there.

Director: True enough. We said that the politician is more concerned with appearances than anything else, did we not?

Friend: We did.

Director: And do you think we were right about this?

Friend: Like I said, that seems pretty good to me.

Director: So when it comes to whether his actions are right or wrong, he is more concerned with whether they appear to be right or wrong.

Friend: Oh, I'm sure about that. Why?

Director: It was something Banker said. He was talking about how his bank presents itself to its clients. One thing led to another and we were talking about dealings between corporate entities when the question of whether they should deal fairly with one another arose. Banker explained that this was why we have regulations, sort of like the rules of a contact sport that prevent things from getting out of hand. Anyway, while we were discussing this I asked whether his bank takes pains about what we call public image. He answered that of course it does, that all businesses do. So I told him, as I'm always telling you, that I have never understood the concern over public image. Would he try and explain it to me? He looked at me rather dubiously.

Friend: No wonder. So what did he say?

Director: That it's better to be aware of being unjust to other corporate entities than to be just to them unaware.

Friend: He didn't say that.

Director: Yes, he most certainly did. Not in so many words, it's true, but after we sifted through what he had said and considered it at length and in detail, even he agreed, when I summarized his position in this manner, that it was truly his position. But there was, of course, a question we had to consider. Given an understanding of the justice or injustice of one's actions is it better to be just or unjust to another corporate entity?

Friend: You're going to have to back up, Director, if you want me to follow this. How the hell did you go from talking about public image to being just or unjust?

Director: Sorry, Friend. I didn't realize I was making too great a jump. It's only right for you to help me cut it down to something that will be better understood or shown to be untrue. We spoke of how a corporate entity represents itself. As we were discussing this I asked Banker whether it is best for a corporate entity to represent itself as it actually is or as it thinks expedient. But as I was asking the question, thinking offence might be taken, I hastened to add that it was also quite possible that a false distinction was being made: it may very well be the case that it is always expedient for a corporate entity to represent itself as it actually is. Banker looked amused by what he seemed to take as naiveté. He asked me whether I could explain how I thought that it could possibly always be expedient for a corporate entity to represent itself as it actually is. Based on what I could make out of his understanding, he took it that by this I meant something like full disclosure or full transparency in all dealings, including those with competitors. So I judged that the best way to make myself clear to both him and his son was to ask whether it is important for a corporate entity to have accurate information regarding the disposition of a competitor or enemy. "Yes, of course," he replied. I next asked, "In obtaining this information, does it suffice to obtain a precise accounting of the strengths and weaknesses of the corporate entity, or must one also obtain information regarding that entity's intentions toward your own corporate entity?" "That, Director," he answered, "is some of the most valuable information to be had." "Well, if," I said, "that is so, how are you to gauge the entity's intentions or disposition toward your own entity if you have dissembled to that hostile or potentially hostile entity what is your own true state?" After some time of further argument, and with a significant amount of reluctance, he admitted that this was problematic. "Then are you willing to consider that it may be true that it is always expedient to represent your entity as it truly is?"

Friend: I still don't believe that Banker went along with this conversation. Student would have, but not his father.

Director: Of course the conversation wasn't exactly as I'm describing it to you now. I'd have to reconstruct it word for word, and not only that, but also reconstruct the entire setting in order to accurately convey the exact conversation. But, I assure you, the conversation was, essentially, exactly along these lines.

Friend: So did you convince Banker that his bank should always make it perfectly clear when they've made a bunch of mistakes and taken on too many bad loans or when they're especially low on cash?

Director: If you're asking me did I ultimately persuade Banker that it is always expedient for his bank to represent itself to competitors in its true state, with nothing to hide: no, I do not think Banker came over to this view.

Friend: Of course he didn't. So I don't see why you went on making that crazy argument.

Director: In making the argument a thing came to light that might not have.

Friend: What?

Director: That which goes with executive or deliberative bodies as they dissemble to outsiders. One of the lines of argument we three pursued in hopes of finding a stable conclusion to our inquiry took us to consideration of the competition or strife between corporate entities. Our attention was turned to those bodies within the corporate entities charged with formulating the communications and actually communicating with the outside entities. Those bodies are necessarily comprised of few in number relative to the entire population and constitute an elite within the organization. The common worker or person is generally not present for the deliberation or action upon that deliberation. He or she is told of the disposition of the outsiders and the decisions and actions of his or her own corporate entity by the deliberative or executive body mentioned. The question is then how these decisions and actions are presented to the common worker or person. It was argued that these things must be presented as just or proper in order that the people, not being privy to the deliberations, will assist in or support their carrying through or execution. To the contrary, it was asserted that the people will not so much care whether the actions or judgments regarding what is to be done are just or proper as they will care that they are expedient, which is to say, that they result in gain. But the basic problem involves trust. Do the people believe that the deliberative or executive body constituted to interface with outsiders is telling the truth, that it is acting in their interests? Now, it is not hard to see if that body is saying that it plans on acting unjustly or improperly in one case it may be assumed that it will do so again on another occasion. One such occasion may quite likely involve internal dealings with the people of the corporate entity. Yet, if the entity is just and proper in dealings with outsiders, is it not likely that the people will tend to have a higher opinion of it and therefore scrutinize it less?

Friend: That does seem likely.

Director: If that is so, the question becomes whether it is just or proper to dissemble or misrepresent oneself to outsiders.

Friend: But, Director, everyone knows you can acquire a reputation for doing the right thing even though that's not what you actually do.

Director: Then, in that case, people would not know the character of their representatives' or leaders' actions unless they were to witness first hand their dealings. But even so, don't you think they also would require expert knowledge in the inter-entity laws, treaties, and regulations in order to judge the justice of an action?

Friend: I guess you're right — that is, if they really cared about that.

Director: But they must care about that. If they don't, wouldn't that be the true path to anarchy and naked rule by force of every sort? Wouldn't their lack of concern for or disregard of justice mark the first step toward anarchy in that it would destroy the possibility of trust or an understanding between the few representatives and leaders and the many people subject to their deliberations, decisions, and actions? Without that understanding what is preserved?

Friend: I think you're overestimating how much people trust their leaders now. But that lack of trust doesn't necessarily cause them to run down the road to anarchy.

Director: But you'd agree that it's better for there to be an understanding between the leaders and the people than not?

Friend: Of course.

Director: So how they establish trust? Is it by making speeches explaining themselves, their thoughts, and actions?

Friend: Ha! That's exactly the sort of thing that makes people distrust them. They're always making speeches.

Director: Would it be better if the leaders were to speak with people individually or engage them in conversation?

Friend: Yes. Then the ones in charge would have to look them in the eyes and be able to explain themselves.

Director: And that would make a big difference?

Friend: All the difference, I think. I don't believe that this would make it so none of them would lie, but I think it would make it harder for them to get away with it, and it least give people a chance to determine for themselves how things really stand.

Director: Don't you think there's another advantage to be derived this proceeding?

Friend: What's that?

Director: If the ones with authority spend too much time worrying about appearance to the people then they won't have the time necessary for understanding those very people, the ones that are so important to them. In speechmaking is the speaker concerned with studying the crowd closely as he speaks?

Friend: How could he be? He's too busy trying to look good.

Director: But by engaging them individually the leader would be able to understand the individual with whom he's speaking?

Friend: If he really wanted to.

Director: You mean if he were not treating the individual as part of the crowd though not at that moment mingled within the larger audience?

Friend: Yeah. Like when you get that feeling that people aren't really looking at you when they're talking to you.

Director: Looking right though you? Yes. What purpose does that serve?

Friend: I think that person is only concerned about his position, making it more secure. He doesn't really care about people.

Director: So in focusing on that he loses sight of the obvious right before his eyes. Yet this makes his position more secure?

Friend: It seems that way.

Director: Then it appears that as the leader's efforts are directed more and more to securing his position they will be less and less directed toward learning: for if what you say is true he thinks he already knows what it takes to obtain his end. Isn't it obvious, Friend, how leaders like these differ from statesmen?

Friend: They're not great.

Director: But do you know why?

Friend: Do you?

Director: When you learn, do you learn about something or about nothing?

Friend: Something, of course.

Director: And would you agree that in order to learn about something you have to be willing to make mistakes?

Friend: Yes.

Director: Would a leader whose only goal is his own security ever really learn anything? Learning involves experimentation, right?

Friend: Right.

Director: Experimentation, if it is to be meaningful or allow for discovery, involves risk.

Friend: That's right.

Director: So experimentation concerning things human, and not merely elements and compounds in laboratory test tubes, must involve a great deal of risk.

Friend: Even more so.

Director: Do you think the leaders feel it a risk to engage in individual conversations with the people?

Friend: I think most of them do.

Director: Yet the leaders' job is to lead people.

Friend: And they don't even really know them.

Director: But suppose for a moment that they do know them yet still do not wish to speak with them. What on Earth could that mean?

Friend: Well, they could be busy. But no one is busy all the time. People would think it's because they've got something to hide.

Director: And that would destroy trust or the understanding among people?

Friend: Of course.

Director: When you wish to know the tensile strength of a rope, what do you do?

Friend: You keep adding weight to it until it breaks.

Director: Surely a leader ought to know the strength of his corporate entity or organization and the individuals that have placed themselves or been placed in it. But we, I think, do not want tension increased to the point of corporate destruction.

Friend: Are you kidding? They would be crazy to want a leader to do that.

Director: So it appears that we don't really want to be known.